WITHDRAWN

THE
PAUL HAMLYN
LIBRARY

DONATED BY
THE PAUL HAMLYN
FOUNDATION
TO THE
BRITISH MUSEUM

opened December 2000

# THE ROMAN OCCUPATION OF BRITAIN

Oxford University Press
*London Edinburgh Glasgow Copenhagen*
*New York Toronto Melbourne Cape Town*
*Bombay Calcutta Madras Shanghai*
Humphrey Milford Publisher to the UNIVERSITY

F. Haverfield

# THE ROMAN OCCUPATION OF BRITAIN

BEING

SIX FORD LECTURES

DELIVERED BY

F. HAVERFIELD

NOW REVISED

BY

GEORGE MACDONALD

---

WITH A NOTICE OF

HAVERFIELD'S LIFE

AND A LIST OF

HIS WRITINGS

---

OXFORD
AT THE CLARENDON PRESS
1924

BEXLEY PUBLIC LIBRARIES
STOCK No 2517
CLASS No 942·01 HAV
WITHDRAWN
St Bc
Cat. Let.
Fletcher. 3. 11. 51. 20/-

942.01 HAV

Printed in England

CVM POST CELEBRATOS TRECENTESIMO ANNO CATHEDRAE CAMDENIANAE NATALES VNIVERSITAS OXONIENSIS DIEI AVSPICATISSIMI MONVMENTVM ALIQVOD FIERI VOLVERIT, NVLLO MODO FELICIVS HOC FACTVM IRI EXISTIMAVIT QVAM SI ILLIVS PROFESSORIS, QVI CAMDENI VESTIGIIS INSISTENDO VIAM EANDEM ALIIS ET MONSTRAVIT ET PROCLIVIOREM REDDIDIT, COLLECTAS INTRA HVNC LIBRVM PRAELECTIONES IPSIVS CATHEDRAE FVNDATORIS MEMORIAE DEDICARET; QVAE RES VT PAR ILLVD NOBILE VIRORVM ERVDITISSIMORVM VELVT EXEMPLAR CETERIS IMITANDVM PROPONAT CVPIDISSIME PRECATVR.

# PREFACE

These lectures were originally delivered in 1907. Their author had always looked forward to publishing them in a revised and considerably expanded form. After his death it was found that at one time he had actually set himself to the task. About 1913 or 1914 he had 'worked over' the first of the series, inserting a number of new paragraphs and even making a beginning with the footnotes. There was thus no doubt as to the scale and character of the book which he contemplated. As his other papers included much material on which he would unquestionably have drawn, it has proved possible to complete the recasting of the whole six on the lines he had marked out, and to do so very largely in his own words. More often than could have been wished, however, there have been gaps to fill, particularly at points where lantern slides were employed, and sometimes the results of the most recent research have rendered alterations or omissions desirable. In all such matters, and indeed throughout, I have perforce had to act on my own responsibility. But I owe much to the valuable advice and assistance of a number of Professor Haverfield's old Oxford friends and pupils, notably Mr. J. G. C. Anderson of Christ Church, Mr. R. G. Collingwood of Pembroke, Dr. H. H. E. Craster of All Souls, and Mr. W. H. Stevenson of St. John's. Professor J. A. Smith and Professor John Fraser have kindly allowed me to consult them on questions relating to Celtic philology and history, while in other departments I have received useful suggestions from Professor Stuart Jones and Mr. N. Whatley of Hertford College, now Head Master of Clifton. Above all, I am indebted to Miss M. V. Taylor for unwearying help of various kinds, especially in the verification of references and in the preparation of the Index. As the account of the 'XXVIII Cities' was a document apart, it appears as an Appendix.

In planning the volume Professor Haverfield aimed at providing the general reader with a trustworthy introduction to the problems of Roman Britain. As now issued, it has a further purpose. The Public Orator explains in his Dedication that it is a tribute from the University of Oxford to the memory of William Camden, and with Camden's name he has conjoined in characteristically felicitous phrase the name of Haverfield himself. With the permission of the Council of the British Academy I have therefore reprinted the biographical notice which I wrote for the Academy's *Proceedings*. A bibliography compiled for the *Roman Journal* seemed an appropriate complement. It will be evident that the Delegates of the Clarendon Press have spared neither pains nor expense to make the memorial a worthy one. On their behalf I desire to thank all those who have lent photographs or blocks for the illustrations, as well as Mr. C. F. Bell, who drew my attention to the portrait of Stukeley, and Dr. Mortimer Wheeler, who supplied fresh information enabling the plan of Caerwent to be supplemented.

GEORGE MACDONALD.

EDINBURGH.
*November, 1923.*

# CONTENTS

# LIST OF PLATES

# LIST OF ILLUSTRATIONS IN THE TEXT

# BIOGRAPHICAL NOTICE

FROM 1500 onwards Haburfelds, Hawberfildes, Haberfeilds, and Habberfields are on record as holding land and making wills in the plain between the Mendips and the Quantocks. It was from this stock that there sprang a certain John Haverfield who, soon after the middle of the eighteenth century, was appointed Superintendent of Kew Gardens by the Princess Dowager of Wales on the recommendation of Lord Bute, a sound judge in all things botanical. John Haverfield *primus* died at a ripe old age in 1784, leaving as his successor in office a son of the same name. A daughter of John Haverfield *secundus* survives in a Gainsborough portrait. His eldest son, likewise a John, held commissions in the 43rd and 48th Foot, and served as Assistant-Quartermaster-General in Spain and Portugal in the year of Talavera. Lieutenant-Colonel Haverfield died in 1830. He had been twice married. His first family continued the name of John Haverfield for one generation and the tradition of soldiering for three; two of his great-grandsons fell in action in 1915. His second wife was Isabella Frances Meyer, daughter of the Würtemberger Jeremiah Meyer, who migrated to England as a lad of fourteen in 1749, designed the bust of George III for the coinage of 1761, and ultimately became one of the foundation members of the Royal Academy; her sister Mary is the 'Hebe' of Sir Joshua Reynolds. William Robert, the only issue of John Haverfield *tertius* and Frances Meyer, was ordained in 1850 after graduating at Oxford. Two curacies in Somerset and a third at Shipston-on-Stour were followed by his presentation in 1864 to the living of Headington Quarry in the immediate neighbourhood of his old University. He had never been robust, and within a year and a half ill-health compelled him to resign and retire to Bath. For a short time he took light duty there. Then he finally broke down, lingering on in invalid seclusion for some seventeen years more. In 1859, while still in the diocese of Worcester, he had married Emily Mackarness, one of whose brothers was afterwards well known as Bishop of Oxford, and another as Bishop of Argyll and the Isles. She died three years later in giving birth to a daughter. A son, born at Shipston on the 8th November 1860, had been christened FRANCIS JOHN.

As the father was seldom well enough to see them in his sickroom, the immediate charge of the motherless children devolved upon a faithful nurse. It was therefore not a normal household from which young Haverfield was sent to a preparatory school at Clifton in January 1872. His new companions were quick to recognize that he was quite unlike themselves. Very shy and somewhat awkward, with little aptitude for games, he received the rather ruthless welcome that might have been expected. But he was content to make his mark after his own fashion, and in the summer of 1873 he rejoiced the whole school by carrying off the first scholarship at Winchester in the same term in which his rival in the top form, Stanley Leathes, won the corresponding distinction at Eton. In the larger society, just as in the smaller, he was confronted by unusual difficulties until grit and character and ability could win him the respect that he deserved. These early experiences undoubtedly left their mark. In self-defence he was driven to don an outer panoply, which he was never able altogether to discard, although long before the end it had worn extremely thin. Inwardly he was in no way embittered. He did not complain and, what is more, he never cherished the slightest personal resentment for what he had endured. Yet he must sometimes have felt it acutely. A passage in a paper which he contributed anonymously in 1884 to the *Lancing College Magazine* is very significant. In the course of a defence of school athletics (of which he was a warm advocate) he draws a sharp line between the mere ' slacker ', on whom he would have no mercy, and the ' duffer ', who has his fullest sympathy. He then proceeds :

> 'Very few boys care much, while boys, for intellectual excellence. But a few such there are. We do not mean those who prefer the society of their elders to that of their companions, for the healthy boy dislikes the society of man. We mean boys who care for something beyond games—for excellence in work, for politics, for literature. Such boys are uncommon in a school, and, being uncommon, unprotected and generally unable to defend themselves, are little tolerated. It is the old story of the Irish dogs snapping at the tidy coat. Of the harm this intolerance does, even in its mildest form, few have any conception. Other boys may express themselves only in casual whispers and gestures ; the victim, however, speedily discovers what those mean ; he loses confidence, and loss of confidence, that is of self-respect, means carelessness in all matters, despondency, and perhaps ruin. The remedy for this we leave to the boys at the head of the School ; they can give, if they will, the necessary protection ; they can understand a little how far superior intellectual is to physical excellence—the mind to the body.'

But his tastes were unconventional as well as intellectual. In 1868, when he was little more than a child, great discoveries of Roman remains were being made at Bath. What he saw of them impressed him deeply, and must have given an unwonted sense of reality to his earliest Latin lessons. At Winchester, under Ridding, he proved himself an indefatigable worker, ' knowledgeable ' all round in many things not generally taught at school, and quick to learn how to distinguish grain from chaff. He was adjudged equal for the Goddard after a Homeric struggle, which old Wykehamists can still recall. At the same time Sir Charles Oman, his friend for forty-six years, remembers him chiefly as " much given to archaeological excursions, and to using German text-books different from the ordinary text-books employed in the class. He always preferred to read off the curriculum and for his own pleasure ". So it was at Oxford, where he matriculated in 1879 as a scholar of New College. Pelham made him a follower of the modern school of Roman historians, and Henry Nettleship lured him into the by-ways of Latin lexicography. Philosophy, on the other hand, did not attract him, and he gave it the minimum of attention. Consequently, while he easily secured his 'first' in Moderations, he missed his proper class in Greats, and with it his immediate chance of a Fellowship. That was in 1883. Next year he accepted a post as sixth-form tutor at Lancing.

This decision can hardly have been a mere *pis aller*. He relished the company of young people more than do most men. During his Oxford vacations, too, he had seen much of the Headmaster of Bath College, Mr. T. W. Dunn, whose manner of handling boys he admired warmly, and whose enthusiasm for teaching he came to share. His choice of a profession, therefore, was probably deliberate. And, if one may judge from casual conversation, he always looked back with satisfaction on his eight years as a schoolmaster. Of these years a vivid picture has been supplied by the Rev. H. W. McKenzie, late Headmaster of Uppingham, who was Headmaster of Lancing during the concluding part of Haverfield's sojourn there:

'It is not easy to place F. H. as a schoolmaster. There was a time when he seriously thought of aiming at a headmastership. But happily the idea faded away. He would have been quite out of his element; and the loss would have been great. He was made for something bigger than a mere pedagogue. Indeed, few men were less like the ordinary schoolmaster. His methods were all his own and not cast in the ordinary mould. He had none of the 'tricks of the trade': even his personal appearance in a classroom was unusual. He had no thought for the conventionalities. He was there not so much to teach as to let all who would learn. With the ordinary sixth-form boy—with his smattering of Classics and his thoughts for the playing-field—he was hardly a success. Not that he cold-shouldered him because of his lack of literary wits. Still, when there are differences about the things that matter, it is not easy to run an easy course. And with him the things that mattered were hardly those of the ordinary schoolboy. But, granted a chosen few with real desire for learning, he was ready to spend himself and all that he had in stirring the lighted fires.

Even so, it must be conceded that he was sometimes difficult. I have in mind two clever boys of whom the one was nursed and trained by F. H. into a fine character, fine in morals and in brain, while the other—they could not draw together, and it was left to his successor as sixth-form tutor to produce the results. Yet no one could come into his class-room without discovering that there was some one there who was out of the common, not only in method but also in largeness of outlook and immensity of knowledge far beyond the ordinary master. He realized, too, the value of illustration. He filled his rather inadequate room with models and maps—many of them self-made—and with everything suggestive and likely to catch and retain the schoolboy's attention.

But I soon found that he required to be 'given his head'. He had his own ways, and was not inclined to change them. Not that I ever had any friction at all: he was wholeheartedly loyal and ready to work beyond what was agreed upon, but it must be according to his own lines, which, as I have said, were not those of the ordinary schoolmaster. And so I suspect he was not always at one with his colleagues. It is unwise for a headmaster to know too much, and I never inquired; but I feel sure things did not always go smoothly. His sitting-room was open to the boys to come in and prowl round and read or borrow books. The literary—nay, even the untidy—look was a great attraction. Boys learned from him by talk and personal contact even more than they learned in the stated hours of teaching. He was no athlete, but none of his pupils could accuse him of lack of interest in that which bulked perhaps too largely in their daily thoughts. When he had passed away from school life, he refused to drop out; he maintained his interest in the boys he knew, and was ready to get hold of and help any one who came up to Oxford and had need of advice. He kept himself young in the sense that he could unfailingly enjoy the society of the young; while his friendship once won was firm to the end. In looking back over my work with him at Lancing College it is impossible to forget the help he gave by his example, in things higher than the mere scholastic round.'

Meanwhile he grew steadily in intellectual stature. As a rule, his vacations were spent abroad. Since one of his objects was to strengthen his hold on foreign languages, he usually travelled alone. Nor, indeed, would it have been easy for him to find a companion of energy and enterprise to match his own. During the summers of the later 'eighties', for instance, he ranged over the whole of Central Europe, exploring even the Bukovina and the Dobrudja, and wandering on foot among the Carpathians. In term-time he devoted his leisure to writing. As early as 1882, while he was still an undergraduate, two important articles had been published over his signature in the *Academy*, then at the zenith of its fame and influence. Now he contributed numerous papers, first to the *Journal of Philology* and the *Berliner philologische Wochenschrift*, and then to an ever-widening circle of other periodicals. As the stream gathered volume, its channel contracted and deepened. Roman epigraphy proved a natural point of convergence for what had been his two main interests at Oxford, Latin lexicography and ancient history. And it so happened that at the moment the epigraphy of Roman Britain was ripe for competent handling.

Haverfield's peculiar qualifications for such a task did not escape the discerning eye of Mommsen, whose personal acquaintance he had made in Berlin. The outcome was that in 1888, five years after he had sat for Greats, he was invited to become one of the editors of the *Corpus Inscriptionum Latinarum*, surely an unprecedented distinction for one so young. His *Additamenta quarta ad Corporis Vol. VII* was ready in 1890, and with its issue his reputation as an epigraphist was made. On laymen the slim brochure of eighty pages may not have left much impression. With scholars it was different. They could appreciate the strenuousness of the labour involved; they could gauge the insight and the skill and the experience that were implicit even in a discussion so terse as '*descripsi et damnavi*'. Two or three sentences from his prefatory note are worth recalling, partly as a specimen of his Latin style, partly for their trenchant account of the chaos out of which order had to be brought: '*Titulos quos quidem adire potui, ipse contuli: libros ad rem spectantes pro viribus excussi. Et horum quidem magna est copia; cum enim nunquam ii fuerint antiquarii qui chartae parcerent, tum prae ceteris hos nostros scribendi quoddam cacoethes invasit. Eduntur societatum archaeologicarum acta, transactiones sive memorias quas vocant, rudis indigestaque moles et sepulcro potius archaeologiae quam monumento futura.*'

These are hard words, and their candour is characteristic. Haverfield was not in the way of mincing matters when he felt that plain speaking was required. Yet the result of his quest was to be more far-reaching than he realized. If it left behind it a disheartening sense of wasted effort, it also served to introduce him to the study of Roman Britain as a whole. The impression that the remains of ancient Bath had made on his boyish imagination was still strong. To his more mature intelligence a much wider vista was now opened up. Here was a definite bit of work to be done, and he felt more and more drawn to the doing of it. Thus it came about that the scholar and the historian developed into the archaeologist. His study of Roman inscriptions broadened into a study of Roman forts and roads and 'villas', of pottery and fibulae, and of the host of 'minor objects' which to the ordinary man may appear to be trifles, but which to him were full of possibilities as links in the chain of evidence. None the less his interest in scholarship and history remained unabated. His acknowledged distinction in these two departments of learning was presently to bring him the offer of a Senior Studentship at Christ Church, and the beginning of 1892 saw him once more in residence at Oxford.

So far as the common round of tutorial duties went, his life during the next fifteen years was but an ampler version of his life at Lancing. From the outset he was universally respected. But his forceful personality did not always adjust itself automatically to the views and the customs of older or more conservative colleagues, and the pupils who got most from him were those who were able to catch something of his own infectious enthusiasm for research. In the sphere of administration his unresting energy found vent in various unexpected directions. While in charge of the Library, he prompted the compilation and issue of a scientific inventory of the many valuable drawings it contains, and initiated similar work for the collection of English music and for the pictures. As Junior Censor, he had the care of the portraits in Hall, and these he catalogued himself after consultation with experts; his *Brief Guide* has run through five or six editions, each an improvement on that which had gone before. He was Senior Censor for a single year, the year before he resigned his Studentship. At Christ Church the two Censors are responsible for internal discipline. The control of a couple of hundred high-spirited undergraduates is not a business for which Haverfield was obviously fitted, or which one would have expected him to enjoy. Yet he found it much to his mind, and he did it uncommonly well. Mr. J. G. C. Anderson, whose opportunities for judging were exceptional, writes to me: "Here he was very successful. Sharp when sharpness was necessary, he was also tactful, discriminating, and reasonable; and his gift of epigram often saved an awkward situation." College tradition has laid firm hold of some of his more memorable *mots*, such as the happy exhortation with which a belated quadrangle-gathering was dissolved in harmless laughter: "Let those who can take those who can't to bed." One other side of his life at Christ Church was conspicuous. To old friends and to new his hospitality was unbounded, and it was shared by even the humblest and least intellectual of his pupils. "Whom would you like to meet?" was his invariable question to non-residents, when a week-end invitation was accepted.

His Christ Church days were also the days when his phenomenal outside activities attained their greatest intensity. He was an indefatigable reviewer. His notices of new books, which appeared regularly in the *Guardian* and elsewhere, were models of their kind, showing a consistent endeavour to keep abreast of the march of knowledge in the whole field of classical scholarship. His reviewing, however, was a mere πάρεργον. There was much besides. In 1895 he saw through the press a posthumous volume of Henry Nettleship's *Essays*, and in 1898 he produced a revised edition of Conington and Nettleship's *Eclogues and Georgics*. In the latter year, too, Robinson Ellis's Velleius Paterculus was dedicated '*Francisco Iohanni Haverfield viro in his studiis exercitatissimo*'. But it was of Roman Britain that he thought most constantly and wrote most assiduously. A multitude of articles in many periodicals, each of them succinct and directly to the point, made his name a household word to students of the subject at home and abroad. Local correspondents flooded him with letters, which he answered with exemplary courtesy and promptitude. Lest he should miss anything of note, he joined innumerable societies and read their publications. Nor was all this enough. Between terms, his chosen recreations were the carrying out of personal examinations of Roman sites and the scrutinizing of Roman remains in museums and private collections. In the late summer of twelve successive years, for example, he settled down with R. P. L. Booker on the western half of Hadrian's Wall, and directed the spade-work that furnished him with material for his annual *Report of the Cumberland Excavation Committee*. When an archaeological expedition was afoot, distance and weather were of no account. Even a mid-winter snowstorm would not deter him from keeping tryst on a bleak Scottish hillside, if a new inscription had come to light.

The earliest public recognition of the position he had attained came from the far north in 1905, when the University of Aberdeen made him an Honorary Doctor of Laws. About the same time he was invited to give a set of Rhind Lectures in Edinburgh. Next followed his nomination to the Ford Lectureship at Oxford. His course of Ford Lectures, delivered in the spring term of 1907, attracted widespread attention as a brilliant summing-up of the most recent results of Romano-British research. Publication was urged upon him, and he readily consented. But happenings of the first importance for his future intervened. In April he married Miss Winifred Breakwell, and crossed to the Continent on an extended holiday. In May, when he was in Florence, he received a telegram informing him that he had been elected Camden Professor of Ancient History, in succession to his old friend Pelham whose death in the preceding February had been so grievous a loss to Oxford and to learning. This involved the severance of his connexion with Christ Church; henceforward he was *ex officio* a Fellow of Brasenose. On his return from abroad he lived for some months in Oxford, while he was building for himself at Headington a house that he called by a name reminiscent of the Northumbrian moors he loved so well. A man of forty-six was bound to find marriage and domesticity a very real adventure. The many for whom Winshields had ever an open door and a more than kindly welcome, know how completely the adventure succeeded. They cannot but feel that all who cared for Haverfield should be grateful to the memory of his wife for the new happiness she brought him. But it can only be to her memory. When he died, the "poison of her grief" proved too potent for an always delicate frame. She followed him in less than a year.

There was a singular fitness in his being called upon to fill the chair that William Camden had founded, for Camden's *Britannia*, published in 1586, represents the first tentative effort to trench the ground which Haverfield tilled to such splendid purpose. Moreover, his promotion came at exactly the right moment. As he sometimes admitted to his friends, the daily routine of college work had begun to be rather irksome. He now breathed an atmosphere where his peculiar qualities could have fuller play. He had the warmest admiration for Pelham's method of exposition; he has said of it that it "commanded attention by an imperious, passionless logic which in its own way amounted to genius". But he had already acquired for himself a method that belonged to nobody else, nor is it likely that he could have changed it, even if he had deemed it desirable to try. In the event his lectures proved magnetic enough to draw and to hold large audiences. The flow of quips and telling phrases sufficed to keep the groundling in good humour. Behind these there was a vast background of solid erudition which secured the initial confidence of all who had come to learn. And this confidence grew insensibly as point after point was driven home with a wealth of apt and novel illustration, on the accumulation of which it was easy to see that endless pains had been lavished.

When business responsibilities came his way, he shouldered the burden cheerfully. For years he served as a Governor of Westminster School and of Roysse's School, Abingdon. He had been a Visitor of the Ashmolean Museum from 1901, and his duties there were specially congenial. He was keenly interested, too, in the School of Geography and in the Association for Promoting the Education of Women in Oxford. On the Hebdomadal Council, which he entered in 1908, he was regarded as a force to be reckoned with. At the same time it would be idle to compare his influence as an administrator with that which Pelham had wielded. Truth to tell, University affairs were not his real *métier*. This is not to say that he was unpractical, or that he lacked dialectical skill. Rather, under conditions that suited him, he had a remarkable knack of putting things through, and on any subject he was a formidable man to argue with. In a general discussion, too, his faculty for keeping himself and others to the point was often of the utmost value. But he was not made for team-work; he was no respecter of persons, and he was too impatient of the unessential, not quite ready enough to compromise or to suffer gladly those whose vision seemed to him less acute than his own. In academic as in national politics he invariably leaned to the liberal side. Sometimes, indeed, he left even his fellow-liberals behind. If he occasionally spoke and wrote as if he were disposed to belittle the strictly educational aspect of University work, that was not because he was blind to its importance; it was because he felt intensely that, "without a basis of profound and accurate knowledge, education of any kind is a sham." In his view a University was valueless as a training-ground, unless it were first and foremost a living well-spring of learning. Under the stress of this conviction it was inevitable that his attitude should now and then have been critical. But Oxford had never a more loyal son. Had there been room for doubt, the terms of his will would have shown where his affections lay. He bequeathed his collection of archaeological books to the Ashmolean. Subject to a life-rent for his widow, the University was to receive the rest of his estate, to be applied for the furtherance of Romano-British studies.

His professorial leisure was abundantly occupied. Of the many societies he had joined, there were four in whose doings he was particularly interested—at one time or another he was either President or Vice-President of them all—the Society of Antiquaries of London, the Society of Antiquaries of Newcastle-upon-Tyne, the Cumberland and Westmorland Antiquarian and Archaeological Society, and the Somersetshire Archaeological and Natural History Society. Through these the leaven of his influence permeated the whole of England. It was equally active to the north of Hadrian's Wall: witness his Honorary Fellowship of the Society of Antiquaries of Scotland. But all the bodies named concern themselves, as a matter of course, with much else than Roman remains, and all of them except the first are avowedly more or less local in their outlook. It seemed to him, therefore, that in this land of group-activity there was room for yet another organization, at once wider and more restricted in its scope. Its principal object would be to provide a focus for the discussion of Roman history and Roman antiquities, Roman art and Roman architecture. Incidentally, however, it would break down the walls of partition between students of the Roman occupation in different parts of the country. An even greater advantage would be that it would bring such students into immediate contact with the main current of Roman research at our own Universities and abroad; one of his *obiter dicta* was that " it is of no use to know about Roman Britain in particular unless you also know about the Roman Empire in general ". The idea appealed strongly to those best qualified to help, and the Society for the Promotion of Roman Studies was formally inaugurated in 1911, with Haverfield as its first President. The fruits of five strenuous years of office are to be found in the earlier volumes of the Society's *Journal*.

It was not surprising that marks of outside appreciation should multiply apace. In 1908 he was invited to serve on the Royal Commission appointed to report on the Historical Monuments of England; in 1910 he was included in a very select band of distinguished men who were made Honorary Doctors by the University of Leeds when its new Chancellor was installed; in 1912, when the British School at Rome was granted a Charter of Incorporation, he was one of the three members of Council nominated by the Crown; in 1914 he was given a seat upon the Board which the Ancient Monuments Act of the previous year had called into existence. Only the first of these involved any real addition to his work. It was well that it should have been so, for both hands were already full; as one of his friends has said, he was for many years " the clearing-house for Roman Britain ". Every discovery was reported to him directly or indirectly, and everything of moment was scrupulously recorded for future use. Sometimes, after a personal visit, he would publish an account of a notable find, more especially if it were an inscription. But he was always ready to leave the task to others, if he were reasonably satisfied of their competence. He was singularly unselfish in such matters; and, when the stage of printing was reached, no one could have been more generous in encouragement or more vigilant and helpful in the reading of proofs.

Nevertheless he was far more anxious that people should dig than that they should write. "To-day the spade is mightier than the pen; the shovel and pick are the revealers of secrets." So ran one of his aphorisms. The digging, however, must be systematic and must be controlled by knowledge, and its results must be promptly and properly recorded. Haphazard and ignorant methods deserved unsparing condemnation; they might do untold harm by destroying priceless evidence. Every well-considered scheme of excavation had, of course, his whole-hearted support—Silchester, Caerwent, Newstead, and Wroxeter, to mention some of the better known. But the one with which he was most closely associated was the uncovering of Corstopitum, the buried Roman settlement at Corbridge-on-Tyne. Operations there began in 1907 and continued until the outbreak of the European War. He was a prominent member of the Excavation Committee, and season after season saw him on the spot, deciphering inscriptions, studying the chronological sequence of Samian and other pottery, impressing on his fellow-workers the vital importance of a careful observation of minutiae. The active assistance of a number of University men, some of them former pupils of his own, gave him much satisfaction. He had often lamented that in England there was such scant opportunity for the young scholar or historian to obtain a real insight into the mechanics of original research; the absence of a proper discipline of the kind seemed to him a grave hindrance to progress. He was sanguine that in the years to come the practical experience gained by these helpers at Corbridge would fructify abundantly. Two or three of those from whom he expected most were ere long to find a grave on the field of battle. The survivors can still justify his hope.

There were other reasons why he welcomed the aid of University men. He deplored the aloofness with which the loftier circles of academic opinion had hitherto been prone to regard the exploration of Romano-British sites, the coldness (as he deemed it) of their attitude to archaeological work as a whole. Even an unofficial indication of sympathy was therefore cause for rejoicing. Again, as was shown by the part he played in bringing the Roman Society to birth, he was a convinced believer in the need for combination among scholars. If the Corbridge undertaking produced substantial results, it would not be amiss as an object-lesson. We in this country required to be taught; organized co-operation in the service of learning was one of the things that they managed much better abroad. That being his view, every effort to remove the reproach could reckon on him as an ally. Hence his unswerving loyalty to the British Academy. Although not a foundation member, he was chosen a Fellow as far back as 1904, and subsequently served on the Council. His essay on *The Romanization of Roman Britain* originally appeared in the *Proceedings* for 1906. In 1910 he began to give to the Fellows each winter a sketch of the discoveries relating to Roman Britain which had been made in the previous twelvemonth. The earlier of these sketches were never printed. But *Roman Britain in 1913* and *Roman Britain in 1914* have both seen the light, and it was his intention to continue the series, thus reviving a custom he had followed from 1891 to 1904, when he published annual or quarterly summaries in the *Antiquary*, the *Athenaeum*, and the *Classical Review*.

But his ideal of co-operation was more than national. It was international. He had correspondents in various

Latin and Slav countries—Cumont, Cagnat, Rostovtzeff, and others. With Germany his relations were more intimate still. As a contributor to the *Corpus Inscriptionum*, he was in regular communication with Berlin. As a Member of the Imperial German Archaeological Institute, he supplied the *Archäologischer Anzeiger* with periodical reports of Romano-British developments. Mommsen had been a personal friend. Dessau, Mitteis, von Domaszewski were among those who maintained the tradition. In the circumstances the shock of the momentous Fourth of August was violent in the extreme. He was too good a historian not to realize all that was at stake when the nations of the world plunged into an orgy of mutual destruction. He knew that the struggle would be bitter, that civilization itself would be imperilled. He foresaw that, whatever the immediate end, the way of reconciliation would be long and hard. He felt as if the entire fabric of his most cherished plans had been irretrievably ruined. For a week or two, indeed, he was stunned. But the mood soon passed, for on the ultimate question of right and wrong he had never wavered for a moment. He was one of the large number of people on this side of the Channel upon whom the violation of Belgium's neutrality reacted most powerfully, leaving the moral issue so stark and clear that doubt or hesitation was impossible.

Before the October term opened, he had pulled himself together and was ready to face the novel task by which he and his contemporaries were confronted. To those who had been familiar with the city under its normal aspect, Oxford during the long years of war presented a strange and a melancholy spectacle. Of the younger generation there remained only the women students, and a handful of undergraduates too young to serve or physically unfit. The lecture rooms were all but empty; the river and the playing-fields were deserted; the Examination Schools were filled with wounded men. And the sounds were as unusual as the sights. The streets echoed to the rumble of army wagons and the tramp of marching feet; the quiet of the most retired of college gardens was broken by the harsh and insistent droning of aeroplanes. The whole atmosphere was depressing in the extreme. In these surroundings the older members of the teaching staff, or such of them as had not been claimed for emergency duty in London, did their best to forget their anxiety as to what was happening overseas, and strove manfully to prevent the total collapse of academic activity. Haverfield took his full share of the work that was going, not despising the drudgery and hoping against hope for the return of normal conditions.

But, when peace did come, he was to have no part in repairing the breach or building the old waste places. In the latter half of the Long Vacation of 1915 the name of Leonard Cheesman, Fellow of New College, appeared among the 'missing' at the Dardanelles. As the weeks wore on, news trickled back that he had fallen on the 10th of August, leading a forlorn hope at Chunuk Bair. Haverfield said little, but those nearest him knew that he had been cut as with a knife. Cheesman had been his favourite pupil, the most brilliant of the little group of 'disciples' that he had gathered round him, the man on whom he hoped that his own spirit would in due time rest. And there was more. A strong personal attachment had grown up between the two; the younger of them was almost as much at home in Winshields as if he had been a brother. The effect of the blow was to increase the strain on Haverfield to the breaking-point. He ended the term in a state of physical exhaustion such as he had never yet experienced. A day or two before Christmas the climax came in an onset of cerebral haemorrhage. In six or eight months he was able to resume his duties, having made what seemed a wonderful recovery. Though he complained that intellectual effort tired him, his mind was as clear and acute as ever. His friends, however, noted with pain the gradual weakening of his bodily powers in the year or two that followed. After the signing of the Armistice he became much happier, and was full of plans for future work. In particular he gave a great deal of thought to a scheme for the publication of a complete collection of Romano-British inscriptions with illustrations and notes. This had been sketched out during the War, and now its realization looked possible. One of the scholars whose collaboration he intended to secure was Rostovtzeff, whom the turmoil in Russia had driven to England. In the early autumn of 1919 he revisited in his company several familiar Roman sites, including Cirencester and Hadrian's Wall, and returned to Oxford full, to all appearance, of fresh vigour. Physically and mentally, in fact, he was more like his old self than he had been for years. On the 30th of September he was exceptionally bright. But towards midnight he had a sudden seizure. Half an hour later he passed away without suffering.

A bibliography of his writings is appended to this Notice. It does not profess to be exhaustive, reviews and anonymous articles being for the most part omitted. Nevertheless, with a total of some 500 entries, the list is sufficiently imposing. The marvel grows, when it is remembered how much labour went to the final shaping of the excellent and seemingly effortless English of which he was a master. If pushed for time, he could write—and write extraordinarily well—with a speed that a trained journalist might have envied. But he had laid to heart the Horatian maxim,

> '*Saepe stilum vertas, iterum quae digna legi sint scripturus.*'

As a rule, his books and more important articles made headway slowly. Despite his beautifully clear hand, he had been one of the pioneers of the typewriter in Oxford. Sometimes he manipulated the instrument himself. Far more frequently he dictated. When a few pages had been drafted, they were generally laid aside for a day or two, then revised and typed out afresh, a process that might have to be repeated three or four times before his fastidious taste was even tolerably satisfied. Nor did he allow what he ultimately accepted as the 'fair copy' to go to the printer, until there had been still further revision, until every unnecessary word had been erased, each phrase adjusted in its proper order. He was all for clearness and simplicity of structure. He had less faith than the majority of classical scholars in the value of Latin prose for the teaching of English composition. It seemed to him too involved, and he thought Greek a better model. His own creed was summed up in the precept he had tried to inculcate at Lancing: "That style is best which attracts least attention".

Besides being an index of his unremitting industry, the list is an unerring reflection of his interests. Lexicography, pure scholarship, textual criticism, geography, even botany, art, and medieval architecture, each had a place alongside of ancient history, epigraphy, and archaeology. In the end, of course, the last three overshadow everything. Equally of course, within these three, the roads all lead to Roman Britain. Thus it is no accident that in his *Ancient Town-Planning*—an enlargement of the Creighton Lecture for 1910—the reader, after being taken to Babylon and distant China, to Greece and Italy, to Africa and Gaul, is brought back at last to Lincoln and Silchester and Caerwent. As might be anticipated, the items in the bibliography vary greatly in length and importance. Had the author been asked to which of them he believed that the most enduring value would attach, he would probably have singled out the *Additamenta quinta ad Corporis Vol. VII*, published in 1913. While it is nominally a reading of new inscriptions and of new readings of inscriptions which were already known, it also contains the essence of his reflections on not a few crucial problems that are more than epigraphical. It is, however, a book for the scholar, or rather for the specialist. Ordinary students will prefer to think of the quite admirable *Romanization of Roman Britain*, or of the lucid and comprehensive chapters that lend an added distinction to the stately volumes of the *Victoria County History*. So long as he was in full vigour, he liked to believe that, after all the counties of England had been dealt with, there would still be time for him to gather the whole of his material up into a definitive *Britannia Romana*. When war and illness interrupted the current of his life, the hope was regretfully dismissed. But, even had the break not occurred, the dream might have lacked fulfilment. Though he was struck down in his prime, the days of his years were passing at too great a speed.

We know that he worked hard. It would be misleading to suggest that he did not also work quickly. But his ideal of thoroughness was high; he was every whit as unwilling to put up with the second-best in matter as we have seen that he was reluctant to be content with it in form. Again, the outside demands upon him were becoming more and more incessant; they increased in direct proportion to the growth of that intelligent curiosity about things Roman which he set himself so sedulously to foster. Yet again, and here is the main point, the farther he himself advanced, the larger did the task that lay ahead of him become; new and unexplored recesses were revealed by every fresh gleam of light that he threw upon the darkness. Such was the penalty he had to pay for making his subject living and progressive. And this is where his real monument must be looked for. As long ago as 1907 he was able to "claim that the inquiry into the history and character of Roman Britain, with all its defects and imperfections, has been carried much farther than the inquiry into Celtic or Saxon Britain, much farther too than the inquiry into any other Roman province; and that our scientific knowledge of the island, however liable to future correction and addition, stands by itself among the studies of the Roman Empire". That Roman

Britain should be to us a thing of substance, is the measure of our debt to Francis Haverfield.

In any endeavour to account for what he accomplished, two or three qualities must emerge couspicuously. His instinct for relevance and his shrewd, penetrating common sense were fundamental; they gave him a rare power of appreciating the value of evidence, and made him as relentless a judge of his own theories as he was of the theories of others. His patience in noting details was balanced by the readiness with which he held the accumulated mass of information at command; the smallest facts, provided they had a bearing on his subject, seemed to have been pigeon-holed in his orderly mind and to be available at a moment's notice. Above all, he had vision, a faculty of synthesis, which enabled him to divine the co nexion between isolated particulars, and to fit each into its appropriate place, until there grew under his hands a picture whose outlines all men could discern. In these respects it might not untruly be said that he resembled Mommsen. No eulogy, however warm, would have pleased him more. As has been pointed out in a singularly felicitous appreciation in the *English Historical Review*,[1] Mommsen's influence was decisive in moulding his career. His admiration for him amounted to reverence: "He was the greatest scholar of the European world since the Renaissance, and his unequalled and amazing achievements stamp the historical research of the nineteenth century with its peculiar feature. It is the age when Roman history was newborn."

These last words recall a criticism that was occasionally made upon Haverfield's own attitude as a historian. It was sometimes hinted that he was too exclusively devoted to the Empire. The explanation is twofold. He held that the 'sources' for the period of the Republic, being almost entirely literary, had probably taught us as much as we are ever likely to know. There was no scope there

[1] Vol. xxxv, pp. 63–70.

for the exercise of his peculiar gifts. "The Republic", he says somewhere, "was one of those states which mark the world, but not individual sites, by their achievements. Such in Greece was Sparta; and, as Thucydides saw long ago, the history of such states must always lack archaeological evidence." The Empire, on the other hand, with its wealth of archaeological material, offered unlimited opportunities for independent inquiry and for the thrill of new discovery. Weightier still was his conviction that, properly understood and interpreted, the story of the Empire had a far more vital meaning for the present generation than had the story of the Republic. Its problems, its possibilities, its dangers were closely analogous to those of to-day. We had much to learn from its methods, and something to learn from its fall. "Even the forces which laid the Roman Empire low", he insists, "concern the modern world very nearly, more nearly indeed than do the causes for the downfall of any other empire about which we have full knowledge." It is worth observing that, in surrendering himself to the spell, he was more or less unconsciously following in the footsteps of his master. As a young man, Mommsen wrote that the Empire had '*wenig Geist, noch weniger Geschmack und am wenigsten Freude am Leben*'. In his old age he is reported to have declared that, if he had to live his life over again, he would begin his study of Roman history with Diocletian.

Thus far I have written of Haverfield as a scholar, a historian, and a teacher. It is desirable to add a few lines on Haverfield as a man, all the more so because in his lifetime he was frequently misunderstood and was, perhaps, not always careful enough to see that it should be otherwise. Simplicity and directness were of the essence of his character. He was singularly fair-minded, and every opinion, every proposal on which he had to pronounce was examined strictly upon what seemed to him to be its merits. On most questions, of course, he had decided views of his own, and these he was slow to abandon unless convinced by reason and argument. It was useless to try to impress him by the weight of eminent names. With him it was things, not persons, that counted. When he felt sure of his ground, he was inflexible. That was probably fortunate, since within his own province he was almost invariably right. But he sometimes provoked a regrettable antagonism by the lightness with which he brushed 'authorities' aside. Moreover, his early experiences had developed a brusqueness of speech that was apt to be disconcerting. In his later years this was rapidly melting away in the sunshine of success and happiness. To the very end, however, he was more concerned to say what was true than to say what was tactful. Personal rancour was utterly foreign to his nature. It would have accorded ill with his genuine sense of humour. He was, in fact, magnanimous to a degree. And he was always willing to help any one, no matter how humble, who was anxious to profit by his guidance. In such circumstances his generosity and his patience were alike inexhaustible. Finally, those who found his manner difficult would have been grievously mistaken to argue therefrom a carelessness for human love. He did not wear his heart upon his sleeve; he had, indeed, a more than average allowance of the educated Englishman's *εἰρωνεία*. But his affections were none the less securely rooted. His enjoyment of hospitality and his delight in the society of the young were surface manifestations. Beneath these was something much deeper. I may venture to quote the testimony of a private letter addressed to myself by one who lost touch with him when he left Lancing, and regained it, after a long interval, in Oxford. "I retain his memory unbroken by the gaps which years made in association, and know that in him it was true 'there is a friend that sticketh closer than a brother'. When I came up here to spend my days of retirement, his kindness was beyond words—and my heart is full of him and his little acts of thoughtfulness—and will always be so." For my own part, I feel this to be the most appropriate note on which a sketch of his life could close.

G. M.

*** In writing the foregoing sketch I have received help from practically all of Professor Haverfield's surviving friends whom I have had occasion to mention by name.

# A BIBLIOGRAPHY

OF

# PROFESSOR HAVERFIELD'S PUBLISHED WRITINGS

THE following abbreviations are used throughout: [1]

*Arch. Ael.* = *Archaeologia Aeliana.*
*Arch. Anz.* = *Archäologischer Anzeiger, Beiblatt des Jahrbuches des kaiserlich deutschen archäologischen Instituts.*
*Arch. Cambr.* = *Archaeologia Cambrensis.*
*Arch. Oxon.* = *Archaeologia Oxoniensis.*
*Arch. Journ.* = *Journal of the Royal Archaeological Institute of Great Britain and Ireland.*
*Arch. Rev.* = *Archaeological Review.*
*Biogr. Jahrb.* = *Biographisches Jahrbuch für Alterthumskunde.*
*Chester Journ.* = *Journal of the Architectural, Archaeological and Historical Society of Chester and North Wales.*
*Class. Rev.* = *Classical Review.*
*C. and W. Trans.* = *Transactions of the Cumberland and Westmorland Antiquarian and Archaeological Society.*
*Derbyshire Journ.* = *Journal of the Derbyshire Archaeological and Natural History Society.*
*Eng. Hist. Rev.* = *English Historical Review.*
*Glouc. Trans.* = *Transactions of the Bristol and Gloucester Archaeological Society.*
*Jour. Phil.* = *Journal of Philology.*
*J.R.S.* = *Journal of Roman Studies.*
*K. Westd. Z.* = *Korrespondenzblatt der westdeutschen Zeitschrift für Geschichte und Kunst.*

[1] They are employed also in the foot-notes to the Lectures.

*Lanc. Trans.* = *Transactions of the Historic Society of Lancashire and Cheshire.*
*Num. Chron.* = *Numismatic Chronicle.*
*P.S.A.L.* = *Proceedings of the Society of Antiquaries of London.*
*P.S.A.N.* = *Proceedings of the Society of Antiquaries of Newcastle-upon-Tyne.*
*P.S.A. Scot.* = *Proceedings of the Society of Antiquaries of Scotland.*
*Somerset Proc.* = *Proceedings of the Somersetshire Archaeological and Natural History Society.*
*Suss. Coll.* = *Sussex Archaeological Collections.*
*Vict. Hist.* = *Victoria County History.*
*Wilts. Mag.* = *Wiltshire Archaeological and Natural History Magazine.*
*Year's Work* = *The Year's Work in Classical Studies.*
*Yorks. Journ.* = *Yorkshire Archaeological Journal.*

The catalogue given below does not profess to be exhaustive. It is, of course, possible that some items of importance have been accidentally overlooked. In the main, however, the omissions are the outcome of a deliberately adopted principle: no systematic attempt has been made to register either the anonymous articles or the reviews of books, whether signed or unsigned. Had all of these been taken into account, the length of the list might well have been doubled. But its practical usefulness would not have been sensibly increased by their inclusion; the great majority of them, like the letters to the daily press, were never meant to be other than ephemeral. An exception has been made in favour of a few that appeared to have a permanent significance as embodying definite pronouncements upon special points, and also in favour of a somewhat larger number to which a biographical interest seemed to attach. The latter belong chiefly to the earlier years of the sequence.

The general arrangement is chronological. But it was obviously impossible to ensure that within each separate year the order of appearance should be rigidly adhered to. In the case of articles in periodicals, too, there may sometimes be a little inconsistency. Wherever possible, such items are catalogued under the year of issue, but in not a few instances all that was ascertainable was the date of publication of the particular volume that contains them.

1882.

‘ The Books of the Ancients ’ [Review of Birt’s ‘ *Das antike Buchwesen* ’]: *Academy*, July 15th.

Review of Wharton’s ‘ *Etyma Graeca* ’: *Academy*, October 28th.

1883.

‘ A Roman Inscription near Broussa ’: *Academy*, May 12th and May 19th.

‘ A Latin Inscription from Nicopolis ’: *Jour. Phil.* xii, pp. 292–296.

1884.

‘ Notes in Latin Lexicography ’: *Jour. Phil.* xiii, pp. 81–84.

‘ Lexicographical Notes II ’: *Ibid.* pp. 299–302.

Review [in German] of Donaldson’s ‘ Culture and Scholarship ’: *Berl. phil. Wochenschrift*, June 7th.

Review [in German] of first part of Felice Rammorino’s ‘ *Frammenti Filologici* ’: *Ibid.*, November 1st.

‘ The Library of Aethelstan, the Half-King ’: *Academy*, July 12th.

1885.

‘ Miscellanea ’: *Jour. Phil.* xiv, p. 132.

‘ Lexicographical Notes ’: *Ibid.* pp. 287 f.

‘ John Henry Parker ’ [in German]: *Biogr. Jahrb.* vii, pp. 7 f.

Review [in German] of B. H. Kennedy’s ‘ *Studia Sophoclea II* ’: *Berl. phil. Wochenschrift*, October 3rd.

1886.

‘ *Purpurei Panni* ’, 22 pp. [Twenty extracts illustrative of English prose style, with a few brief notes and “ N.B. That style is best which attracts least attention ”: compiled for the use of the Sixth Form at Lancing College.]

‘ Words from Cicero ’, 28 pp. [No title-page or date, but obviously of the same character and period as the foregoing.]

Topographical Model of Syracuse [with J. B. Jordan]: Teachers’ Guild Educational Museum.

‘ On Aurelius Victor ’: *Jour. Phil.* xv, pp. 161–163.

1887.

‘ Five-Hundredth Anniversary of Winchester College ’: *Guardian*, March 30th.

‘ The Servian Elections ’ [Letters from Belgrade]: *Ibid.* September 29th and October 5th.

‘ Grote’s Maps of Syracuse ’: *Academy*, March 19th.

‘ A Misread Roman Inscription from Hungary ’: *Ibid.*, August 13th.

‘ Gomme’s Romano-British Remains ’: *Ibid.*, October 22nd and November 1st.

‘ Roman Dacia ’: *Eng. Hist. Rev.* ii, pp. 734–736.

1888.

‘ Lexicographical Notes ’ : *Jour. Phil.* xvi, pp. 193–195.
‘ Miscellanea (Tacitus, etc.) ’ : *Jour. Phil.* xvii, pp. 268–271.
‘ Scholia on Claudian ’ : *Ibid.*, pp. 271–273.
‘ Notes from Krain, Croatia and Serbia ’ : *Ibid.*, pp. 274–288.
‘ Discovery of Roman Coins at Brighton ’ : *Suss. Coll.* xxxvi, p. 244.
‘ Roman Remains in Sussex ’ : *Arch. Rev.* i, pp. 434–440.
‘ Roman Inscriptions in Britain ’ [intimating that he had been asked to edit British inscriptions for the Berlin *Corpus*, and appealing for co-operation] : *Ibid.* ii, p. 267.
Review of R. Ellis's edition of Orientius : *Academy*, April 21st.
‘ The Lost Decades of Livy ’ : *Ibid.*, June 16th.

1889.

‘ Notes on Roman Britain ’ [(*a*) The Founding of Viroconium. (*b*) Roman Roads in Sussex. (*c*) Epigraphica.] : *Arch. Journ.* xlvi, pp. 65–72.
‘ An Inscribed Stone at Colchester ’ : *Arch. Ael.* (2nd ser.) xiii, p. 358.
‘ The Roman Inscriptions of Brough under Stainmore ’ : *Ibid.*, pp. 358–360.
‘ Further Remarks on the Ring of Senicianus ’ [Silchester] : *Glouc. Trans.* xiii, pp. 203 f.
‘ Roman Remains at Scarborough and Chichester ’ : *Arch. Rev.* iii, pp. 71 f.
‘ Roman Remains in Carniola, etc.’ : *Ibid.*, pp. 272–275.
‘ Roman Inscriptions ’ [1. The Cliburn Inscription. 2. A lead ‘pig’ found at Saint Valery in France. 3. A Dutch Inscription. 4. Milestone of Constantine from Crindledykes] : *P.S.A.N.* (2nd ser.) iv, pp. 34 f.
‘ Notes on records of Roman Inscriptions relating to the North of England, discovered in the manuscripts of the Bodleian Library (Codd. Rawl. B. 206) ’ : *Ibid.*, pp. 116 f.
‘ A Roman Plant at Chesters ’ [*Erinus Hispanicus*] : *Ibid.*, p. 164.
‘ The forged figure found near Brough ’ : *Ibid.*, p. 165.
‘ Abolition of the Dictatorship ’ : *Class. Rev.* iii, p. 77.
‘ Two Notes on Syracuse ’ [1. Achradina. 2. Ἡ ἔξω πόλις] : *Ibid.*, pp. 110–112.
‘ The Gold Bars of Kraszna ’ : *Ibid.*, p. 186.
‘ Roman Inscriptions from Sardinia ’ : *Ibid.*, pp. 228–234.
‘ Thuc. iv, 98 ’ : *Ibid.*, p. 372.
‘ Eur. Hec. 595 ’ : *Ibid.*, p. 418.
‘ Portus Adurni and the River Adur ’ : *Academy*, April 20th.
‘ Roman Inscriptions ’ [France and Holland] : *Ibid.*, May 11th.
Review of J. P. Earwaker's ‘ Recent Discoveries of Roman Remains in Chester ’ : *Ibid.*, June 22nd.
Review of H. Nettleship's ‘ Contributions to Latin Lexicography ’ : *Ibid.*, December 7th.

1890.

'Extracts from the *Gentleman's Magazine* relating to Oxford, 1731–1800': Oxford Historical Society's Publications, *Collectanea* ii, pp. 421–448.

'Roman Inscriptions from Sardinia, II': *Class. Rev.* iv, pp. 65–67.

'Roman Inscriptions in Britain, 1888–1890': *Arch. Journ.* xlvii, pp. 229–267.

'An inscribed lead plate said to have been found at Hylton': *P.S.A.N.* (2nd ser.) iv, p. 230.

'A bronze bowl found at S. Shields inscribed *Apollini Anextiomaro*': *Ibid.*, pp. 272 f.

'Find of Roman Coins in Roumania': *Num. Chron.* (3rd ser.) x, p. 282.

'A forged Roman tile': *Academy*, March 8th.

'Provisional Account of Roman Inscriptions found at Chester (North Wall)': *Athenaeum*, December 13th.

1891.

Translation of a passage of Swinburne's *Erechtheus* into Greek iambics: *Class. Rev.* v, pp. 65 f.

'Thuc. ii, 11': *Ibid.*, p. 67.

'Tragic Tribrachs': *Ibid.*, p. 67.

'Re-excavated Relics': *Ibid.*, pp. 240 f.

'Notes on some Museums in Galicia and Transilvania': *Arch. Journ.* xlviii, pp. 1–13.

'Notes on Roman Britain': *Antiquary* xxiii, pp. 9–11.

'Quarterly Notes on Roman Britain': *Ibid.*, pp. 146–149; *Ibid.* xiv, pp. 19–22, and pp. 212–214.

'Roman Remains in Local Museums': *Antiquary* xxiv, pp. 168–172.

'Roman Remains at Chester': *Athenaeum*, May 16th.

'Roman Remains in Chester': *Ibid.*, October 31st.

'Roman Inscriptions found at Chester': *Arch. Cambr.* (5th ser.) viii, pp. 78–80. [Reprinted from *Athenaeum*, 1890.]

'The Brough Idol': *C. and W. Trans.* xi, pp. 296–299.

'The Roman Inscription at West Park': *Academy*, August 29th.

'The Chester Pigs of Lead': *Ibid.*, November 7th.

'On the Binchester inscription': *P.S.A.N.* (2nd ser.) v, pp. 39 f.

'Ollototae' [in German]: *K. Westd. Z.* x, 90.

1892.

'Thuc. ii, 11, 4': *Class. Rev.* vi, p. 123.

'*Additamenta quarta ad Corporis Vol. vii.*': *Eph. Epigr.* vii, pp. 273–354.

'Quarterly Notes on Roman Britain': *Antiquary* xxv, pp. 21–23 and pp. 155 f.; and xxvi, pp. 24–26 and 169–171.

'Roman Inscriptions in Britain, 1890–91': *Arch. Journ.* xlix, pp. 176–201. [Also reprinted separately with additions and corrections.]

'Some Notable Romano-British Inscriptions': *Ibid.*, pp. 215–234. [Included in reprint.]

'An Altar to the *Matres Ollototae* discovered at Binchester': *Arch. Ael.* (2nd ser.) xv, pp. 225–227.
'The Mother Goddesses': *Ibid.*, pp. 314–339.
'A New Altar from Wallsend dedicated to Jupiter': *Ibid.*, xvi, pp. 76–80.
'On the Matribus Africanis or Afliabus, Ollototae': *P.S.A.N.* (2nd ser.) v, pp. 143 f.
'On the recent discovery at Wallsend of fragments of an inscription to Mercury, and on a new centurial stone from Sewingshields': *Ibid.*, pp. 187 f.
'Notes on the epigraphic evidence as to the date of Hadrian's Wall': *P.S.A.L.* (2nd ser.) xiv, pp. 44–55.
'Note on a Roman inscribed bronze tablet, lately found at Colchester': *Ibid.*, pp. 108–112.
'Additional Remarks [on the same]': *Ibid.*, pp. 183–187.
'On the site of *Portus Adurni* and the river Adur': *Ibid.*, pp. 112–116.
'The Administration of the Roman Mines': *Chester Journ.* iv, pp. 80–95.
'MS. Materials for Romano-British Epigraphy': *Arch. Oxon.* i, pp. 15–22.
'Roman Remains at Chester': *Athenaeum*, April 16th and July 9th.
'An Inscription in the Eifel': *Ibid.*, July 23rd.
'Hardknott Castle': *Ibid.*, October 22nd.
'A Roman Inscription from Carlisle': *Academy*, December 24th.
'On the Site of Portus Adurni and the river Adur': *Suss. Coll.* xxxviii, pp. 217–221. [Reprinted, with additions, from *P.S.A.L.*]

1893.

'Nasidienus (Horace, *Sat.* ii, 8)': *Class. Rev.* vii, p. 359.
Obituary Notice of Prof. Nettleship: *Ibid.*, pp. 369 f.
'Discoveries of Roman Remains in Britain, I': *Ibid.*, pp. 430 f.
'Quarterly Notes on Roman Britain': *Antiquary* xxvii, pp. 23–25, and xxviii, pp. 159–163.
'Romano-British Inscriptions 1892–1893': *Arch. Journ.* l, pp. 279–307.
'Three Notable Inscriptions' [1. The Cirencester Dedication. 2. The Carlisle Gravestone. 3. The Lanchester Altar]: *Ibid.*, pp. 308–321.
'On a Roman Inscription found near Carlisle': *P.S.A.L.* (2nd ser.) xiv, pp. 263–267.
'On a fragment of Roman tile, found at Carlisle': *C. and W. Trans.* xii, pp. 280–282.
'On the Roman Altar to the Goddess "Garmangabis" found at Lanchester': *Arch. Ael.* (2nd ser.) xvi, pp. 321–327.
'A new Roman Inscription from South Shields': *Ibid.*, pp. 157–161.
'A walk along the Pfahlgraben' [Letter to Dr. Hodgkin]: *P.S.A.N.* (2nd ser.) vi, pp. 78–80.
'Romano-British Remains in Berkshire' [with A. J. Evans]: *Athenaeum*, August 26th.
'A new Roman Inscription at Lanchester': *Academy*, August 19th.
'Hadrian's Wall': *Ibid.*, October 28th.

1894.

'Discoveries of Roman Remains in Britain, II': *Class. Rev.* viii, pp. 227 f.

'Maps of Roman Britain, etc.': *Ibid.*, pp. 324 f.

'Quarterly Notes on Roman Britain': *Antiquary* xxix, pp. 55–57 and 244 f.; and xxx, pp. 207–209.

'On the Discovery of a fourth Inscribed Pig of Roman Lead in Derbyshire' [with J. Charles Cox and E. Hübner]: *Ibid.* xxix, pp. 218–223.

'On two Roman inscriptions found at Carlisle, and on a third in the Cardiff Museum': *P.S.A.L.* (2nd ser.) xv, pp. 119–122.

'On an Inscribed Pig of Lead from Matlock (Derby)': *Ibid.*, pp. 188 f.

'On a Roman milestone found at Carlisle': *Ibid.*, pp. 263 f.

'On an inscription at Wallsend': *P.S.A.N.* (2nd ser.) vi, p. 223.

'A new theory of the *Vallum Romanum* and *Murus* by Prof. Mommsen of Berlin': *Ibid.*, pp. 223–225.

'Notes on a Visit to the German *Limes*' [Letter to Dr. Hodgkin]: *Ibid.*, pp. 246–248.

Review of Traill's 'Social England': *Eng. Hist. Rev.* ix, pp. 724–726.

'A Roman Inscription from Cirencester illustrating Fourth Century Britain': *Arch. Oxon.* iv, pp. 215–226.

'The North Wall of Chester': *Athenaeum*, January 27th.

'The Foundation of Silchester': *Ibid.*, December 15th.

'A Roman Tile from Gloucester': *Academy*, March 10th.

'Roman Britain' [Note on Traill's 'Social England']: *Ibid.*, March 24th.

'A Roman Pig of Lead' [Derbyshire]: *Ibid.*, April 21st.

'Exploration of Hadrian's Wall' [An appeal, signed also by H. F. Pelham and J. L. G. Mowat]: *Ibid.*, June 23rd.

'The "Limes" in Germany': *Ibid.*, October 13th.

'Legionary Tiles at Carlisle': *Ibid.*, October 27th.

'Inschrift zu Carlisle' [in German]: *K. Westd. Z.* xiii, 32.

1895.

'Quarterly Notes on Roman Britain': *Antiquary* xxxi, pp. 37 f., 201 f., and 299 ff.

'Tacitus, *Agricola* 24': *Class. Rev.* ix, pp. 310 f.

'Note on Hoards of Roman Silver Coins found in Britain, with special reference to the Silchester Hoard': *Archaeologia* liv, pp. 489–491.

'On a Roman inscription at Shirburn (Oxon.)': *P.S.A.L.* (2nd ser.) xv, pp. 456 f.

'A Fourth-Century Roman Tombstone from Carlisle': *C. and W. Trans.* xiii, pp. 165–171.

'On two Roman Inscriptions recently found at Carlisle': *Ibid.*, pp. 224–226.

'On a Milestone of Carausius and other recent Roman finds': *Ibid.*, pp. 437–439.

'Report of the Cumberland Excavation Committee for 1894': *Ibid.*, pp. 453–469.

'The Origins of Deva': *Chester Journ.* v, pp. 99–103.

'The Characteristics of Roman Chester': *Ibid.*, pp. 353–360.
'English Topographical Notes': *Eng. Hist. Rev.* x, pp. 710–712.
'On the *Historia Augusta*': *P.S.A.N.* (2nd ser.) vii, p. 135.
'On Excavations at Appletree' [Turf-Wall]: *Ibid.*, 137.
'Discoveries on the line of Hadrian's Wall at Greatchesters and Birdoswald': *Arch. Oxon.* vi, pp. 321 f.
'The Roman Army in the Acts of the Apostles': *Guardian*, October 16th.
'A Milestone of Carausius' [Carlisle]: *Academy*, January 12th.
'A Milestone of Carausius and a Welsh Tombstone': *Ibid.*, November 2nd.
Edited H. Nettleship's 'Lectures and Essays, Second Series' (Clarendon Press).

1896.

'Quarterly Notes on Roman Britain': *Antiquary* xxxii, p. 53.
'Discoveries of Roman Remains in Britain, III': *Class. Rev.* x, pp. 73 f.
'On the Roman Town of Doclea in Montenegro' [with J. A. R. Munro, W. C. F. Anderson, and J. G. Milne]: *Archaeologia* lv, pp. 33–92.
'Notes on Excavations at Aesica in 1894': *Ibid.*, pp. 195–198.
'An Archaeological Survey of Herefordshire' [with J. O. Bevan and J. Davies]: Soc. of Antiq. of London (16 pp.).
'On a Roman bronze vessel from Herringfleet (Suffolk)': *P.S.A.L.* (2nd ser.) xvi, pp. 237–240.
'On the supposed *Mithraeum* discovered at Barham, Kent, in 1894': *Ibid.*, pp. 248 f.
'Report of the Cumberland Excavation Committee for 1895': *C. and W. Trans.* xiv, pp. 185–197.
'On the names of Carausius': *P.S.A.N.* (2nd ser.) vii, pp. 174 f.
'Excavations in the Vallum': *Ibid.*, pp. 283–285.
'The Antiquity of Place-names' [Magnae]: *Chester Journ.* vi, pp. 36–41.
'Roman Altar discovered in 1896': *Ibid.*, pp. 76–78.
'Early British Christianity': *Eng. Hist. Rev.* xi, pp. 417–430.
'The Roman Army in the Acts of the Apostles: A Further Note': *Guardian*, June 10th.
'Chester' [The place-name]: *Athenaeum*, August 8th.
'Romano-British Place-names in Inscriptions' [Neath, Kenchester]: *Academy*, August 1st.
'Die Hadriansmauer in Nordengland' [in German]: *K. Westd. Z.* xv, 81.
'Introductory Note' to posthumous "Notes on Nonius" by Prof. Nettleship: *Jour. Phil.* xxiv, pp. 212 f.

1897.

'Note on Aesch. *Pr. V.* 358': *Class. Rev.* xi, p. 98.
'Tacitus, *Agricola* xxiv': *Ibid.*, p. 447.
'Quarterly Notes on Roman Britain': *Antiquary* xxxiii, pp. 16–20, 103–105, 230–232, and 360–362.

‘On a Roman lamp of terra-cotta found at Bradfield, Berks.’: *P.S.A.L.* (2nd ser.) xvi, pp. 276 f.
‘On a Roman bronze prow found in London’: *Ibid.*, p. 308.
‘Report of the Cumberland Excavation Committee, 1896’: *C. and W. Trans.* xiv, pp. 413–427.
‘The Vallum’: *Ibid.*, pp. 427 f.
‘The Name “Maiden Way”’: *Ibid.*, pp. 428–433.
‘A new Roman Inscription from Chesters’: *Arch. Ael.* (2nd ser.) xix, pp. 179–181.
‘Roman Inscriptions from Aesica’: *Ibid.*, pp. 268–274.
‘Roman Inscription, etc. at Carrawburgh’: *P.S.A.N.* (2nd ser.) viii, p. 95.

1898.

Revised edition of ‘The Works of Virgil’ by J. Conington and H. Nettleship. Vol. I, *Eclogues* and *Georgics* (Bell and Son).
‘Ancient Gaul’: pp. 1–20 of Jervis's ‘History of France’, ed. by A. Hassall.
‘Quarterly Notes on Roman Britain’: *Antiquary* xxxiv, pp. 70–72, and 232–234.
‘Discoveries of Roman Remains in Britain, IV’: *Class. Rev.* xii, pp. 83 f.
‘Roman Shoe found at Birdoswald’: *Ibid.*, p. 142.
‘Notes on the Inscribed Tubs found at Silchester (Hants)’: *Archaeologia* lvi, pp. 122 f.
‘Report of the Cumberland Excavation Committee, 1897’: *C. and W. Trans.* xv, pp. 172–188.
‘Notes on Samian Ware’: *Ibid.*, pp. 191–196.
‘Inscriptions preserved at Birdoswald’: *Ibid.*, pp. 197–200.
‘Newly discovered Roman Inscription at Housesteads’: *P.S.A.N.* (2nd ser.) viii, pp. 208 f.
‘Further Inscriptions from Housesteads’: *Ibid.*, pp. 253 f.
‘The Roman “Limes” in Germany’ [Abstract of a paper by Prof. Schumacher in *Neue Heidelberger Jahrbücher*]: *Ibid.*, pp. 207 f.
‘Roman Uses of Roman Tombstones’: *Chester Journ.* vi, pp. 137 f.
‘An Inscribed Fragment from Shoemaker's Row [Chester]’: *Ibid.*, pp. 139 f.
‘On the name “Watling Street”’: *Ibid.*, pp. 249 f.
‘Military Aspects of Roman Britain’: Traill's ‘Social England’ (2nd ed.) i, pp. 42–64.
‘The English before England’: *Ibid.*, pp. 110–114.
‘Roman Roads in Britain’: *Athenaeum*, November 12th.
‘Die Hadriansmauer in Nordengland’ [in German]: *K. Westd. Z.* xvii, 9.
Topographical Model of Syracuse (2nd ed.).
‘Henry Nettleship’ [in German]: *Biogr. Jahrb.* xxii, pp. 79–81.

1899.

'A Catalogue of the Sculptured and Inscribed [Roman] Stones in the Cathedral Library, Durham': (Thomas Caldcleugh, Durham).

'The Roman World': D. G. Hogarth's 'Authority and Archaeology, Sacred and Profane', pp. 296–331.

'Roman Britain': *Edinburgh Review* clxxxix, pp. 369–390.

'The Fall of the Western Roman Empire': *Ibid.*, cxc, pp. 170–189.

'Quarterly Notes on Roman Britain': *Antiquary* xxxv, pp. 39–41, 70–72, 248–250, and 364 f.

'On an Altar to Silvanus found near Barr Hill, and on the Roman Occupation of Scotland' [with list of coins]: Glasgow Archaeological Society's 'Antonine Wall Report', pp. 153–168.

'Did Agricola invade Ireland?': *Class. Rev.* xiii, pp. 302 f.

'On *Eques* for *Equus*': *Ibid.*, pp. 305 f.

'Five Years' Excavation on the Roman Wall': *C. and W. Trans.* xv, pp. 337–344.

'Report of the Cumberland Excavation Committee for 1898': *Ibid.*, pp. 345–364.

'Roman Altar at Bewcastle': *Ibid.*, pp. 459 f.

'Roman Inscribed and Sculptured Stones preserved at Tullie House, Carlisle': *Ibid.*, pp. 461–503. [Also published separately.]

'Romano-Gaulish Statuette found in Carlisle': *Ibid.*, pp. 504–6.

'On a Roman Altar from Bewcastle (Cumberland)': *P.S.A.L.* (2nd ser.) xvii, p. 296.

'On the excavation of a Roman Road in Blenheim Park': *Ibid.*, pp. 333–335.

'On a Greek inscription from Oxfordshire': *Ibid.*, xviii. pp. 9 f.

'Account of some Romano-British remains in the Upper Thames Valley': *Ibid.*, pp. 10–16.

'Notes on the discovery of a Roman Building in Northgate Street, Chester': *Chester Journ.* vi, pp. 281 f.

'Notes on the Roman Origin of a Mediaeval Charm' [Cirencester]: *Journ. of the Anthropological Institute* xxix, pp. 306 f.

'The Roman Milestone found at Castleford': *Publications of the Thoresby Society* ix, pp. 97 f. [Reprinted from *Report of the Leeds Philosophical and Literary Society* 1897–98, pp. 19 f.]

'On the ΣΤΡΑΤΗΓΟΙ of Philippi': *Journ. of Theol. Studies* i, pp. 434 f.

'Eine Britannische Inschrift von Agricola' [in German]: *K. Westd. Z.* xviii, 103.

1900.

'Romano-British Hampshire': *Vict. Hist. Hants* i, pp. 265–349.

'Catalogue of the Roman Inscribed and Sculptured Stones in the Grosvenor Museum, Chester': *Chester Journ.* vii, pp. 128, with many illustrations.

'The Roman Conquest of Gaul': *Edinburgh Review* cxcii, pp. 427–449.

'Quarterly Notes on Roman Britain': *Antiquary* xxxvi, pp. 6–8, 105–106, and 334–336.
'Agricola's Invasion of Ireland (?)': *Class. Rev.* xiv, p. 53.
'The Bridge at Aricia': *Ibid.*, pp. 86 f.
'The Census of Sulpicius Quirinius': *Ibid.*, p. 309.
'On an inscribed Roman ingot of Cornish tin, and Roman tin-mining in Cornwall': *P.S.A.L.* (2nd ser.) xviii, pp. 117–122.
'A Roman Charm from Cirencester': *Arch. Journ.* lvi, pp. 319–322.
'The Sepulchral Banquet on Roman Tombstones': *Ibid.*, pp. 326–331.
'Report of the Cumberland Excavation Committee for 1899': *C. and W. Trans.* xvi, pp. 80–99.
'The Place-name Drumburgh, with List of Spellings': *Ibid.*, pp. 100–103.
'Note on the Antiquity of the Wheel Causeway': *P.S.A. Scot.* xxxiv, pp. 129 f.
'On a Hoard of Roman Coins found at Carhayes, Cornwall': *Num. Chron.* (3rd ser.) xx, pp. 209–217.
'Roman Britain in 1899': *Athenaeum*, January 13th.

1901.

'Roman Britain in 1900': *Athenaeum*, January 5th.
'Roman Remains at Inchtuthil': *Ibid.* September, 7th.
'Henry of Huntingdon and Geoffrey of Monmouth': *Ibid.*, April 6th.
'Romano-British Norfolk': *Vict. Hist. Norfolk* i, pp. 279–323.
'Romano-British Worcestershire': *Vict. Hist. Worcestershire* i, pp. 199–221.
'Quarterly Notes on Roman Britain': *Antiquary* xxxvii, pp. 12–14 and 341–343.
'Tac. *Germ.* 13': *Jour. Phil.* xxvii, p. 228.
'Report of the Cumberland Excavation Committee for 1900': *C. and W. Trans.* (n.s.) i, pp. 75–92.
'Excavations at Rudchester': *P.S.A.N.* (2nd ser.) x, pp. 81 f.
'On a Hoard of Roman Coins found near Eastbourne in 1899': *Sussex Arch. Coll.* xliv, pp. 1–8.
'Funde aus England' [Gellygaer, Birdoswald, Chesters, etc.: in German]: *Arch. Anz.* xvi, pp. 80 f.

1902.

Map of Roman Britain (with introductory note and list of places) in Poole's 'Historical Atlas of Modern Europe' (xv).
'Excavations at Chesters in September, 1900': *Arch. Ael.* (2nd ser.) xxiii, pp. 9–21.
'Note [on the same]': *Ibid.*, p. 268.
'Roman Britain in 1901': *Athenaeum*, March 15th.
'Quarterly Notes on Roman Britain': *Antiquary* xxxviii, pp. 107–109, 175 f. and 376 f.
'Romano-British Northamptonshire': *Vict. Hist. Northants* i, pp. 157–222.
'Report of the Cumberland Excavation Committee for 1901': *C. and W. Trans.* (n.s.) ii, pp. 384–392.

'Two Hoards of Roman Coins found in Somersetshire in 1666': *Arch. Journ.* lix, pp. 342–345.
'Two Hoards of Roman Coins [from Sussex and Norfolk]': *Num. Chron.* (4th ser.) ii, pp. 184–186.
'Find of Roman Silver Coins near Caistor, Norfolk': *Ibid.*, pp. 186–188.
'Funde aus Grossbritannien' [Caerwent, Gellygaer, Hadrian's Wall, etc.: in German]: *Arch. Anz.* xvii, pp. 105 f.
'Roman Walls (Recent Excavations)': *Encycl. Brit.* (10th ed.) xxxii, pp. 279–81.
'Silchester': *Ibid.*, pp. 625–627.
Map of Roman Britain: Frontispiece to illustrated ed. of Traill's 'Social England', vol. i.
'The Roman Army in Britain': *Ibid.*, pp. 76–106.
'The Art of Roman Britain': *Ibid.*, pp. 136–161.
'The English before England': *Ibid.*, pp. 161–167.

1903.

'Roman Britain in 1902': *Athenaeum*, April 18th.
'A Roman Inscription at Caerwent': *Ibid.*, September 26th.
'The Aucissa Fibulae': *Arch. Journ.* lx, pp. 236–246.
'Liskeard, Legio': *Ibid.*, pp. 285–288.
'Report of the Cumberland Excavation Committee for 1902': *C. and W. Trans.* (n.s.) iii, pp. 328–349.
Review of Rice Holmes's 'Caesar's Conquest of Gaul': *Eng. Hist. Rev.* xviii, pp. 332–336.
'Roman Forts in South Wales': *Arch. Cambr.* (6th ser.) iii, pp. 12–15.
'The Forts and the Hyginian Camp compared': J. Ward's 'The Roman Fort of Gellygaer', pp. 99–101.
'A Roman Inscription from Worthing': *Suss. Coll.* xlvi, pp. 155–162.
'Cornish Tin': *Mélanges Boissier* (Paris), pp. 249–253.
'Funde aus England' [Merthyr, Castlecary, etc.: in German]: *Arch. Anz.* xviii, p. 109.
'Römische Inschriften aus Britannien: neuer Statthalter' [in German]: *K. Westd. Z.* xxii, 86.
'Theodor Mommsen': *Athenaeum*, November 7th.

1904.

'Roman Britain in 1903': *Athenaeum*, February 6th.
'Romano-British Warwickshire': *Vict. Hist. Warwickshire* i, pp. 223–249.
'Report of the Cumberland Excavation Committee, 1903': *C. and W. Trans.* (n.s.), iv, pp. 239–249.
'On a Roman Inscribed Slab from the Tyne': *Arch. Ael.* (2nd ser.) xxv, pp. 142–147.
'Theodor Mommsen' [obituary notice]: *Ibid.*, pp. 185–188.
'Excavations at Housesteads: The Inscriptions': *Ibid.*, pp. 277–281.
'On Julius Verus, a Roman Governor of Britain': *P.S.A. Scot.* xxxviii, pp. 454–459.

'The Ribchester Temple': *Lanc. Trans.* liv, pp. 197–202.
'Theodor Mommsen': *Eng. Hist. Rev.* xix, pp. 80–89.
'The Last Days of Silchester': *Ibid.*, pp. 625–631.
'Notes on the Inscribed Tablet [at Brough], and on the Romano-British Name of Brough': *Derbyshire Journ.* xxvi, pp. 197–204.
'Funde aus England' [Silchester, Caerwent, London, Brough, Wall of Pius, etc.: in German]: *Arch. Anz.* xix, pp. 145–147.
'Brief Guide to the Portraits in Christ Church Hall, Oxford': Oxford (30 pp.).
'The Roman City of Silchester': *Pearson's Magazine* (Eng. ed.) xviii, pp. 9–17.
'Roman Chester': *Ibid.*, pp. 355–362.
'The Roman City of Bath': *Ibid.*, pp. 484–489.
'Note' to 'Supplement to Catalogue of Roman Inscribed and Sculptured Stones preserved at Tullie House, Carlisle' [see under 1899].

1905.

'Roman Britain in 1904': *Athenaeum*, February 25th.
'Late Celtic': *Ibid.*, November 4th.
'Romano-British Derbyshire': *Vict. Hist. Derbyshire* i, pp. 191–263.
'Notes on Roman Britain': *Class. Rev.* xix, pp. 57 f.
'Recent Literature on Orientius': *Ibid.*, pp. 126–128.
'Caesar *De Bello Gallico* v. 12': *Ibid.*, pp. 206 f.
'Notes on Fibulae': *Arch. Journ.* lxii, pp. 265–269.
'On a small bronze vase of Early Italian work, said to have been found in Bath': *P.S.A.L.* (2nd ser.) xx, pp. 265 f.
'On Roman brooches, and on an inscribed stone found at Caerwent (Mon.)': *Ibid.*, pp. 319 f.
'Caerwent (Römische Inschrift)' [in German]: *K. Westd. Z.* xxiv, 16.
'Funde in England' [Silchester, Caerwent, Benwell, Bar Hill, etc.: in German]: *Arch. Anz.* xx, pp. 97–99.

1906.

'The Romanization of Roman Britain': *British Acad. Proc.* ii, pp. 185–217.
'On two Marble Sculptures and a Mithraic Relief of the Roman period, found in London': *Archaeologia* lx, pp. 43–48.
'Notes on the Mural Problem': *P.S.A.N.* (3rd ser.) ii, pp. 304 f.
'Romano-British Somerset': *Vict. Hist. Somerset* i, pp. 207–371.
'The Roman Occupation of Derbyshire': pp. 9–14 of *Melandra Castle* (Report for 1905 of the Manchester and District Branch of the Classical Association).
'Relics of Roman Defences': *Pearson's Magazine* (Eng. ed.) xxii, pp. 496–500.
'The Ordnance Survey Maps from the Point of View of the Antiquities on them': *Geographical Journ.* xxvii, pp. 165–172.
'Brief Guide to the Portraits in Christ Church Hall, Oxford' (2nd ed.).

1907.

'Henry Pelham': *Athenaeum*, February 16th.
'Three Notes': *Class. Rev.* xxi, pp. 105 f.
'On a fragment of Arretine ware found at Bicester': *P.S.A.L.* (2nd ser.) xxi, pp. 461 f.
'Greek Coins at Exeter' [with G. Macdonald]: *Num. Chron.* (4th ser.) vii, pp. 145–155.
'Late Celtic': *Reliquary* xiii, p. 216.
'Note on Roman Armour found on Tynemouth Bar': *Northumberland County History* viii, pp. 278–80.
'Latin Inscriptions' in *Year's Work* (1906), pp. 75–77.
'Introduction' (pp. 9–13) to A. J. Taylor's 'Catalogue of Roman Remains in Bath'.
'Brief Guide to the Portraits in Christ Church Hall, Oxford' (3rd ed. revised).

1908.

'Romano-British Shropshire' [with M. V. Taylor]: *Vict. Hist. Shropshire* i, pp. 205–278.
'Notes on portions of three Inscriptions found at Silchester': *Archaeologia* lxi, pp. 215–218.
'Henry Francis Pelham, 1846–1907': *British Academy Proc.* iii, pp. 365–370.
'Latin Inscriptions' in *Year's Work* (1907), pp. 78–80.
'Roman Britain': *Ibid.*, pp. 126–131.
'Account of the Corbridge Excavations in 1907, with special reference to the Corbridge Lion': *P.S.A.L.* (2nd ser.) xxii, pp. 300 f.
'Report of Excavations at Corstopitum, 1907': 'Inscriptions': *Arch. Ael.* (3rd ser.) iv, pp. 262–271.

1909.

Revised edition of the English Translation of Mommsen's 'Provinces of the Roman Empire', 2 vols. including 'Appendix: Roman Britain' (ii, pp. 347–354).
'Report on the 1908 Excavations at Corstopitum': 'Inscriptions. Notes on the Smaller Objects': *Arch. Ael.* (3rd ser.) v, pp. 395–424.
'A Roman Tombstone': *Lincolnshire Notes and Queries* x, pp. 193–6.
'Note on a detail in the architecture of Christ Church, Oxford': *P.S.A.L.* (2nd ser.) xxii, pp. 424–429.
'On the Corbridge Excavations in 1908': *Ibid.*, pp. 521 f.
'Note on the Backworth Find': *Northumberland County History* ix, pp. 26–32.
'Roman Dolaucothy': *Trans. of Carmarthenshire Antiq. Soc.*, v, pp. 14 ff.
'Britannien' [Newstead, Corstopitum, Castleshaw, Silchester, 1905–8: in German]: *Arch. Anz.* xxiv, pp. 230–251.

1910.

'Military Aspects of Roman Wales' [with Appendix: 'On the Chronology of Decorated Samian Ware']: *Trans. of the Hon. Soc. of Cymmrodorion* 1908–9, pp. 53–187.

'Ancient Imperialism: Introduction, Roman Empire': *Class. Rev.* xxiv, pp. 105–107.

'On a Roman inscribed tile from Plaxtol, Kent': *P.S.A.L.* (2nd ser.) xxiii, pp. 109–112.

'The Corbridge "Pottery Shop", and other Notes on Samian Ware [Pan Rock]': *Ibid.*, pp. 112–120.

'On the Corbridge Excavations of 1909': *Ibid.*, pp. 213–215.

'Note on the date of part of the great quadrangle of Christ Church, Oxford': *Ibid.*, p. 284.

'On some pieces of Roman pierced (or filigree) bronze work bearing inscriptions': *P.S.A.N.* (3rd ser.) iv, p. 225.

'Report on the 1909 Excavations at Corstopitum': 'Smaller Finds (except coins)': *Arch. Ael.* (3rd ser.) vi, pp. 269–272.

'Sir Robert Sibbald's "Directions for his Honoured Friend Mr. Llwyd how to trace and remarke the Vestiges of the Roman Wall betwixt Forth and Clyde"': *P.S.A. Scot.* xliv, pp. 319–327.

'Romano-British Period [in Herts.]': *Inventory of the Historical Monuments in Hertfordshire*, pp. 3–5.

'Roman Verulam': *Ibid.*, pp. 190 f., with plan.

'Brief Guide to the Portraits in Christ Church Hall, Oxford' (4th ed.).

Various Articles in *Encycl. Brit.* (11th ed.), viz.—'Boadicea' (iv, p. 94); 'Pre-Roman Britain' (iv, p. 583); 'Roman Britain' (iv, pp. 583–589, with map); 'Caerleon' (iv, p. 937); 'Caledonia' (iv, p. 987); 'Cassiterides' (v, p. 460); 'Ermine Street' (ix, p. 750); 'Fosse Way' (x, p. 731); 'Gaul' (xi, pp. 532–534); 'Icknield Street' (xiv, p. 271); 'Roman Army' (xxiii, pp. 471–474); 'Silures' (xxv, p. 109); 'Ancient History of Spain, to A.D. 406' (xxv, pp. 537 f.); 'Thule' (xxvi, pp. 897 f.); 'Trimontium' (xxvii, p. 284); 'Trinovantes' (xxvii, p. 287); 'Watling Street' (xxviii, p. 412).

1911.

'Essays by Henry Francis Pelham', collected and edited with notes and biographical introduction (Clarendon Press: pp. xxiv + 328).

'Roman Britain': *Cambridge Mediaeval History* i, pp. 367–381.

'Roman Scotland': *Edinburgh Review* ccxiii, pp. 468–490.

'Inaugural Address to the Roman Society': *J.R.S.* i, pp. xi–xx.

'Roman London': *Ibid.*, pp. 141–172.

'Note on the Quinquennium Neronis': *Ibid.*, pp. 178 f.

Review of 2nd ed. of Rice Holmes's 'Caesar's Conquest of Gaul': *Class. Rev.* xxv, pp. 257 f.

'Town Planning in the Roman World': *Transactions of the Town Planning Conference, October 1910*, pp. 123–132.

‘ Roman Inscriptions at Bitterne and Minsteracres ’ : *Arch. Journ.* lxviii, pp. 139–148.
‘ On Roman Coins found near Brougham Castle ’ : *C. and W. Trans.* (n.s.), xi, p. 211.
‘ Cotton Julius, F. vi. Notes on Reginald Bainbrigg of Appleby, on William Camden and on some Roman Inscriptions ’ : *Ibid.*, pp. 343–378.
‘ Roman Inscriptions from Cumberland ’ : *Ibid.*, pp. 469–473.
‘ The Corbridge Excavations ’ in *Year's Work* (1910), pp. 122–124.
‘ On the Corbridge Excavations of 1910 ’ : *P.S.A.L.* (2nd ser.) xxiii, pp. 478–489.
‘ A new Roman Inscription found at Corbridge ’ : *P.S.A.N.* (3rd ser.) v, pp. 102–104.
‘ Report of the 1910 Excavations at Corstopitum ’ : ‘ Smaller Objects ’ : *Arch. Ael.* (3rd ser.) vii, pp. 176–202.
‘ Britannien 1909–11 ’ [Wall of Pius, Corbridge, Hadrian's Wall, Silchester, Caerwent, etc. : in German] : *Arch. Anz.* xxvi, pp. 288–307.

1912.

‘ The Romanization of Roman Britain ’ : 2nd ed., greatly enlarged (Clarendon Press, 70 pp.).
‘ Roman History since Mommsen ’ : *Quarterly Review* (217), pp. 323–345.
‘ The Study of Ancient History in Oxford ’ [Lecture to Undergraduates reading for the Lit. Hum. School] (Clarendon Press, 32 pp.).
‘ Representative Examples of Romano-British Sculpture ’ [with H. Stuart Jones] : *J.R.S.* ii, pp. 121–152.
Illustrated Catalogue of the foregoing : 46 pp.
‘ Four Notes on Tacitus ’ [*Annals* i, 2 ; i, 10 ; xii, 35 ; i. 14] : *J.R.S.* ii, pp. 195–200.
‘ Notes on Roman Coast Defences of Britain, especially in Yorkshire ’ : *Ibid.*, pp. 201–214.
‘ Noviomagus ’ : *Vict. Hist. Surrey* iv, pp. 347–349.
‘ On a Roman Altar at Tunstall ’ : *C. and W. Trans.* (n.s.) xii, p. 432.
‘ Roman London ’ : *Proc. Class. Assoc.* ix, pp. 103–111.
‘ On (1) a fragment of Samian ware from Fenny Stratford, and (2) the site of Magiovinium ’ : *P.S.A.L.* (2nd ser.) xxiv, pp. 35–37.
‘ Roman Corbridge ’ in S. F. Dixon's ‘ History of the Saxon Royal Town of Corbridge on Tyne ’, pp. 9–14.
‘ On the Excavations at Corbridge in 1911 ’ : *Ibid.*, pp. 261–272.
‘ Note on an Inscription from Corbridge ’ : *Arch. Journ.* lxix, pp. 524 f.
‘ Note on Bloom of Roman Iron found at Corbridge ’ : *Journ. of Iron and Steel Institute* lxxxv, pp. 132 f.
‘ The Chesterholm Milestone ’ : *P.S.A.N.* (3rd ser.) v, pp. 184 f.
‘ On a Roman Inscription from Mucklebank ’ : *Ibid.*, p. 222.
‘ Report of the 1911 Excavations at Corstopitum ’ : ‘ Smaller Objects ’ : *Arch. Ael.* (3rd ser.) viii, pp. 186–209.

'The Corbridge Excavations' in *Year's Work* (1911), pp. 157–159.

'Ancient Ireland': *Athenaeum*, October 19th.

'H. F. Pelham' in *Dict. Nat. Biogr.* 2nd Suppl. iii, pp. 96 f.

'Brief Guide to the Portraits in Christ Church Hall, Oxford' (5th ed.).

'Roman Remains [in South Bucks.]': *Inventory of the Historical Monuments in Buckinghamshire* i, pp. xxii. f.

'Zur Zeitbestimmung der Sigillatagefässe' [in German]: *Römisch-germanisches Korrespondenzblatt* v, pp. 29 f.

'Britannien 1911–12' [Cappuck, Corbridge, Hadrian's Wall, Saltburn, Wallsend, Castell Collen, etc.: in German]: *Arch. Anz.* xxvii, pp. 483–495.

1913.

'Ancient Town-planning' (Clarendon Press: 152 pp.).

'*Additamenta quinta ad Corporis Vol. vii*': *Ephem. Epigr.* ix, pp. 509–690.

'Ancient Rome and Ireland': *Eng. Hist. Rev.* xxviii, pp. 1–12.

'Portus Itius': *Class. Rev.* xxvii, pp. 258–260.

'Note on the dating of Casterley Camp': *Wilts. Mag.* xxxviii, pp. 82 f.

'On the Excavations at Corbridge in 1912': *P.S.A.L.* (2nd ser.) xxv, pp. 146–157.

'Voreda, the Roman Fort at Plumpton Wall': *C. and W. Trans.* (n.s.) xiii, pp. 177–198.

'Notes on Finds [on line of Roman Wall in Cumberland, 1909–12]': *Ibid.*, pp. 332–335.

'Report of the 1912 Excavations at Corstopitum': 'Inscriptions, Sculptures, Small Objects': *Arch. Ael.* (3rd ser.) ix, pp. 263–276.

'Ambleside Roman Fort': *Ambleside Roman Fort Exploration Committee's First Report*, pp. 1 f.

'Castell Collen': *Times*, October 1st.

'List of Periodicals taken by Oxford College Libraries, the Ashmolean, the Taylorian, and the Indian Institute' (Clarendon Press: 24 pp.).

'Roman Period [in North Bucks.]': *Inventory of the Historical Monuments in Buckinghamshire* ii, pp. 8–11.

'Britannien 1912–13' [Wroxeter, Caerwent, Casterley, Yewden, Corbridge, Balmuildy, Hadrian's Wall, etc.: in German]: *Arch. Anz.* xxviii, pp. 283–304.

Articles [in German] in Pauly-Wissowa's *Real-Encyclopädie* Bd. viii, viz.—'Hibernia' (1388–92), and 'Hunnum' (2615).

1914.

'Roman Britain in 1913': *British Academy Supplem. Papers* ii, 60 pp.

'Notes on the Agricola': *Class. Rev.* xxviii, pp. 43–45.

'Portus Itius'; *Ibid.*, pp. 82–84.

'Legions and *Auxilia*': *Ibid.*, pp. 226 f.

'Roman Silver in Northumberland': *J.R.S.* iv, pp. 1–12.

'On an Inscription of the Alban Salii': *Ibid.*, p. 148.

'Report of the Exploration of the Roman Fort at Ambleside' [with R. G. Collingwood]: *C. and W. Trans.* (n.s.) xiv, pp. 433–465.

'Note on Isolated Bath Buildings': *Festival Book of Salisbury: Salisbury Museum* 1864–1914, pp. 24 f.

'On the Excavations at Corbridge in 1913': *P.S.A.L.* (2nd ser.) xxvi, pp. 185–188.

'Report of the 1913 Excavations at Corstopitum': 'Inscriptions and Sculptured Stones', and 'Potters' Stamps and Small Objects': *Arch. Ael.* (3rd ser.) xi, pp. 306–310.

'An Account of the Roman Remains in the Parish of Corbridge-on-Tyne': *Northumberland County History* x, pp. 457–522. [Also published separately with 31 additional illustrations.]

'Roman Sculpture at Nettleton Scrub, near Castlecombe': *Proc. Bath and District Branch of Somersets. Arch. and Nat. Hist. Soc.* pp. 50 f.

'The Battle between Boadicea and Suetonius': *Antiquary* l, pp. 439 f.

'Britannien 1913–14' [Ythan Wells, Wall of Pius, Traprain Law, Corbridge, Ribchester, Wroxeter, Colchester, Lowbury, etc.: in German]: *Arch. Anz.* xxix, pp. 392–408.

Articles [in German] in Pauly-Wissowa's *Real-Encyclopädie* Bd. i A, viz.—'Raeba' (39); 'Rat(a?)' (258); 'Ratae Coritanorum' (258 f.); "'Ρατοστάβιος" (266 f.); 'Ravius' (310); 'Ravonia' (310); 'Regia' (469); 'Regni' (509); 'Regnum' (509); 'Regulbium' (511 f.); 'Repandunum' (602); "'Ρεριγόνιον" (615); 'Ricina' (799); 'Riduna' (802); 'Riga' (803); "'Ριγόδουνον" (804); 'Robogdii' (951); 'Rutunium' (1283 f.); 'Rutupiae' (1284); 'Sabrina' (1608 f.); 'Sacrum promuntorium' (1688); 'Salinae' (1902); 'Sambis' (2122).

## 1915.

'Roman Britain in 1914': *British Academy Supplem. Papers* iii, 68 pp.

'The Romanization of Roman Britain'; 3rd ed., further enlarged (Clarendon Press, 92 pp.).

'Herodotus and Babylon': *Class. Rev.* xxix, pp. 169 f. and 239.

'The Romano-British Names of Ravenglass and Borrans (Muncaster and Ambleside)': *Arch. Journ.* lxxii, pp. 77–84.

'Note on a Roman Milestone found near Appleby in 1694, and lately refound': *C. and W. Trans.* (n.s.) xv, pp. 132–134.

'Catalogue of Roman Inscribed and Sculptured Stones, Coins, Earthenware, etc., discovered in and near the Roman Fort at Maryport and preserved at Netherhall' [with J. B. Bailey]: *Ibid.*, pp. 138–172.

'The Roman Road in the Upper Duddon Valley': *Ibid.*, pp. 191 f.

'Newly Discovered Roman Altars': *Arch. Ael.* (3rd ser.) xii, pp. 201–205.

'On a Roman Inscribed Tile found at Corbridge': *Ibid.*, pp. 272 f.

'Conspectus of Potters' Stamps on plain Samian Ware found at Corbridge, 1906–1914': *Ibid.*, pp. 273–286.

'Leonard Cheesman': *J.R.S.* v, pp. 147 f.
'The Name Augustus': *Ibid.*, pp. 249 f.
'Leonard Cheesman': *Class. Rev.* xxix, pp. 222 f.
'Slack, Greetland, Cambodunum': *Yorks. Journ.* xxiii, pp. 395–398.
'Old Sarum and Sorbiodunum': *Wilts. Mag.* xxxix, pp. 22–29. [Reprinted, with a few additions, from *Eng. Hist. Rev.* xxx, pp. 1–5.]
'The Ancestry of Albrecht Dürer': *Burlington Magazine* xxvii, p. 78.

1916.

'Roman Notes': *C. and W. Trans.* (n.s.) xvi, pp. 282–286.
'Modius Claytoniensis: The Roman Bronze Measure from Carvoran': *Arch. Ael.* (3rd ser.) xiii, pp. 85–102.
'Tacitus during the late Roman period and the Middle Ages': *J.R.S.* vi, pp. 196–201.
'Roman History, with Inscriptions' in *Year's Work* (1915), pp. 63–70.
'Some Roman Conceptions of Empire': *Occasional Publications of the Classical Assoc.* no. 4 (18 pp.).
'Holt': *Arch. Cambr.* (6th ser.) xvi, pp. 222–232.
'Pre-Roman and Roman Remains [in Essex]': *Inventory of the Historical Monuments in Essex* i, pp. xxi–xxv.
'Roman Country-House by the Evenlode River, Northleigh (East End), Oxon.': Leaflet (4 pp.).
'Introduction' (pp. iv–viii) to 'The Romano-British Site on Lowbury Hill in Berks.' by Donald Atkinson (Univ. Coll. Reading Studies in Hist. and Archaeol.).
Review of Bushe-Fox's 'Excavations at Hengistbury Head': *Man* xvi, pp. 45–48.
Articles [in German] in Pauly-Wissowa's *Real-Encyclopädie* Bd. ix, viz.—'Iceni' (820 f.); 'Icht Mare' (830); 'Iciani' (850); 'Ictis' (857 f.); 'Idumania' (918); 'Iena' (922); 'Iernus' (928); 'Ila' (996); 'Isaca' (2048); 'Isca' (2056); 'Isca Dumnoniorum' (2056 f.); 'Isca Silurum' (2057); 'Iscalis' (2057); 'Isurium Brigantum' (2282 f.); 'Itis' (2366); 'Itius Portus' (2368–70); 'Ituna' (2377).

1917.

'The First Days of Carlisle': *C. and W. Trans.* (n.s.) xvii, pp. 235–250.
'Roman History, with Inscriptions': *Year's Work* (1916), pp. 53–56.
'Arretine Fragments in Cambridgeshire' [Barrington and Foxton]: *Cambridge Antiq. Soc. Proc. and Communic.* xx, pp. 53–59.

1918.

'The Roman Name of Birdoswald Fort': *C. and W. Trans.* (n.s.) xviii, pp. 223–228.
'Early Northumbrian Christianity and the Altars to the Di Veteres': *Arch. Ael.* (3rd ser.) xv, pp. 22–43.
'Roman Leicester': *Arch. Journ.* lxxv, pp. 1–46.

'Roman History' in *Year's Work* (1917), pp. 75–77.
'Agricola and the Antonine Wall': *P.S.A. Scot.* lii, pp. 174–181.
'Centuriation in Roman Britain': *Eng. Hist. Rev.* xxxiii, pp. 289–296.
'On a Roman Inscribed Bronze Plaque, in the Taunton Museum': *Somerset Proc.* lxiii, pp. 60–62.
Review of 3rd ed. of Codrington's 'Roman Roads in Britain': *Eng. Hist. Rev.* xxxiv, pp. 245 ff.

1919.

'Augustus': *Class. Rev.* xxxiii, pp. 65 f.
'Catalogue of Romano-British Fibulae in the Museum, Tullie House, Carlisle': *C. and W. Trans.* (n.s.) xix, pp. 1–16.
'Note' on the Roman Road in the Duddon Valley: *Ibid.*, pp. 28 f.
'The Character of the Roman Empire as seen in West Somerset' [Presidential Address]: *Somerset Proc.* lxiv, pp. xxiii–xxxvii.
'Roman Christian Inscriptions on Exmoor': *Ibid.*, pp. xxxviii f.
'The Place-name "Chester" in Somersetshire': *Ibid.*, pp. xxxix–xlii.
'Centuriation in Roman Essex': *Trans. of the Essex Archaeological Soc.* xv (n.s.), pp. 115–125. [Reprinted, with Appendix, from *Eng. Hist. Rev.* xxxiii.]
Articles [in German] in Pauly-Wissowa's *Real-Encyclopädie* Bd. x, viz.—'Kairener' (1507), and "Κασσιτερίδες" (2328–32).

1920.

'The Roman Empire in the First Century': *Peake's Commentary on the Bible*, pp. 612–617.
'Roman Cirencester' [with appendices by W. H. Stevenson, H. Stuart Jones, and M. Rostovtzeff]: *Archaeologia* lxix, pp. 161–209.
'The Provisioning of Roman Forts' [with R. G. Collingwood]: *C. and W. Trans.* (n.s.) xx, pp. 127–142.
'Old Carlisle': *Ibid.*, pp. 143–150.

1921.

Articles [in German] in Pauly-Wissowa's *Real-Encyclopädie* Bd. ii A, viz.—'Saudonium' (255), and 'Saxonicum Litus' (327–334).

PLATE I WILLIAM CAMDEN

## LECTURE I

# THE STUDY OF ROMAN BRITAIN: A RETROSPECT

No Empire has left so great a name as Rome. None has so thoroughly conquered its barbarian conquerors and set so deep a mark on the memory of succeeding generations. When it fell, barbarian statesmen copied its administrative forms, barbarian writers learnt its language, barbarian genealogists set themselves seriously to prove that their own races, if they only knew it, were lost tribes, perhaps of that Trojan stock from which the Romans themselves were sprung. All origins were traced to Rome, and historians opened their narratives by connecting their subject with the Roman Empire. Even in Britain, where the English conquest broke the Romano-British tradition sharp across, and where Celtic legends (if they be Celtic) told of native resistance to Rome, men were eager from early days to preface the story of England by a Roman foreword. The *Historia Brittonum* and Bede and the Saxon Chronicle and many other books and writers gave the Roman Empire a place in their first chapters.

This was only a beginning. The actual study of Roman Britain by writers who possessed some kind of historical and antiquarian interest dawns, faintly enough, in the twelfth century. Then the fusion of Norman and English learning and sentiments and traditions produced a little group of mostly monkish historians, tinged with a nascent antiquarianism. It is not very easy to appraise this twelfth-century antiquarianism. Its traces are few, and it has been too little regarded by modern scholars. But the evidence is clear that, in the reigns of Henry I and his successors, men began to note ancient remains, to tell each other about them, to record in their histories what they had heard or seen, and to look on it as historical material. This may be observed in all the important chroniclers who published during the twelfth century—Florence of Worcester and William of Malmesbury and Henry of Huntingdon in its earlier half, Giraldus Cambrensis and Roger Hoveden nearer its close. It may be seen also in their more illustrious contemporary, Geoffrey of Monmouth, who lived for years in Oxford just before the teaching elements there coalesced into a guild, and who probably wrote his *British History* during his sojourn.[1]

The antiquarianism of these men did not limit itself to things Romano-British. It was not in any sense specialized. Nor have its fruits great value, if judged by modern standards. I may cite a specimen from William of Malmesbury.[2] In his account of Carlisle he mentions a '*triclinium*'—I suppose, a large room—made of exceedingly hard Roman work and inscribed in front MARII VICTORIAE. It was, no doubt, the common dedication MARTI ET VICTORIAE, of which examples have been found in many places; William, however, suggests that Cimbri, defeated by the Roman general Marius, had fled to Cumberland and set it up. We may look with a melancholy pleasure at the first copy of a Roman inscription made by any English antiquary. But the Cimbri who fled to Cumberland and recorded their defeat in Latin, are an example of the irrational etymologizing common to the antiquaries of nearly all ages.

Nor again had these writers valuable documents or traditions now lost to us. Once or twice, as in Henry of Huntingdon's story of King Coel at Colchester, we get a piece of what may be local folk-lore or local

[1] See note on 'Geoffrey of Monmouth and Oxford' by the Rev. H. E. Salter in *Eng. Hist. Rev.* xxxiv (1910), pp. 382–5.

[2] *Gesta Pontificum*, iii. 99.

patriotism.[1] But of true record or direct tradition of Romano-British times, preserved in no other older source, there is not the slightest trace either in Henry or in any of his contemporaries; they tell us things familiar from other and older writers. Geoffrey of Monmouth, of course, had (as he asserts) the "very ancient book in the British tongue" in which he found all manner of things otherwise unknown. The statement is by no means improbable. But, for all that, the pages of Geoffrey contain no new 'fact' about Roman Britain which is also true. It has, indeed, been suggested by so good a judge as the late Bishop Stubbs—though only in an *obiter dictum*—that Geoffrey's references to Silchester show that he possessed some authority now lost who called his attention to the place as one suitable for use in his fiction. Yet the mere circumstance that he knew only the English name Silchester is sufficient to disprove the idea. Had he used a genuinely ancient authority, he would have employed the Roman name according to his general custom. It is much more likely that he was indebted to some fellow-antiquary for his information. The ruins of Roman towns were being noted at the time when he wrote; he seems to have heard of the remains of Silchester—the ruined walls, we may suppose, that still stand in sombre state some thirty miles from Oxford

[1] Mr. W. H. Stevenson considers it improbable that even local folk-lore or local patriotism was responsible for the connexion of King Coel with Colchester (O.E. *Colneceaster*, from the river *Colne*, O.E. *Coln*(*e*)). Rather it is an invention of Geoffrey of Monmouth (v. 6). Mr. Stevenson adds: "Geoffrey identified Colchester with the Caer Colun of the Welsh list of cities [see *infra*, pp. 290 ff.], which the inaccurate printed text reproduces as Kaercolvin. This cannot be derived from the Middle Welsh *Coel*, which descends through Old Welsh *Coil* from a British **Caelos*. If it had been a local tradition taken over by the English in the fifth or sixth century, the name would have resembled the British, not the Middle Welsh form. If taken over as *Coil*, we should have expected an O.E. *Cel* to have resulted. That Henry derived the story and the preposterous assertion that Helen was of British birth from Geoffrey is shown by the fact that both appear in the abstract that he made of Geoffrey's pretended history at Bec in 1139, printed in the Chronicle of Robert of Torigny, ed. Howlett (Rolls Series), p. 72."

—and he inserted the place in his narrative under the only name by which he knew it. Thus it became a city where mythical British princes were crowned or were buried, and a contemporary writer, either inspired by Geoffrey's tales or using his own knowledge of the ruins, gave it, as we shall see, an ancient (though not a Roman) name.

The real importance of these twelfth-century antiquaries lies in their influence on succeeding writers. Many of the incorrect statements in later archaeological books—far more than most readers suspect—date from one or other of them. From this point of view the most significant among them is probably Henry of Huntingdon. He was born in the Fens about 1084, published his *Historia Anglorum* in various editions between 1130 and 1154, and died as archdeacon of Huntingdon in 1155. His history, describing his own and earlier times, is a dull heavy work which has won little praise from those best able to judge. But he knew something of local antiquities ; he was aware of ruins such as those of Silchester, or of Chesterton and Castor in his own country near Peterborough, and he makes occasional references to Roman Britain. These references are based partly upon his own knowledge, partly upon earlier writers like his contemporary Geoffrey of Monmouth [1] or like Bede, and partly perhaps upon his own invention. Two or three instances will show how he has handed on to later writers incorrect and misleading ideas.

The *Historia Brittonum* enumerates in an appendix

[1] The first edition of the *Historia Anglorum*, issued in 1130 and preserved in the Hengwrt and All Souls MSS., lacks several statements which occur in the later editions from 1139 onwards. They are plainly taken from Geoffrey's book, which had been published in the interval ; see F. H.'s note in *Athenaeum*, April 6, 1901. Mr. W. H. Stevenson points out that even the two MSS. of the 'first edition' are already contaminated with the pseudo-history of Geoffrey : they contain the statement about Coel and Colchester. Mr. Arnold has shown (Rolls Series ed. of Henry of Huntingdon, p. xlii) that both MSS. are derived from a copy of the first edition that was written in 1163.

twenty-eight or (according to a later version) thirty-three '*civitates*' or 'cairs' of Britain. The origin of the list is unknown; it seems post-Roman in date and probably refers mainly to Wales.[1] Thanks to Henry, it has been applied to all Britain. He was the first who set himself to identify the 'cities',[2] and some of his identifications, however worthless, recur in later writers to this day. Thus, he identified Cair Segeint—possibly Segontium, now Carnarvon—with Silchester, apparently (as Bishop Stubbs thought) for no better reason than that Segeint and Silchester both began with 'S', and that he had somehow heard of the ruins of Silchester. Again, he interpolated into the list a Kair-Dorm and equated it with Dormeceastre, that is, with the Castor and Chesterton whose ruins he knew. Such identifications have died hard; rather, they are not yet dead.[3]

A still more notable example of antiquarian invention is supplied by Henry's dealings with the four great roads of Saxon England. The Laws attributed to Edward the Confessor and the *Leges Willelmi*, both of them documents later than the Conquest, mention four privileged Royal Roads (*Chimini Regii*) as a special group of highways—Foss Way, Icknield Street, Watling Street, Ermine Street; and the statement is repeated in many later writers. It appears to be a Norman figment. The individual names of these four roads do indeed occur in pre-Conquest documents. But no reference to them, or to any four roads, as a special class has been cited from any pre-Conquest source; and it is significant that the later writers who speak of the group or class were not agreed as to where two out of the four roads really ran. Apparently the grouping of the four names is due to the antiquaries or the lawyers of the twelfth century, who conceived the idea of Four Roads having a special legal

[1] For a detailed discussion of this list, see Appendix, *infra*, pp. 289 ff.
[2] *Hist. Angl.* i. 3.
[3] Thus, one of them has even found its way into a recent volume of Pauly-Wissowa's *Real-Encyclopädie* (ii. A. 1086).

status, and selected names for them from road-names used in older charters. That in itself would not much matter. But Henry put the Four Roads into his book [1] and assigned them definite or, rather, indefinite courses: Icknield Street, he says, ran from east to west, Ermine Street from south to north, Watling Street from Canterbury to Chester, and the Foss Way from 'Totenes' in the far west to 'Catenes' or Caithness at the other end of Scotland.[2] Whether he invented these routes or whether he borrowed them, is not quite certain; probably there is room for something of both explanations. But his account has in either case no authority. Yet it forms the basis of much subsequent discussion on the 'Four Roads'. Hence come the frequent statements that the chief roads of Roman Britain were the four mentioned above, and the frequent efforts of antiquaries to fit the actual Roman roads into a category of four main highways. As a matter of fact, the real road-system of Roman Britain, as we shall learn by and by, differs markedly from the alleged *Chimini Regii*, and the Icknield Street is not a Roman road at all.[3] Henry has merely misled succeeding scholars down to our own day. Even Guest in his well-known paper on the Four Roman Ways [4] did not quite realize the truth.

Another fiction for the dissemination of which Henry

[1] *Hist. Angl.* i. 7.

[2] *Scilicet a principio Cornugalliae in finem Scottiae*, as he explains; or from Land's End to John O'Groats, as we should put it nowadays.

[3] That part (if it be a part) of its course which follows the crest of the Berkshire Downs and the Chilterns is older than the Romans and was probably very little used by them. Only a section near Dunstable and another near Little Kimble (*Inventory of the Historical Monuments of Buckinghamshire* i, p. xxiii, and ii, p. 2) can be called in any sense Roman. But the actual line is very uncertain at many points. Mr. W. H. Stevenson remarks that the boundaries of the pre-Norman charters in the Abingdon Chartulary prove that the Icknield Way was not the Ridge Way but the Port Way at the foot of the Downs. Cf. Prof. Stenton in Atkinson's *Romano-British Site on Lowbury Hill*, pp. 29 f., and, more recently, G. B. Grundy in *Arch. Journ.* lxxv, pp. 124 f.

[4] *Origines Celticae* ii, pp. 218 ff.

is mainly responsible concerns an important detail of Romano-British Christianity. It is commonly said that a bishopric or archbishopric existed at Caerleon-on-Usk in Monmouthshire. This is the invention of Geoffrey. He had seen the ruins of Caerleon. He was ready, as Welshmen and all other true patriots are, to glorify his native land, and in his *History*, and possibly also in another document, he ascribed the ecclesiastical primacy of Roman Britain to his own country.[1] Henry, too, had heard of the ruins of Caerleon, presumably from Geoffrey, and in the second edition of his book he borrowed from the Welshman two references to the archbishopric of Caerleon.[2] As a matter of fact, Caerleon in Roman times seems to have been a legionary fortress with very little in the way of a town or other civilian settlement attached to it, and it is a most unlikely spot for a bishop or archbishop to choose as his seat, to say nothing of the fact that archbishops were unknown in Western Europe till the seventh century. However, the story passed into regular history, and it still survives even in works of established learning.

[1] *History*, ix. 12. The other document is the *Liber Landavensis* or *Book of Llan dâv*. J. Gwenogvryn Evans in his edition of the latter (Oxford, 1893) argues (pp. xviii ff.) that the oldest MS., which he considers to be the original copy, was written about or after 1150, certainly after 1133 and before 1154. He suggests that the text was composed by Geoffrey of Monmouth, but his reasons are not very definite. On the other hand, this theory is rejected on stylistic grounds by Loth in *Rev. Celtique* xv (1894), pp. 101 ff. So, too, H. Williams in his *Christianity in Early Britain* (Oxford, 1912) declines to admit the possibility of Geoffrey having been the compiler (p. 124). He assigns the work to the ten years between 1140 and 1150 (p. 299), and believes (p. 120) that the author and Geoffrey borrowed independently from the *Liber Pontificalis*. Mr. W. H. Stevenson adds that Geoffrey gives the names of the envoys sent by the fictitious British King Lucius to the pope as Faganus and Duvianus (iv. 19), whereas the *Liber Landavensis* (ed. Evans, p. 68) calls them Eluanus and Meduuinus; and that Geoffrey copied Bede and not the *Liber Pontificalis*, echoing his phraseology and accepting his erroneous date. All that is certain is that the *Book of Llan dâv* must have been written after the *History*. Its archbishoprics, etc., are Galfridian.

[2] *Hist. Angl.* i. 3 and 5.

This twelfth-century antiquarianism and romance set the fashion for four hundred years. The chroniclers of the thirteenth and fourteenth centuries copied—not seldom they copied out—their predecessors, and even the earliest histories of England which appeared in print, Holinshed, Harrison and others, kept much of the old tradition. A new era dawned with the Renaissance, and in particular with the Elizabethan age. Then Englishmen became proud of their own country and curious about her, and histories and topographies were written with a new inspiration and on new methods. Then, too, books that had hitherto lain virtually unknown in manuscript, emerged into the publicity of printed circulation, and provided the needful matter for students, encouraged by the new patriotism and the new learning.

The great scholars of the Renaissance were foreigners, and the first steps were taken abroad. Two works of great value for Romano-British as for all ancient topography, the *Geography* of Ptolemy and the *Itinerary of Antoninus*, were now edited on the Continent, the former towards the end of the fifteenth century,[1] and the latter at the beginning of the sixteenth (1512). Both works, so far as they here concern us, are mere lists of names. Ptolemy enumerates—in a style which manuals of geography still sometimes employ—the towns, rivers, capes, estuaries, tribes of the various parts of the world known to him, and among them those of the islands which he calls Ivernia and Alvion, and adds to each its latitude and longitude. The *Itinerary* sets forth the names of towns or posting-stations along selected Roman roads and, save that these roads are chosen on no now discoverable plan, it is very much like an eighteenth-century

[1] The *editio princeps* was produced at Vicenza, 13 Sept. 1475, by Hermann Lichtenstein. Others followed rapidly. The first of the various Rome editions, the earliest to be published with maps, was issued in 1478. In the same year or in 1480 an Italian metrical paraphrase in terza rima by Francesco Berlinghieri appeared at Florence. See Wilberforce Eames, *List of Editions of Ptolemy's Geography*, 1475–1730 (New York, 1886).

coaching guide. The ordinary references to Roman Britain in ancient writers—Tacitus, Caesar, Dio—contain very few place-names. Such lists as those of Ptolemy therefore assume an even greater importance for Britain than for other lands. Their influence upon Romano-British research has been enormous.

Both Ptolemy and the *Itinerary* obviously require a commentary. The *Itinerary* found at first no commentator. But Ptolemy received some sort of elucidation in 1535 from a scholar who is best known for other and more serious reasons, Michael Servetus of Villanova in Spain, physician, physiologist, theologian and, in the end, victim of Calvin. When barely twenty-six years old, this versatile and original thinker issued at Lyons an edition of Ptolemy in which " obsolete names of cities are set forth in modern fashion " by means of brief marginal identifications. His British identifications, seventy-seven in number, do not carry us very far forward. He explains correctly a dozen familiar names—Londinium, Eburacum, and the like; that he could hardly help, for they had been known throughout the Middle Ages. But the rest of his guesses are as bad as those of Henry of Huntingdon. Doubtless he knew little of England; probably he took a contemporary map of it, and connected Ptolemy's place-names with any modern names thereon which began with the same initial letters and fell within the proper districts. This method was less irrational than it sounds. In Italy, Spain and France, the lands where Servetus was most at home, modern towns frequently stand on Roman sites and their names preserve fragments of the Roman appellations. Unfortunately it was useless in Britain. Here the towns rarely stand on Roman sites, and the Roman appellations have seldom survived, except in obscure and distorted forms not likely to be known to a Spaniard in 1535. A few examples will show how he went astray. Thus, he interpreted Dunum, according to Ptolemy a bay, as Durham; Bremenium, now recognized to be Rochester in Northumberland, as Berwick;

Cataractonium, Catterick in Yorkshire, as Carlisle; Mediolanum as Manchester; Victoria, put by Ptolemy in Scotland, as Wigton in Cumberland. But, bad as we now see them to be, his guesses passed into later sixteenth-century works, such as the great Latin and English Dictionary issued by Sir Thomas Elyot in 1538, and the Geographical Lexicon which Abraham Ortelius published at Antwerp in 1578; they have even influenced later theories on Roman Britain. Thus, quite apart from the fact that it was a pioneer effort, his edition has left its mark.

Foreign scholars have rarely mastered English geography. Success in Romano-British studies began only when Englishmen took up the task. Robert Talbot, a Wykehamist of Winchester and New College, was the first to edit and comment upon a portion of the *Itinerary* (1547).[1] Humfrey Lhuyd from North Wales, William Harrison, and others followed quickly.[2] All of them—*fortes ante Agamemnona*—were soon obscured by a greater man. William Camden, born in 1551, graduate of Christ Church and afterwards founder of the Camden Chair of Ancient History in Oxford, nevertheless made his home and found his inspiration away from the University. In the intervals of a schoolmaster's life—he was Usher and then Headmaster of Westminster from 1575 to 1597—and in the leisure which his friends secured for his later years, he travelled up and down England, examined antiquities, searched libraries, corresponded with many helpers in England and abroad, and prepared his *Britannia*, a "chorographical description of the flourishing kingdoms of England, Scotland, Ireland, and the islands adjacent", grouped by counties. The first edition came out in 1586; it is a tiny book, easily slipped into a small

[1] His '*Annotationes*' dealt with the British portion of the *Itinerary*, and were first printed '*e codice MS in Bibliotheca Bodleiana*' in Hearne's *Itinerary of John Leland the Antiquary*, 'intermixed with divers curious Discourses', iii (1711).

[2] Lhuyd's *Commentarioli Britannicae Descriptionis Fragmentum* was published at Cologne in 1572, four years after the author's death. Harrison's *Description of England* appeared in 1577.

coat-pocket. Its success was rapid. Though written in Latin, it quickly ran through six editions, and in 1607 it appeared as a stately folio.[1] Scaliger, the greatest scholar of the day, hailed the work with joy and styled its author the British Strabo. The title is not inapt, so far as it refers to the contents of the *Britannia*. But in everything else Camden far outstripped Strabo. The Greek geographer became famous two or three generations after his death. Camden's vogue began with his first year of publication.

The triumph was deserved. In the *Britannia* he condensed, in brief, masterful, perhaps inelegant style, all that was then knowable about our national antiquities, Roman or medieval. He wove together the medieval chronicles and what his own researches had taught him; he took up the study of inscriptions, hitherto unknown in England, rose to the level of contemporary continental learning, and wrote a great book. Much of his popularity, we may admit, was due to the outburst of national pride in Elizabethan England. He described, as no man had done before him, our national antiquities, and the nation welcomed him. But he was no mere child of the moment. He created an organic whole out of a vague, incoherent, ill-understood material. The scholar who does this creates an epoch in historical writing as surely as a Vergil or a Tennyson creates an epoch in literary style.

Doubtless, if we look closely, we find defects—defects, indeed, which matter more to us, who use his results as part of our scientific *data*, than they mattered to average contemporary readers. He was, in the first place, conjectural beyond the verge of unscrupulousness. Everyone knows how, in his wish to prove Oxford older than Cambridge, he interpolated into Asser's *Life of King Alfred* a whole chapter on Oxford University, a chapter which is proven false alike by external evidence and by its own diction.[2] Not every one realizes that he allowed

[1] This folio is the volume which Camden has open before him in the portrait reproduced in Plate I.

[2] Chap. 83 B. See W. H. Stevenson's ed. of Asser (Oxford, 1904), pp. xxiii ff.

himself equal licence in minor details. His texts of Roman inscriptions, for example, are not infrequently adorned with his own guesses. It is not wholly surprising. He must often have had before him an imperfect copy, with no post to bring him rapid corrections and few local correspondents to verify details. The temptation to emend was natural. Unfortunately he emended silently and emended frequently.[1]

Again, he had no hesitation in altering place-names which he wished to explain. I will give two or three instances. There is in Northamptonshire a small town called Towcester, where Roman remains have been found, on the Roman road, Watling Street. There was in the same district a Roman posting-station, Tripontium, mentioned in the *Itinerary* as on Watling Street. Camden thought to identify the two. So he declared that the true form of Tripontium—the harmless Three Bridges—was 'Torpontium', and that the original name of Towcester was 'Torcester'. He had no evidence on either head. He produced, triumphantly, a disastrous conjecture. For we know now that the Roman name of Towcester was Lactodurum, and that Tripontium was elsewhere.[2] So, again, he wished to identify Thetford in East Anglia with the Sitomagus mentioned in the *Itinerary* as apparently 85 miles north-east of London. He had no evidence that Thetford was a Roman site, and no more that Sitomagus was actually near Thetford.[3] But that was no hindrance. He rechristened the river Thet as 'Sit', and then found no trouble in proving where Sitomagus was. So, once more, when dealing with a Bomium in South Wales, he renamed it 'Bovium' and identified it as Cowbridge in Glamorgan. It is a mercy that he was not attracted by the names of Oxford, Cowley, and Bullingdon to place 'Bovium' on the Isis.

[1] See F. H.'s 'Cotton Iulius F. vi, Notes on Reginald Bainbrigg of Appleby, on William Camden and on some Roman Inscriptions' in *C. and W. Trans.* (n.s.) xi, pp. 343 ff.

[2] *Vict. Hist. Northants* i, pp. 184 and 187, and *Vict. Hist. Warwickshire* i, pp. 230 f.

[3] *Vict. Hist. Norfolk* i, p. 321.

These are faults which the better scholars of Camden's age, the Casaubons and the Scaligers and the de Thous, did not commit, and they have meant a legacy of error to many of Camden's successors. He has left us another legacy for which he may be less reasonably blamed but which, under modern conditions at least, yields unsatisfactory results. He initiated (unless it be that he borrowed from Harrison) the treatment of English antiquities by counties. Such grouping was natural enough in his day and to one who had collected much of his material by his own travels, and his contemporaries accepted it willingly; even before his *Britannia* appeared, the Kentish antiquary, William Lambarde, had issued a *Perambulation* of his own county (1576) and planned a similar account of others. The method still survives. Most of our local archaeology is based on county divisions, and it suits our social and administrative arrangements well enough; for the study of medieval churches and castles it is sometimes even an advantage. But for the Roman period it is harmful. The divisions of our English counties correspond in no single case to any known division of Roman days. The Roman remains of Derbyshire or of Somerset or of Kent are artificial and meaningless groups. They have still to be treated by their counties because the literature and the local societies and perhaps even the readers are also grouped by counties. But the necessity of the practice does not lessen its evils, and we must trace them back to Camden.

Camden's influence ruled throughout the seventeenth century. The greater antiquaries of that period, Dugdale, Ashmole, Ussher and others, so far as they dealt with Roman things, depended largely on Camden, and such books as William Burton's *Commentary on Antoninus his Itinerary* (1658)—a curious product of the Puritan epoch, but notable as being concerned solely with Roman antiquities—are based almost wholly upon him. Eighty or a hundred years later, however, a new movement begins. The first half of the eighteenth century was an age of considerable intellectual life, more vivacious than profound, but redeeming its shallowness by its manifold interests and open sympathies. English antiquities, of whatever period, now found numerous students, and permanent institutions and journals were the solid fruit. The Royal Society had come into existence in 1662, and still included within its scope the works of man; it had not yet learned, and did not learn till after 1750, to limit itself to things which were not the products of human intelligence. The Society of Antiquaries of London was instituted or, as it prefers to say, revived in 1718.[1] The *Gentleman's Magazine*, which was meant for readers of educated and not least of antiquarian taste, first appeared in 1731. The British Museum, by no means the oldest of our English museums, was opened to the public in 1759.

Specially noteworthy among such efforts and interests were those of a band of men who knew one another, corresponded freely on antiquarian and particularly on Roman subjects, travelled together, and kept alive each other's enthusiasm in less formal ways than by meetings at the Society of Antiquaries, to which most of them belonged. They were, as a rule, men of University education, but they had very little connexion with the Universities in their archaeological work. Among the best known of them are Thomas Gale (1635–1702), Dean of York, and his son Roger (1672–1744), who edited

[1] A very full 'Historical Account of the Origin and Establishment of the Society of Antiquaries' is given in *Archaeologia* i, pp. i–xli. It was founded by Archbishop Parker in 1572 and maintained its activities for more than forty years, Camden being its most distinguished member. In 1604, or shortly after, it was dissolved by James I, "alarmed for the arcana of his government, and, as some think, for the established church" (*l.c.*, p. xv). The reorganization of January 1717–18, at which Stukeley was appointed Secretary, had had as its prelude a long series of informal weekly meetings. These were begun as early as 1707 at the Bear Tavern in the Strand, but were soon removed to the Young Devil Tavern in Fleet Street and subsequently to the Fountain Tavern, also in Fleet Street, over against Chancery Lane.

together an edition of the *Itinerary*.[1] Roger Gale's letters, partly existing in collected manuscript form,[2] partly published by Nichols [3] and by the Surtees Society,[4] are among the most useful archaeological productions of his day. He formed the centre of a circle of active correspondents which included Browne Willis, Stukeley, Hearne, and many of the other principal antiquaries of the time. Thomas Hearne deserves a sentence or two of particular notice here. He was born in 1678, son of a day labourer, owed his education to the charity of a friend, and was for seventeen years an assistant in the Bodleian.[5] Suspicious beyond even the wont of self-made men, quarrelsome beyond even the worst standard of antiquaries, *difficile* about publishing his books as few scholars have ever been, he spent his life at war with the authorities of the University and the Bodleian, forfeited promotion and pay, and at the end won from Pope the chief place as a dull man in the *Dunciad*. But it stands to his credit that he took a keen interest in the Roman remains of the Oxford district, and that he was one of the first to combine a more than amateurish attention to local antiquities with a real learning.[6]

[1] The book appeared in 1709, seven years after the father's death.

[2] F. H. himself possessed an interesting volume of this correspondence, now in the Haverfield Library in the Ashmolean, and there are various others extant, in the library of the Society of Antiquaries of London and elsewhere.

[3] *Reliquiae Galeanae* in *Bibliotheca Topographica Britannica* vol. iii (1790).

[4] In *Stukeley's Diaries and Letters* vols. ii and iii.

[5] He was appointed in 1699. In 1716 he was ejected for refusing to take the oath of allegiance to George I, and he never entered the Library afterwards.

[6] An interesting account of Hearne by the Dean of Winchester was published in the *Edinburgh Review*, April 1922. One of the specimens of his style there quoted (p. 365) is very characteristic: "James Parkinson A.M. & Fellow of Linc. Coll. a rank stinking Whigg, who us'd to defend ye Murther of King Charles 1st & recommend Milton & such other Republican Rascalls to his Pupills. . . . In King Wm's Reign (when ye sneaking Villains, like Worms upon a Rain, crawl'd out of yeir lurking holes) he appear'd in Print in a small Pamphlett against Dr Halton." That his career should have been stormy is hardly surprising.

For the most part these men concerned themselves with almost any antiquarian subject and with much else besides. This was in entire harmony with the spirit of the time. Sir Robert Sibbald (1641–1722), for instance, first professor of medicine in the University of Edinburgh, who was responsible for the 'Additions' relating to Scotland in Gibson's edition of Camden's *Britannia* (1695), has left a strange medley of miscellaneous works, mainly antiquarian and geographical but including a treatise on the *Liberty and Independence of the Church and Kingdom of Scotland*. He belonged to a rather older generation than Roger Gale, with whom he does not seem to have been personally acquainted. More directly connected with Gale was another Scotsman, who did good work on Roman Britain, Alexander Gordon, a native of Aberdeen. He was a man of many activities,—student of music, artist, traveller in Italy, promoter of a Forth and Clyde canal, author of a comedy, partner in a bookselling business in the Strand, some time Secretary to the London Society of Antiquaries and to sundry other learned societies, and finally to a colonial Governor.[1] He died in South Carolina about 1754. His *Itinerarium Septentrionale*, issued in 1726, described his own observations of the monuments and other remains of the Walls of Hadrian and of Pius, and appears to have been of considerable assistance to his much abler contemporary Horsley.

John Horsley, from our point of view the most important of the group, stood a little apart from the rest and confined himself to Roman work. Born in Northumberland in 1685 and educated at Edinburgh, he was by profession a Presbyterian minister and a teacher of natural science in his native region. In the intervals of teaching and preaching he travelled up and down England, noting

[1] The list leaves a rather uncomfortable impression that 'Sandy' Gordon—Galgacus, as some of his friends always called him—was a man who lived by his wits. He certainly seems to have quitted England under a cloud (Nichols, *Literary Anecdotes* v, p. 699).

antiquities and copying inscriptions and sculptures with remarkable accuracy and no less remarkable clumsiness. Just before his death in 1732 he completed his *Britannia Romana*, a folio volume of peculiar value, which transformed the whole study of Roman Britain. It is entirely devoted to the Roman period; there is nothing about earlier or later antiquities, as there is in Camden's *Britannia* and other works. Nor, again, is the material arranged exclusively or mainly by counties. If part of it is thus treated, far more is taken in its natural connexion. The work has other merits and other advantages worthy of note. It is based to a quite unusual extent on definite personal knowledge of the monuments. It is based also on a real conception of what a Roman province was. Camden and his contemporaries looked on Roman remains as interesting objects scattered up and down the land. Horsley understood that he was dealing with a part of the Roman Empire. His researches led him—he was after all a Northumbrian—to a much clearer conception of the military element in Roman Britain and of the northern frontier defences than of the civil life of towns and country houses and farms in the south. The importance of the latter aspect of the subject has, however, only been tentatively realized in our own times, and it lay outside the range of one who died nearly two centuries ago. Certainly, Horsley's *Britannia Romana* was till quite lately the best and most scholarly account of any Roman province that had been written anywhere in Europe.

Beside Horsley, as specially illustrating the Romano-British archaeology of the period, we may set the figure of William Stukeley, who married as his second wife a daughter of Thomas Gale. Born in 1687 and educated at Cambridge to be a doctor, he was a mixture of simplicity and drollery and superstition, of agreeable kindliness, unbounded conceit, and real ability and width of interest. His first tastes were scientific. He was indeed known even in his childhood for stealing out to catch dogs and dissect them. Later on he turned his attention to every form of antiquity and even to mechanics. As the '*Ipse f.*' of PLATE II[1] shows, he could use his pencil as well as his pen. He studied, and believed he had solved, such biblical problems as the nature of Manna, of the Shekinah, and of Aaron's breastplate. He invented new musical and astronomical instruments—none that are now in use. He cast his own horoscope and did the same for any friend who would let him. Like all such men, he was inaccurate. Hearne remarked in his usual manner that "it is observed by all that I have talked with that what he does has no manner of likeness to the original". One example will show the extent of his perverted ingenuity. He acquired a coin of Carausius bearing the head and name of Fortuna. In the legend the F was rubbed out and the T blurred. Stukeley decided that the legend was ORIVNA, that Oriuna was the wife of Carausius, and that the head on the coin was hers, and accordingly he wrote and printed the life of that lady.[2] He went on to write a life of Carausius, and every name in England that began with 'Car'—Carfax, for instance,—was used to prove the journeys of the great monarch.[3]

But he had other and better qualities. He was, for instance, the first who had any correct idea of the course of the Foss Way; before Stukeley it had often been mentioned by chroniclers and antiquaries, but no one knew its precise course from end to end. The growth of accurate knowledge of actual remains, as one antiquary

[1] Although this drawing, now published for the first time, is dated 1727, it suggests a somewhat younger man than does the well-known Kneller portrait of 1721, in which Stukeley wears a full-bottomed wig. The two subjects are nevertheless obviously identical, and the inscription (on the back of the drawing) reproduced in PLATE II is clearly in Stukeley's hand.

[2] *A Dissertation upon Oriuna* (1751), reprinted in *Palaeographia Britannica* iii (1752).

[3] *The Medallic History of Marcus Aurelius Valerius Carausius*, 2 vols. (1757 and 1759).

Ipse W: Stukeley f.
1727.

after another saw them for himself and planned them, is indeed characteristic of the seventeenth and eighteenth centuries. Camden was familiar with the general line of the Roman Wall, thanks mainly to his own visit to it and to the letters of a Cumberland correspondent, Reginald Bainbrigg, Schoolmaster of Appleby.[1] But his ideas of the forts that defended it were vague. Some of them he identified correctly, at least in his later editions. Others he found in strange places, not even on the Wall. Thus Segedunum was located at Seghill instead of at Wallsend, Pons Aelii at Ponteland instead of at Newcastle, Gabrosentum at Newcastle instead of somewhere in Cumberland, Uxellodunum at Hexham instead of at Maryport on the west coast. These ideas prevailed during the seventeenth century; they occur, for example, in the earliest printed account of Newcastle, issued by William Gray in 1649.[2] It was not till Gordon and Horsley themselves walked along the Wall, and Edward Lhuyd and Warburton and Hunter and others examined various parts of it, that its course was properly mapped out and the ancient names of most of its forts recovered.

Unfortunately, towards the close of his life Stukeley made one fatal blunder, no more surprising perhaps than many of his other blunders, but far more disastrous for his successors. In 1747 a young Englishman, by name Charles Bertram, teacher of English at Copenhagen, sent to Stukeley an account of a manuscript on Roman antiquities which he had found in Denmark. This manuscript was alleged to contain a description of Britain in eight chapters, a number of *itinera* resembling the Antonine list, and a rough map of the British Isles in the Roman period. Stukeley was much interested in the work, induced Bertram to publish it at Copenhagen, published it himself in London, and persuaded the

[1] See F. H. in *C. and W. Trans.* (n.s.) xi, pp. 345 ff.

[2] *Chorographia or a Survey of Newcastle upon Tine, and a Relation of the County of Northumberland*: see the reprint published by Andrew Reid in 1883.

Society of Antiquaries to endorse it and Bertram by unanimously electing him a Fellow. It was almost an undergraduate's joke. Bertram had found no manuscript at all. He had merely forged a description of Roman Britain from the works of Camden and Stukeley and the rest, with due use of Caesar and Tacitus and Ptolemy and other ancient authorities. Stukeley was naturally pleased to find his own views supported by the description which Bertram attributed to Richard of Cirencester, and he did not stop to inquire whether the manuscript existed. As we know now, the manuscript was never forthcoming. Every one of the details said to be taken from it can be explained from the sources mentioned above, and many of these details are such as are credible in no ancient writer.[1]

But the result has been untold confusion. The forgeries of Bertram have been taken as gospel by many subsequent writers, and they have frequently been repeated by men who knew that Bertram was a forger but did not know that they were repeating Bertram's fiction. Almost all that was written on Roman Britain between 1757 and the middle of Queen Victoria's reign is tainted from this source. Inquirers have been set on wrong tracks, and attention has been diverted into wrong channels. A few of the greatest among local archaeologists saw through the fraud: T. D. Whitaker the historian of Whalley, Hodgson the historian of Northumberland, and one or two others freely expressed their scepticism. But even foreign scholars fell victims to

[1] The treatise was first printed in *Britannicarum gentium historiae antiquae scriptores tres: Ricardus Corinensis, Gildas Badonicus, Nennius Banchorensis. Recensuit . . . Carolus Bertramus* (*Havniae, 1757*). In the same year Stukeley's *Account of Richard of Cirencester, Monk of Westminster, and of his Works: with his Antient Map of Roman Brittain: and the Itinerary thereof* appeared in London. The latter, together with Bertram's entire text, notes, and map, was reprinted in 1776 in Part II of Stukeley's *Itinerarium Curiosum* (pp. 79–168). For later editione and for a full exposure of the forgery see J. E. B. Mayor's *Ricardi de Cirencestria Speculum Historiale* ii (Rolls Series, 1869), pp. xvi–clxiv.

Bertram's skill, and the errors which have been derived from him still figure in serious publications of to-day.[1]

It may be well to give a few instances of these errors. From Bertram's *De Situ Britanniae* comes the common assertion that in Roman Britain eleven cities had the Roman municipal franchise, an assertion which more than doubles the number of such cities and proportionately overstates the civilization of the province. Hence, too, the idea that Bath and Chester and Caerleon were the sites of large and civilized Roman cities instead of being, the first a spa, and the two others fortresses occupied only by legionary soldiers. Hence, again, many errors about the provincial divisions of Britain—the boundaries assigned to the five provinces of the fourth century, Britannia Prima and the rest, the existence in North Britain of a province called Vespasiana, and much else besides. Hence many inaccurate place-names, mere inventions of Bertram,—'Dorocina' the supposed name of Dorchester on the Thames, 'Ad Fines' a title ascribed to several Romano-British sites, 'Aelia Castra' meant for Alchester near Bicester, and so forth. No less than forty-eight of the names in the *Itinerary* of Bertram, very nearly a third of the whole total, are of his own coining. Stukeley died in 1765. He had lived eight years too long.

Despite this unhappy chance, the first half of the eighteenth century saw two great steps taken forward in the study of Roman Britain. In the first place, as has been already pointed out, men's actual acquaintance with extant remains was widened by travels, not confined to Horsley and Stukeley. In the second place, the conception of the subject was made more precise: it was marked off from the study of other periods in the history of Britain and was recognized as in some way connected with an empire of which Britain formed only a part.

[1] In one particularly glaring case F. H. was moved to make a formal protest. See *Athenaeum*, Nov. 12, 1898.

The years which followed did not continue this progress. Horsley's profound and learned volume aroused no one to similar study. Indeed his merits were very little understood by his contemporaries. The antiquaries who from the first months of 1718, according to our reckoning, met on Thursday afternoons in the apartments of the London Society, were able and accomplished men, but they were not specialists; curiosity, not learning or training, was their motive force, and few of them cared, like Horsley, to acquire a particular knowledge of a particular period. Their services to the study of Roman Britain were the services of registering and recording, either in print or in their still unpublished Minutes, new discoveries, and sometimes they even promoted excavations.[1] They formed also a focus, which in its turn radiated influence; the *Gentleman's Magazine*, as it was throughout the eighteenth century and indeed almost continuously till 1868, exhibits an even less specialist but a much more widely spread interest in antiquities.

This interest lasted on through all the miseries and excitements of the French Revolution and the Napoleonic wars. Nothing, perhaps, declares so eloquently the confidence of the British nation and the security ensured by its island home, as the unbroken series of peaceful antiquarian notes and letters which were printed in the *Gentleman's Magazine* throughout this terrible age. England between 1806 and 1814 was pressed hard. Its King was insane, its Regent discredited; its capitalists were in distress, its people without bread, its trade declining; it could hardly at first continue the struggle in the Peninsula, and a party cried out for the recall of Wellesley to the defence of the home-land. Yet just at this time Samuel Lysons produced his stately folios of Romano-British mosaics and other antiquities, perhaps

[1] A notable instance of their interest in Roman Britain is their publication in 1793, in a splendid folio, of Roy's *Military Antiquities of the Romans in North Britain*, the plans in which are still of value: see *Archaeologia* lxviii, pp. 161 ff.

the most magnificent volumes ever published on the Roman antiquities of this country, and he and his brother Daniel began their *Magna Britannia*, a series of quarto county histories of exceptional size and excellence. It was in 1806, too, that the final edition of Camden's *Britannia*, with the vast collections of Gough inserted, was issued in four tall folios. Archaeology at least had no reason to complain of the Great Wars.

The French Revolution and the French wars failed to disturb the English antiquaries of the moment. But they changed the whole future of the study of Roman Britain. They roused intellectual interests throughout Europe. The freer political life, the new national feelings, the new consciousness of both peoples and nationalities, coupled with the new chances for research in libraries no longer closed to scholars, inspired an outburst of historical writing. The nineteenth century, the age of Buckle and Grote and Stubbs, of Niebuhr and Mommsen and Ranke, was an age of historians. Still more it was an age of Roman historians. Mommsen, born in 1817, published his first book in 1843 and his last in 1903, when he died. His colossal activity, maintained for sixty continuous years, marked an epoch in Roman history and in every branch, every nook and corner of that wide subject. In particular his studies of the remains of the Roman provinces worked a complete change in our idea of what those provinces were. Our horizon broadened beyond the Curia and Palatine in Rome to wide lands north and east and south of the Mediterranean, and we began to realize the true genius of the Roman Empire.[1]

This was one current of intellectual movement. But it did not affect England so directly or so quickly as it affected the continent. The study of Roman Britain in the earlier part of the nineteenth century in England was of a different order. There was new life enough in the country. The reforms of the franchise and the poor law, the developments of churchmanship, of elementary

[1] See F. H. in *Eng. Hist. Rev.* xix (1904), pp. 80–9.

education and of the public schools are obvious examples of it. In archaeological matters the new growth is perhaps most closely connected with the new religious movement. The antiquary and the tractarian have much in common. The ascertainment of primitive practice must or, at least, ought to be dear to both, and the two movements, though not in origin the same, probably helped one another. There is, however, this difference. The tractarian worked in a University, though in an unfriendly one. The antiquaries were for the most part men who neither cared for the Universities nor found any encouragement within their walls.

Two special features seem to mark the new growth in archaeology. It moves along lines characteristic of the early Victorian age through the formation of societies. This social tendency towards groups is, indeed, one of the most striking features in the educated life of England during the last seventy or eighty years, and its effects are plain in the institution of societies in almost every town. It was in the early forties that the London Society of Antiquaries roused itself to a keener life and began to print its *Proceedings*; it was then, and indeed before that, that new societies were formed all over England, often entitled 'philosophical' but always much concerned with archaeology. Most of these belonged to special towns or counties. Others, like the British Archaeological Association and the Archaeological Institute, were meant to be more broadly based. Now, too, museums were erected. At first they were planned as temples of the Muses, club-houses of intellectuals, rather than as stores of ancient remains. Still a step was taken which did provide local homes for local discoveries, and homes which would not pass away at the death of a private owner. Now also the newly founded societies, and sometimes even the museums, swelled the literature of the subject by their journals.

A second feature is more temporary. The antiquarian zeal of the early Victorian age touched all classes. Aristocracy and archaeology have never shaken hands so warmly as they did in those days. Archaeology was not a little helped by the social prestige of this alliance. It was not a little hindered by the gulf which too often sunders rank and serious learning; the nobleman who takes up archaeology as an interest and a hobby is seldom willing to spend weary days in research. Nor indeed was the movement one which was likely to produce much serious inquiry; the new societies and the new museums were not created for specialists. Exceptions, however, existed. John Hodgson, from his country parish in Northumberland, described the Roman Wall in a volume which, however amorphous,—much of it is the longest foot-note in literature—is a work of scientific research and immense learning.[1] The fourth Duke of Northumberland, far in advance of his time, had both the Wall and the Roman road which crosses its eastern section surveyed by competent engineers,[2] and he meditated its excavation; it was the archaeologists who discouraged him.

Nevertheless the very dilettantism of the movement gave it a character which involved archaeological advance. It paid much attention, as amateurs do, to the objects of ancient daily life—ornaments, pottery, bronzes, hypocausts, mosaics. Neither Horsley nor Stukeley had cared for these things. We owe to the early Victorian period the beginnings of that investigation into the forms and developments of Roman provincial pottery and other small objects which to-day, on a much more scientific method, is about to yield very valuable historical and economic conclusions. Probably this was to some extent accidental. Most of the men directly concerned came from the south of England—that is, from districts where military remains, such as forts and inscriptions, were

[1] *History of Northumberland* vol. iii, part ii (1840). The foot-note begins on p. 157 and ends on p. 322.

[2] *The Roman Wall and Illustrations of the Principal Vestiges of Roman Occupation in the North of England.* By Henry Maclauchlan (Privately printed: 1857).

somewhat uncommon, but where potsherds and brooches and enamels and glass were turned up almost daily. Mr. Charles Roach Smith (1807–90), resident first in London and afterwards in Kent, lived in two regions where these smaller objects were extraordinarily frequent, and worked at a time when they were being found in London in peculiar abundance. It was natural that he should take up the study of Roman pottery, and it was not very difficult for him to cast his eye across the Channel and compare the Samian ware of England with the Samian ware of Gaul and recognize, in some dim fashion, the great importance of the Auvergne potteries in the Allier Valley at Lezoux.

The wave soon spent itself. Mr. Roach Smith sold his collection of London antiquities to the British Museum in 1856 and had finished his best work before 1875. In 1868 the *Gentleman's Magazine*, which had hitherto been maintained as a journal for archaeologists by various editors (among them Joseph Whitaker, founder of the Almanack), was entirely divested of its archaeological elements. Now, too, the aristocrat and the archaeologist began to part company, and the local societies to decline in numbers and in social importance. We may here turn aside and attempt to sum up the main characteristics of the three centuries of research which we have been describing. That its results have been great, a mere glance at any good archaeological library will show. The county histories, the long series of the periodical publications of societies, the array of miscellaneous works large and small, which deal to a greater or less extent with Roman Britain, may well impress the casual spectator. There has assuredly been no lack of interest in the subject. In this country, indeed, remains of the Roman period have, throughout, received a fuller share of general public attention than has fallen to them anywhere on the continent. Thanks to our system of classical education, nearly every one—until the most recent times—has read a little Latin literature, some Caesar if nothing else, and has thus learnt something of Roman Britain, and people who in any other country would give no heed to such things are in Britain deeply interested in them. Interest, however, is not science nor can it take the place of scientific work. It may be well to analyse this long interest and to appraise its real strength and weakness.

It is characteristic of Englishmen that their efforts should be individual. Admirable explorers, pioneers, single workers, they have no capacity for co-operation, and they cannot organize. Even the societies which sprang up in the nineteenth century did not provide any real combination of forces. They brought lonely students together and furnished the means of publication for learned articles. But of real organization, of men working in unselfish union for a common end, they show scarcely a vestige. They have possibilities which may develop some day into collective effort. At present we can only call them the loose framework for a number of individualist workers. The best publications on Roman Britain have in every case proceeded from single scholars, from men who, like Horsley or Hodgson, wrought by themselves with little aid even from friends and correspondents. At the present day co-operation is peculiarly needed in scientific work, and its absence from the methods of Romano-British study is perhaps the gravest evil which hampers progress.

Another evil feature is no less English. The Englishman, explorer and pioneer, individually capable and self-reliant, disbelieves not only in co-operation but also in training. We in England have an almost disastrous conception of learning. It is not merely that we think the learned man a social nuisance or an oddity; we have a particular indifference to learning as such. In the field of natural science we perhaps allow the value of a specialized knowledge. Elsewhere we find no use for it, and believe that any Englishman can go where he likes and achieve what he wants, without training and without special knowledge. The English archaeologist has been like the ordinary Englishman. Our students have had plenty of native ability and have firmly declined to improve it by training. They have been deemed able to go anywhere and do anything—and they have done it freely.

This indifference to training has been accentuated by a further cause. It will have been noticed that, throughout the sketch which I have given, the Universities are hardly mentioned. The greatest of our archaeologists have had nothing to do with them. Camden quarrelled with Oxford. Horsley, so far as we know, was never inside of either Oxford or Cambridge, and, though he and Bentley were both members of the Royal Society and were probably the two greatest scholars of their age, it is improbable that they ever met. So, too, with Hodgson and all the lesser men. The one great name in the list which concerns Oxford is Geoffrey of Monmouth, and he lived in Oxford before the University fully began. This gulf between Universities and archaeologists is partly geographical. Oxford and Cambridge, however near London under modern conditions, are distinct from it. Meetings held in London are not easily attended by University men, and the British Museum cannot have the connexion with University learning which, for example, supports the museums of Berlin, Paris, or Vienna. Hence the national instincts, which burn brightest in a capital, have been somewhat wanting in our Universities. They have had it as their aim to be the nursery of statesmen, and perhaps it is a quality of a good nursery that it is detached from the interests of grown-up life. Certainly they have cared nothing for our national antiquities.[1]

But there is a still more potent educational reason. Our dominant education has been classical and linguistic.

[1] In a petition drafted in 1589 for presentation to Queen Elizabeth, praying her to grant a charter of incorporation to the Society of Antiquaries, one of the reasons urged in support of the request is: "This Society will not interfere with the Universities, as tending to the preservation of History and Antiquities, whereof the Universities, long buried in the arts, take no regard" (*Archaeologia* i, p. iv).

Even history has been taught hitherto as a matter of words. There has been little care for things, and in consequence archaeology is in our Universities a somewhat novel study to-day, still regarded with a faint suspicion and occasional jealousy. The Universities are antiquarian enough when you ask them to change one of their old customs. But their care for ancient things has gone no farther in the centuries which I have been reviewing. The result has been as decisive as it has been unfortunate. Roman Britain has been the playground of the amateur—often, no doubt, of the amateur who has great abilities and has trained himself well, but more often of the man who, whatever his abilities, has had no training at all. Abundant work has been produced, but its value rests rather on its being a record than on its being a critical account. Frequently, indeed, such work is valuable to us only because of some detail to which the writer plainly attached little weight. Much has been printed which has not even this value. Our antiquarian journals have been prone, when they mentioned remains exhibited to this or that society, to record the exhibitors rather than to describe the exhibits; they tell us who brought an object for inspection; they do not say precisely what it was or where it was found or what was found with it.

Two causes have tended to conceal the weakness of this literature. One is a further result of the classical education which has so deeply influenced Romano-British archaeology. When every one knows a little Latin, it is easy for an ignorant writer to give an impression of expert knowledge, and many of the archaeological works in our libraries appear to be based on a better education and sounder methods of criticism and wider learning than they can really pretend to. The wealth of England has added to the deception. A rich nation has been able to afford subscriptions to societies and expenses on private printing which would hardly have been possible in most foreign countries. Archaeological publications in England have had, not only a classical tinge, but a fine outward dress. And, though the best print and the best paper go as naturally with second-rate work as a smart hunting-coat with a third-rate horseman, critics have shrunk from believing that these stately volumes are of mixed worth.

For three centuries the individual untrained Englishman has done good work. In the nineteenth century foreign scholars, and above all Mommsen, have carried out reforms in learning, and particularly in Roman history, which make it doubtful if the amateur can in the future do any real good. Those who to-day study a province of the Roman Empire have before them a region which is in part much better known and in part much more open to exploration than had any of their predecessors, and they have to employ far more delicate instruments and far more complicated methods. The whole subject has become much harder. Sixty or eighty years ago it did not matter greatly if a writer on Roman York or Roman Lincoln had any clear idea of what a Roman legion or a Roman *colonia* was. As a rule, indeed, he had none, and the descriptions of these important sites which I have before me—from Drake's folio on York, issued in 1736, down to the most readable modern sketch of Lincoln I have met with—are quite innocent of the accurate use of those terms. To-day, unfortunately, accuracy is necessary. The accounts which local antiquaries have written, with much local knowledge and nothing more, may contain helpful records. But, judged as historical accounts of Roman York or Roman Lincoln, they are devoid of any value.

PLATE III THE BATHS AND BASILICA OF WROXETER

# LECTURE II

## THE GEOGRAPHY OF BRITAIN AND THE ROMAN CONQUEST

In the preceding lecture I endeavoured to summarize the salient features of previous archaeological and historical research into Roman Britain. I pass on now to the province itself, and first to the geographical conditions which affected its Roman occupation. A short review of these will lead naturally to a sketch of the history of the Roman conquest. The earlier part of the present lecture will thus form a brief essay in historical geography. To most of us the term 'historical geography' probably suggests nothing very precise. We are aware that it somehow concerns history and maps, and we have a comforting feeling that it is 'up to date'. But we do not try to define it. It seems, however, to have two distinct senses. To the authors of ordinary historical atlases it implies a list of political boundaries, arranged chronologically and described pictorially on a series of vari-coloured sheets. This is certainly useful enough in its way. But it hardly deserves so fine-sounding a name as 'historical geography'. There are others who take a different and, as I think, a wider and a wiser view. If we would understand the relations of geography and history, we must (they tell us) begin by studying the physical features of the world by themselves, neglecting for the moment all historical or political divisions. We may then proceed to deduce the influence of these physical features in any special period with which we are occupied.

The following paragraphs are to be regarded as an abbreviated exercise in the method indicated by the second view. They will not seek to describe the whole physical geography of Britain. Indeed, the historian of a special epoch hardly needs so profound a study. They will merely bring into relief those facts of British geography which are known to have been of real consequence in Roman times. Very little will be said about boundaries and political divisions—partly because I do not consider these the chief element in historical geography, and still more because there are none to discuss. The internal divisions of Roman Britain were few, and their boundaries are almost entirely unknown. Too many modern histories talk of them with pathetic unanimity and unanimous inaccuracy; much repetition has set a spurious seal of authenticity on what is simply conjecture or slenderly founded, if plausible, theory.[1] It will be better to restrict ourselves to the features that are at once certain and important.

These features are not quite what one might at first sight expect. Nor are they the same as concern the student of later Britain. They are, in the main, broad and general features. It is possible that the smaller geographical facts which mattered much in the Middle Ages produced their effect on Roman Britain also. But, if they did, the slightness of our knowledge hinders our recognition of the outcome. And the supposition is not very likely. In the Middle Ages England was, at least at times, a small self-contained state. Throughout the Roman period Britain was a part of an enormous whole—a single province in an empire which stretched out over

[1] See F. H. in *Archaeologia Oxoniensis* 1892–5 (1895), pp. 221 ff., for an analysis of current views. To the references there given may be added one to the very interesting inscription discovered at Bordeaux in December 1921 (*Rev. des Études anciennes* xxiv (1922), Pl. III, and *J. R. S.* xi, pp. 101–7). It proves that Lincoln, as well as York, was in Lower Britain. This is important as showing that the boundary line between Upper and Lower Britain cannot have been drawn (as has usually been supposed) from the Humber.

three continents. This empire was constituted on a scale which dwarfs details into insignificance. Its history contains none of that quick succession of momentous incidents and that continuity of the individual life which mark the little nations of ancient Greece or modern Europe. Single men, single events are the least factors in its true annals: they vanish in the wide movement of the whole mass. Similarly the smaller features of geography do not seriously affect the course of Imperial history. The great processes of conquest, of civilization, of the spread of religions and language and political franchise move forward like an engulfing flood. Only the tallest hills remain uncovered. The boundaries of some provinces may, as in Spain, be based chiefly on geographical considerations. The prosperity of a few towns like Carthage or Antioch or Alexandria may depend upon them. The division of the Empire into East and West may have its geographical justifications. But, when one seeks geographical reasons for smaller issues, the case alters, other forces interfere. In Britain, accordingly, only the broader aspects concern us.

In the first place, then, Britain is an island, but an island which is firmly linked to continental Europe. Under modern conditions, particularly of steam navigation, its insular position has greatly helped to its unique status in the world, as the cradle of a widespread race and the centre of a proverbial empire. That, however, is a modern phase, made possible by modern machinery. It has not existed long. It may not last. During all its earlier history Britain has belonged closely to the opposite mainland. The two together form one vast flat-bottomed valley—almost on the scale of the flat-bottomed valleys of the American Mississippi or Missouri—which slopes slowly up from the sea to the Derbyshire and Welsh hills on the north-west, and on the south-east to the succession of ranges which connect the Auvergne and the Eifel. This geographical character of Britain was stamped on it by irresistible agencies in an antiquity whose remoteness cannot be measured in years. We can trace the great valley far back into geological time. In the Pleiocene and Pleistocene ages it was drained by two rivers. The one flowed north into the Arctic Ocean, the other south-west into an Atlantic that was much more distant than the Atlantic of to-day. Between them ran a low watershed of chalk hills connecting the sites of Dover and Calais. The watershed has long since vanished. The two rivers are lost in the unquiet waves of the North Sea and the Channel. The level country through which they made their way is submerged. But the geographical result endures. The lowlands of south-eastern England, of northern France, and of Belgium and Holland form a single geographical area.

To-day the essential unity of the area is obscured by racial and political divisions which have for once proved stronger than geography. In ancient times, both pre-Roman and Roman, it showed itself distinctly. A civilization of the type which we may call Celtic covered the whole region between the Rhine and the western ocean. The same Celtic tribes dwelt on both shores of the Channel and, at least in or about Caesar's day, the same chiefs sometimes ruled on both sides of the water.[1] There were Parisii round Paris and also near the Humber, Atrebates round Arras and also in Berkshire, Menapii in Flanders and also in Ireland, Belgae all over North Gaul and also in Hampshire and Wiltshire. The same Celtic dialects were spoken in Britain and in Gaul. The same Celtic types of house-plans, of pottery and of metal work prevailed, and the products of the same 'Late Celtic' art were in use. Then, as in Norman and Angevin days, England was part of the mainland which it fronts.[2] It has indeed counted as an island only in the Saxon period and in the centuries since 1300.

[1] *De Bell. Gall.* ii. 14. Cf. *Archaeologia Oxoniensis* 1892–5, p. 159, where Sir Arthur Evans fixes "somewhere about 300 B.C." as the date from which "Belgic princes, like Roman emperors and Norman dukes, reigned on both sides of the Channel".

[2] As to the lines of communication, see F. H. in *Man* xvi, pp. 45 ff.

It is a further consequence of this geographical unity that each side of the valley still lies exposed to attack from the other. The invasions of Britain by Celt and Roman and Saxon and Norman merely reflect the fact that the easily invaded area of England lies in the east, near the bottom of the ancient river-valley. Had the uplands of Britain been placed, not in the west, but on the other side, we may believe that the Roman (and any) conquest would have taken much longer to complete and perhaps would never have been attempted at all. Britain, in short, is an island which lies by nature uncomfortably open to the opposite continent, and it is not surprising that its history consists largely of more or less violent foreign infiltrations. Invasions occurred because they were easy movements within closely related parts of the same geographical area. The tide has indeed generally flowed from continent to island. But it has not always been so. Witness the struggle to maintain the English rule over various parts of France, which lasted for five hundred years from 1066 till the reign of Queen Mary. In the end it is a matter of population. Were Britain larger and its people more numerous, we should long ago have realized that Holland and Germany are as exposed geographically to invasion from us as we are from them. As it is, Britain has usually been the invaded, and its own special conformation has helped its fate. Its plains are in the east. Its most navigable rivers flow out on the eastern coast. Its hills rise gently up from the south-east and reserve their steeper slopes for their northern or western faces. The land is, as it were, made for invasion from Europe.

If we turn to the interior, a third conspicuous characteristic is immediately apparent—the manner in which the island is divided into uplands and lowlands. The uplands lie to the north and west. They are the British hillside of the great valley of which I have just been speaking. But it is a broken discontinuous hillside, composed of three dissevered pieces—the west-country moors of Dart and Exe and Bodmin, the Welsh hills, and the Pennine Chain and northern highlands. The lowlands, on the other hand, are compact. They comprise the midland plain and the counties of the southern and eastern coast. A line drawn from York through Derby to Chester, and from Chester through Shrewsbury to Gloucester, would form a rough boundary between the two areas. Hills do occur to the south and east of this line, just as low ground occurs to the north and west of it. But with obvious exceptions it divides two very different kinds of country. Expressed geographically, the division might almost be said to follow the 600-foot contour-line. What is lowland is mostly and predominantly lower than 600 feet. What is upland is as generally higher. Let us look at each area more closely.

The lowlands form a level or more often a slightly undulating expanse. Like northern France, they are noticeable for the low scale of their physical features. Little of them is absolutely flat, but there are few high hills and few continuous tracts of moorland. Rivers flow through them, but the streams of these rivers are not broad or deep, their valleys are small and shallow, and even their watersheds are ill-defined. Between Oxford and Banbury, for instance, a narrow strip divides the head waters of a small river-system, and a trifling change might—and some day perhaps will—divert the current of the Oxfordshire Cherwell to Northamptonshire, and cause the water that now runs past Oxford and London to reach the sea at the Wash. Soil and climate generally favour peaceful life and a rural population and the pursuit of agriculture or of pasturage of sheep or cattle. Within the area, however, the different districts vary as to the amount of population they can carry. Neither the midlands, in such regions as Warwickshire, north Oxfordshire, and Leicestershire, nor the downs of Berkshire and north Hampshire are capable of dense inhabitation, and it is probably true to say that the fringe of the midlands is more suited to the higher developments, whether of town or of country-house or farm, than is the central plain.

Such being their character, the lowlands naturally contain few strategic points (if one may borrow a military term), few sites or passes or regions that soldier or merchant must use or must avoid. A general, starting at any point on their edge, could easily march through them in any direction that he wished. He would doubtless march easiest from the south or east; he could then utilize the more navigable of the rivers and their valleys, and the gradients of the hills would favour him. But, even if he marched otherwise, he would encounter few substantial obstacles. In some periods of history woodland regions, like the Weald, the Chilterns, Arden, Wyre Forest, may have counted in warfare. But their influence has probably been overrated. They are not all true forests. Nor are they so very extensive, if we take care to exclude from them those medieval hunting-spaces which were called forests but were not necessarily uninhabited or woodlands. In the Roman period they certainly did not so count. Then they had none of that strategic importance which Mr. J. R. Green assigned to them in the history of the Anglo-Saxon conquest.[1] More definite obstructions are the marshes of the Wash and the Humber estuaries—Holland and Hatfield Chase—as they were in the old days before the Dutchmen came over and taught us to drain them. But these lie on the fringes of the lowlands, and besides they can readily be turned.

Only one site in the lowland area can claim definite strategic importance. That is London.[2] London is the greatest expression of the primeval geographical bond between England and the opposite lands. Here many advantages combine. Here is a harbour, not only capacious and accessible in all weathers, but also handy to the continent whence all early and medieval trade necessarily came. Here is, further, a crossing over the one tidal

[1] See *The Making of England*, Introduction and Chap. ii, *passim*.

[2] See 'Roman London' in *J.R.S.* i, pp. 143 f.

estuary which cuts deeply into south-eastern England. Kent and Sussex here most easily join hands with East Anglia ; and Norfolk, hemmed in by fen and sea, here finds its proper door. The rest of the midlands, too, are grouped accessibly—Oxford has always been within easy reach of London—and the river which flows out through the estuary opens a path into the heart of the island. Our modern railways radiate from London because it was the capital before railways began. As we shall learn presently, the Roman highways radiated in the same manner, but that was because geography commanded it. It is often the greatest of the Fates, our Mother Earth, that orders the rise and fall of cities.

No other site in England can match the advantages which London enjoyed under early and medieval conditions. The vicinity of Southampton is perhaps its most formidable rival, and it may be no geographical accident that Winchester was at one time a capital city. But Southampton is farther from the continent and farther from the midlands. Its river is a mere chalk stream. Its position commands no important passage such as that which London provided between north and south Saxons, and all the western side of it is shut in by a vast heath that was barren and uninhabited even during the Roman occupation. Hull, Plymouth, Manchester, Bristol were still less able to vie with London in the things that were of real moment then. Each lies in a corner, compassed about by rivers, marshes, or hills. Each owes its present importance to steamships and the interchange of goods with distant lands which steam has made possible. In the Roman period the whole of the region on the west, looking out over the Atlantic, was neither adapted to civilization nor connected with any trade route. To-day Liverpool is the beginning of the world ; in ancient times it was the end. In the natural geography of the British lowlands London holds the one central place.

Very different is the picture presented by the uplands. In position they are scattered. I have already pointed out that they lie in three great pieces—in Devon and Cornwall, in Wales, in northern England. In character they have a general likeness. Usually, as we have seen, they rise above 600 feet, and they are often considerably higher. Though the hills are seldom lofty enough to be styled mountains, the three districts are nevertheless mountainous. Deep ravines scar them, as in Derbyshire, and sudden valleys and tortuous gorges and sharp precipices. Soil and climate forbid agriculture, and their grazing lands cannot support a large population. Here was little place in early days for civilized life. Tactically, too, they are difficult and tangled regions, where hill tribes might hold out for many years. At the same time, since they do not reach the height and configuration of true mountains, they do not offer the inevitable barriers or passages which confront us as we approach the Pyrenees or the Alps, or journey over the central plains of France. Roads can be carried easily across them and were so carried in Roman times. Neither the heights near Buxton nor the Pennine Chain nor the Cheviots offered serious hindrance to the Roman roadmaker. Even the higher Lake hills were traversed by a pitched and permanent roadway, climbing over 2,500 feet.

At the same time these uplands have certain strategic lines of less resistance, valleys along which roads and railways can be carried with infinitely less trouble than across the hills—with so much less indeed that only military necessity or commercial competition would lead men to forsake them. Thus the great mass of the Pennine Chain forms a long upland belt down the centre of northern England. This belt is hard to cross. The two gaps in it known to geographers—the Tyne and the Aire gaps—were little used in early days. But on each side of it is a strip of lowland, and these two strips formed and still form the two readiest ways of passing the uplands. The traveller from the south may cross the midlands as he likes. But, if he wishes to go farther northwards, he must proceed by one of the two lines known to-day as the West and East Coast routes.

The western line begins with the gap of Crewe, well marked between the Welsh and the Derbyshire hills, and immediately north of that it reaches a strategic point which was early seized by the Romans, the site of Chester. Under ancient conditions of navigation Chester, planted beside the tidal waters of the Dee, had a sea-borne trade. A twelfth-century writer, preserved in a Bodleian MS.,[1] records that in his day ships came from Ireland, from Aquitaine, from Spain, from Germany to Chester, and doubtless it was not only at that time that the harbour was used. Chester also looks out from its sandstone rock across a stretch of marsh to the wild Welsh hills, and from Chester these hills can be watched more closely than from any other fortress in this corner of England. And thirdly it serves—though perhaps other sites in the same neighbourhood might equally well have served—to hold the north end of the gap of Crewe and the further road thence along the lower lands of Lancashire, past Preston and Lancaster to the north. The route indeed is not well marked out by nature in this part of its course. The Lancashire lowlands are ' heavy going ', and beyond them rise the Lake hills. By the Lune valley, past Sedbergh and Tebay, a tolerable access can be gained to the Eden basin, but no one specially easy line exists. The objective, however, is plain—Carlisle, the ancient Luguvallium, child of the fertile Solway lowlands, guardian of a ford across rivers of local importance, and of the western end of the Tyne and Solway Isthmus. At this place any general must aim in a northward advance, and this he must secure if he plans permanent occupation.[2]

By comparison the eastern route is far simpler and easier. It lies through the Vale of York, a rich, open country, encumbered only by too much river water, and

[1] *Liber Luciani de Laude Cestrie* (Bodley MS. 672). See the extracts transcribed and edited by Miss M. V. Taylor in *Lancs. and Ches. Record Soc.* vol. lxiv (1912).

[2] See F. H. in *C. and W. Trans.* (n.s.) xvii, pp. 239 ff.

thence across Durham to the estuary of the Tyne and the eastern end of the isthmus, at Newcastle or its neighbourhood. This isthmus is the central fact of the north country of England. Here the span narrows to some seventy miles between open sea and sea ; a valley runs across it and forms at present the principal link between the east and west coasts ; and harbours lie open, especially on its eastern side. Its narrowness, perhaps even more than its valley and its harbours, has made it always peculiarly important, alike as a line of defence and as a base for further advance to the northward.

An army undertaking such an advance would find that the country immediately in front of it resembles that in its rear, but is more difficult. Nature has marked out no obvious tracks across Cheviot or the hills of southern Scotland. But here again the objective is plain. Seventy miles north, or (if you will) north-west, the land again contracts. The span between Forth and Clyde is only thirty-five miles, just half of the southern span ; here, too, a broad valley runs from sea to sea, and at each end are admirable harbours. It is thus, like the longer southern line, a necessary base for further progress northwards and a no less necessary line for one who meditates frontier defences. And for him who would still press forward, the way beyond is plain. Nature once more points out the course. It runs north-east from the head of the Forth estuary. The gap of Stirling, the crossing of the Tay near Perth, and the long valley between the Grampians and the Sidlaw hills, all form part of a route which runs through much lowland country, rich and well inhabited. Any general advancing from the Edinburgh and Glasgow base would find here both easy passage and a desirable land to conquer. Elsewhere he might look in vain for either. The Highlands rise sheer in front of the isthmus, and they prevent all attempt to turn west from the route just indicated. A little to the north of Perth the Tay and Isla meet. It is a simple matter to follow the course of the Isla north-eastwards. He who marches to the north-west along the Tay speedily finds himself in a deep and difficult valley among lofty hills. Hither the Roman never came, and we may leave the unconquered Highlands unexplained.

How far can we trace in the history of the Roman conquest the influence of the physical features we have been considering? We have seen that our island was always accessible to continental influences. Caesar's subjugation of Gaul opened Britain to Roman culture. During the century which followed Caesar's Gallic wars, the Mediterranean civilization flowed freely into the Atlantic land across the intervening strip of sea. Vases and brooches of bronze as well as fine pottery, all of Italian pattern, were imported. Roman coin legends and devices were adopted on British gold and silver money. Roman suzerainty was accepted by British chiefs. The process was apparently favoured by the man who, during the reigns of Augustus and Tiberius, ruled all the part of Britain that was nearest to Gaul—Cunobeline, "the radiant Cymbeline, which shines here in the west". His capital seems to have been Camulodūnum, now Colchester. Cunobeline, as the details of his coins testify, was no enemy of Roman ways. On some of the pieces which he struck he actually used the title *Rex*.[1] We may think that under him the south-east of the island was becoming gradually and peacefully Romanized. But with his death in or about A.D. 42 there came a change. In A.D. 43 the Roman government determined to invade and annex the country.

The exact motives for the step are not recorded. The earlier Claudian rule is, however, marked by a forward provincial policy, hardly noticed by historians, which produced the annexation of several outlying suzerainties, such as those of Mauretania and Thrace. With this the annexation of Britain must be connected. It is significant that, when the soldiers of the invading army showed a mutinous reluctance to quit the shores of Gaul, the

[1] Evans, *Coins of the Ancient Britons*, Pl. XII, 5.

freedman Narcissus, one of the chiefs of the imperial bureaucracy, was dispatched post-haste from Rome to induce them to embark.[1] Something, too, must be allowed to the position of the Emperor. He was generally ridiculed and despised, and he might naturally desire to meet the ridicule by surpassing the military achievements of all his predecessors and extending the Empire (as contemporary poetasters put it) even beyond the waves of the Atlantic.[2] Events in Britain also gave cause for action. Cunobeline's death may have produced internal wars, dangerous to Roman trade and traders; or a nationalist party hostile to Roman things may have gained the upper hand. Suetonius gives us some hint of dissensions and a repudiation of the Roman suzerainty.[3] But the details are obscure. All that can be said with certainty is that in some way there was confusion in the isle, and that this coincided with the predominance of a 'spirited' foreign policy at Rome.

The invasion itself is a credit to the home Government. The invading force combined in a rare manner the elements of success. The army was large, the troops good, the officers numerous and well-selected, the commander competent. Their triumph was complete and speedy. The details unfortunately can only be recovered by conjecture. Cassius Dio, our main authority, is brief and vague. We know that the troops sailed—apparently from Boulogne and neighbourhood—in three divisions and in a westerly direction.[4] We may presume that they landed at the three ports of Richborough, Dover, and Lymne. Thence moving forward along the fertile and easy plains

[1] Dio, lx. 19.

[2] '*Oceanus medium venit in imperium.*' See the anonymous *De laudibus Claudii Caesaris*, reprinted in *Mon. Hist. Brit.* p. lxxxix.

[3] '*Britanniam . . . tunc tumultuantem ob non redditos transfugas*' (*Divus Claudius*, 17). Mommsen (*Rom. Prov.* i. 174) follows O. Hirschfeld in connecting this with the flight of one of Cunobeline's sons, Adminius, to the continent in the reign of Caligula, as recorded by Suetonius (*C. Caligula*, 44), and sees in *tumultuantem* a reference to raids, actual or projected, on the coast of Gaul.

[4] Dio, lx. 19.

of north Kent and never losing touch with their base, they quickly forced the Medway and pushed on to the Thames. Here, according to Dio,[1] they met with a momentary check. The vanguard reached the farther bank, and slew many of the enemy. But in a too eager pursuit they became entangled in trackless swamps, and had to fall back with heavy loss. A halt was therefore called. In conformity with a pre-arranged plan, Claudius himself was summoned. His arrival, and the accession of the reinforcements which we may suppose him to have brought,[2] gave a fresh impetus to the advance. The Thames was crossed once more, and Essex and the native capital at Colchester were seized almost immediately. Thus in a few weeks (Claudius was only sixteen days in the island altogether [3]) the invaders possessed a new base round the Thames estuary—a base which was in easy communication with the continent and which commanded the whole British midlands. Meanwhile the native princes of Cunobeline's family were dead or in flight.

Another view, adopted and popularized by Hübner,[4] calls for a word of notice. Dio mentions incidentally, as one of the early episodes of the invasion, the submission to the Romans of a section of a tribe called the Boduni who were subjects of the Catuvellauni.[5] The name of the Boduni is otherwise unknown. Camden, however, identified them with the Dobuni of Ptolemy, whose capital was Corinium or Cirencester.[6] This identification, which has been widely accepted,[7] involves a transference of the Roman operations from Kent to the vicinity of Gloucestershire and a landing, not in the

[1] lx. 20.

[2] After describing the arrangement for the summoning of Claudius, Dio says (lx. 21): *καὶ παρασκευή γε ἐπὶ τῆς στρατιᾶς πολλὴ τῶν τε ἄλλων καὶ ἐλεφάντων προσυνειλεκτο.*

[3] Dio, lx. 25.

[4] See particularly *Römische Herrschaft in West-Europa*, pp. 16 ff. Cf. *Hermes* xvi, pp. 528 ff., and Pauly-Wissowa, *Real-Encycl.* iii, pp. 868 ff.

[5] Dio, lx. 20.

[6] Ptol. ii. 3, 12.

[7] It was, however, emphatically rejected by Mommsen (*Rom. Prov.* i, p. 175, foot-note).

south-east of England, but somewhere on the southern coast. One spot has found special favour among antiquaries. Bitterne, on the east bank of the Itchen opposite Southampton, is without doubt the Clausentum of the Antonine Itinerary. Hübner chose to regard the name as a corruption of 'Claudientum', and to find in it a clue to the actual port at which the Emperor had disembarked. Others, following the same train of thought, have preferred to connect it with Attus (or Atta) Clausus, the legendary founder of the Claudian family. In point of fact, this ingenious etymologizing is beside the mark. Clausentum is good Celtic.[1] The whole theory of a landing in or about Hampshire rests ultimately on Camden's more than doubtful conjecture as to the Boduni. It ignores all strategic advantages of geography and all convenience of communications, for it implies that, in order to attack Colchester, the Romans first made for the head waters of the Thames and then marched down the river-valley into Essex. We may dismiss it without more ado.[2]

From the base round the Thames estuary a rapid advance was made. It is quite clear that within four years, by A.D. 47, the Roman arms were definitely established on the border of South Wales and on the edge of the Yorkshire and Derbyshire hills. That is proved by what Tacitus records[3] as to the operations of Ostorius Scapula, governor from 47 to 51. His narrative shows that the Icĕni, who dwelt in Norfolk and Suffolk, had accepted Roman ascendancy before Ostorius arrived. The first scenes of conflict with tribes beyond the pale were the hills of Monmouthshire and the lead-mines of Flintshire, the territories, respectively, of the Silŭres and of the Deceangi or Deceangli, and the fighting at once spread to north-west Wales, the territory of the Ordovices. In other words, the whole of the lowland area

[1] See *Vict. Hist. Hants* i, p. 332.

[2] For a fuller discussion see Furneaux's edition of the *Annals* of Tacitus, ii, pp. 134 ff.

[3] *Annals* xii. 31–3.

had been already overrun. The frontier, as Tacitus seems to say in an unfortunately corrupt passage,[1] was the Severn and the Trent, with Chester added. But the methods by which the conquest had been won are less plain. Many theories have been advanced, and (so far as I can judge) all of them to no purpose; for their authors have without exception [2] misunderstood the elements of the problem. For instance, a recent writer on the subject plants his Second Legion at Gloucester, his Ninth at Leicester, and his Fourteenth and Twentieth at Cirencester, as a first stage in the advance.[3] Yet there is neither evidence nor probability that any of these brigades was ever stationed at any of these places. The materials for decision are indeed few. Literature fails us completely; the light from archaeology is feeble and flickering. But the salient facts appear to be as follows.

The regular army of occupation is known to have been composed of four legions—brigades, each of some 5,000 heavy infantry—and of auxiliary troops of the second grade, perhaps in all some 40,000 men. The legions were the II Augusta, the IX Hispana, the XIV Gemina, and the XX Valeria Victrix. Not improbably this constituted the original expeditionary force, which crossed under the supreme command of Aulus Plautius.[4] Tem-

[1] *Annals* xii. 31 '*cunctaque castris Antonam et Sabrinam fluvios cohibere parat*', where *cis Trisantonam* (see Dr. H. Bradley in *Academy*, April 28th and May 19th, 1883) seems an almost certain emendation. Cf. *Vict. Hist. Northants* i, p. 213, and F. H.'s Appendix to Mommsen's *Rom. Prov.* (1909) ii, p. 348.

[2] This was written in 1907. A year or two later Dr. G. Teuber published his *Beiträge zur Geschichte der Eroberung Britanniens durch die Römer* (Breslau, 1909), an admirable little study, the results of which agree, in the main, with those here reached. About the same time a summary of F. H.'s views appeared in the Appendix which he contributed to the revised edition of Mommsen's *Rom. Prov.* (ii, pp. 347 ff.).

[3] *Eng. Hist. Rev.* xviii (1903) pp. 1 ff.

[4] As Teuber points out (*op. cit.* p. 19), this was certainly the case with the Second Legion, since its commander Vespasian, the future emperor, is expressly mentioned by Dio (lx. 20) as having distinguished himself at the forcing of the Medway, and almost certainly the case with the Ninth, since it proceeded direct to Britain from Pannonia, of which province Plautius was governor when he was selected as generalissimo.

porary reinforcements, presumably brought by Claudius, appear to have included a contingent of the Praetorian Guard, and a detachment of the Eighth Legion. Dio tells us[1] that Rubrius Pollio, one of the Praetorian prefects, was among the officers on whom signal honours were bestowed at the close of the campaign, and from an inscription found at Rimini in the fifteenth century we learn that a certain Vettius Valens, who had been orderly to a Praetorian prefect, was decorated '*torquibus, armillis, phaleris*' for his services in "the British war".[2] Distinctions were conferred rather freely on this occasion, doubtless because it was a very exceptional thing for the Emperor to take the field in person. Hence our knowledge of the presence of at least part of the Eighth Legion, as a special draft.[3] Such special drafts did not usually stay long in the region to which they were sent. In all likelihood the temporary reinforcements which Plautius received were soon withdrawn. The contingent of the Praetorian Guard may have left Britain with the Emperor.

According to the rules of the Roman military system, an army acting independently usually comprised not legionaries only nor auxiliaries only, but legionaries and auxiliaries together. We may therefore assume that, if the general army just described were broken up into independent forces, the separate portions would not be all legions or all *auxilia*, but each would contain both legions and *auxilia*. There is evidence that the army was thus broken up. Definite traces—many of them tombstones—show us, in times later than A.D. 47, the Second Legion posted at Caerleon-on-Usk, near Newport in Monmouthshire, the Fourteenth at Wroxeter (FIG. 1)[4]

[1] lx. 23.

[2] *CIL.* xi. 395 (Dessau, *Inscr. Sel.* 2648).

[3] See *CIL.* v. 7003, *C. Gavio L. f. Stel. Silvano [p]rimipilari leg. VIII Aug. . . . [d]onis donato a divo Claud. bello Britannico [to]rquibus armillis phaleris corona aurea. . . .* (Dessau, *Inscr. Sel.* 2701). Cf. Dessau, *op. cit.* 967.

[4] The stone, which was found in 1752, reads: **M PETRONIVS**

and perhaps afterwards at Chester, the Twentieth at Chester, and the Ninth at Lincoln.[1] Other more scanty remains—mostly inscribed tiles—show vestiges of the Ninth Legion at Hilly Wood in east Northamptonshire on one of the roads to Lincoln ; vestiges of the Twentieth at Whittlebury in west Northamptonshire on the Watling Street, which ran towards Chester ; vestiges of the Second Legion on Mendip in Somerset, in Nero's reign, and also at Honeyditches near Seaton in east Devon ; and, finally, a hint of the Eighth at Leicester.[2] The dates of most of these evidences are uncertain. But we find no other sign of Roman troops in the lowlands which can be dated after A.D. 47 ; we know from recent German discoveries that legionary tiles were used as early as this period ; and to this period we may therefore refer at least the traces of the Second Legion in Devon and of the Ninth and Twentieth in Northamptonshire.

A further argument is supplied by the chief Roman roadways of southern Britain. These fall into three distinct groups. One runs westward from London, crosses the Thames at Staines, and at Silchester (Calleva Atrebatum) divides into branches running to Winchester,

L(VCI) F(ILIVS) MEN(ENIA TRIBV) VIC(ETIA) ANN(ORVM) XXXVIII MIL(ES) LEG(IONIS) XIIII GEM(INAE) MILITAVIT ANN(OS) XVIII SIGN(IFER) FVIT H(IC) S(ITVS) E(ST). That is : 'Here lies M. Petronius, son of Lucius, of the Menenian tribe, born at Vicenza, aged 38, soldier in the Legion XIV Gemina. He served for eighteen years and reached the rank of standard-bearer.' From internal evidence it is clear that the inscription was set up during the earliest years of the Roman occupation, probably in the reign of Claudius : see *Vict. Hist. Shropshire* i, p. 244.

[1] For Caerleon see *CIL*. vii. 100 ff. ; for Wroxeter, *ibid*. 154 f., and *Vict. Hist. Shropshire* i, pp. 244 f. ; for Chester, *Ephem. Epigr.* ix, pp. 535 ff., with references ; and for Lincoln, *CIL*. vii. 183 f. and *Ephem. Epigr.* ix, p. 557.

[2] For Northamptonshire see *Vict. Hist. Northants* i, pp. 214 f. ; for Somerset, *CIL*. xiii. 3491 = Dessau, *Inscr. Sel.* 8709 (a pig of lead found at S. Valery-sur-Somme), and *Vict. Hist. Somerset* i, pp. 338 ff. ; for east Devon, *Arch. Journ.* xlix, p. 180, and *Ephem. Epigr.* ix. 1268*a* ; and for Leicester, *Ephem. Epigr.* vii. 1124 and *Arch. Journ.* lxxv, pp. 25 f.

Fig. 1. TOMBSTONE OF A SOLDIER OF THE FOURTEENTH LEGION FROM WROXETER

See foot-note 4 on pages 105–6

Bath and Exeter, Cirencester, Gloucester and South Wales. A pig of lead found on Mendip, bearing the name of Britannicus and letters which indicate that it was smelted in the consulship of Veranius and Pompeius,[1] justifies the inference that this road was undoubtedly carried as far west as Somerset before A.D. 49. A second runs north-west from London past the municipality of Verulam—whose remains are still visible at St. Albans—to Wroxeter and Chester, and it also can be shown to have been pretty certainly in existence very soon after the invasion. The third route runs either from London or from Colchester, past Cambridge and the outskirts of Peterborough, to Lincoln, and was supported by a subsidiary line from the second route through Leicester. These are the roads which seem the most important and the earliest in the south of Roman Britain.

This, so far as I am aware, is the evidence. It is scanty and incoherent enough. But it seems to point to a definite scheme of conquest. The army, we know, when it sailed from Gaul, was organized in three divisions. Later on, it appears in three detachments in three different stations in Britain; three different groups of roads lead from the Colchester–London base to the three stations; and traces of each of the appropriate legions occur on each of the road-systems—in places where we should hardly expect troops except during the earliest years of the occupation. It seems probable, therefore, that the conquest of the lowlands was carried out by three armies. The Second Legion under the future emperor Vespasian, which as we chance to know was the left wing,[2] dealt with the south and ended in the fortress

[1] See *Vict. Hist. Somerset* i, p. 341. The pig itself is illustrated, *infra*, Fig. 66 *a*, where the letters giving the date (**V · ET · P · C**) will be found upon the side.

[2] *Duas validissimas gentes superque viginti oppida et insulam Vectem Britanniae proximam in dicionem redegit* (Suetonius, *Divus Vespasianus*, 4). The mention of the Isle of Wight puts the sphere of operations beyond doubt.

at Caerleon (Isca Silŭrum). The Fourteenth and the Twentieth formed the centre and went north-west to Wroxeter (Viroconium) and Chester (Deva). The Ninth, the right wing, moved north to Lincoln (Lindum). By A.D. 47 all four legions were planted in fortresses on the edge of the lowlands. Three watched the Welsh hills—from Caerleon, Wroxeter,[1] and Chester. Two—from Chester and Lincoln—kept the frontier against the Brigantes. The limits of the province were very much those which Tacitus describes, the Severn and the Trent.

One more event was required to complete the conquest of the south. The Romans, like other invaders, were wont to annex first and subdue afterwards. They did this in Britain, just as they had done it a century earlier in Gaul. The Icĕni, whose territory (as I have indicated) lay well within the lowlands, had apparently submitted to Plautius without a struggle. As the grip of Rome tightened, they grew restive. Ostorius had to read them a sharp lesson before he was free to turn his arms against the tribes of Wales. Hardly a decade later, in A.D. 61, heedless of what they had learned, they again rose in revolt. The whole land was instantly aflame. The gravity of the danger is best measured by the prominence given to the story in the narratives of Tacitus and Dio.[2] The causes of the outbreak are not obscure. Ill-treatment and exaction had goaded the provincials beyond endurance. The philosopher Seneca seems to have been personally responsible for a peculiarly usurious demand.[3] The death of Prasutagus, the ruling prince, brought matters to a head. In the hope of preserving for his family his kingdom and with it a share of his extensive private fortune, he had named Nero, now Emperor, as

[1] No trace of the fortress at Wroxeter has survived except a few tombstones of its soldiers. It was garrisoned for only a brief period, being superseded by Chester. Whether the two were ever simultaneously occupied, is perhaps doubtful. See *Vict. Hist. Shropshire* i, p. 216, and *Chester Journ.* vii, p. 11.

[2] Tacitus, *Agricola* 15 f., and *Annals* xiv. 31–9; Dio, lxii. 1–12.

[3] Dio, lxii. 2.

one of his heirs. The subservience was unrewarded. He left no son, and the spoilers laid hands on the entire heritage. His daughters were outraged. His widow Boudicca, better known to us as Boadicea, had to submit to the indignity of scourging. Stung to desperation, she took the field, drawing after her the great mass of the native population. Her personality, like that of Vercingetorix, made a profound impression on the imagination even of her foes. Dio dwells on the picture she presented as she addressed the rebel host—her commanding stature, the fierceness of her appearance, the keenness of her glance, the masculine accents of her voice, and (above all) the wealth of golden hair that flowed down over her shoulders and covered her whole back.

She had chosen an opportune moment to deliver her blow. Suetonius Paulinus, the governor, was fighting far away in Anglesey. Those of the legionaries who were not with him were in their frontier-fortresses. The first point threatened was the newly founded *colonia* at Colchester. Two days sufficed to wipe it out. Flushed with success, the insurgents immediately faced round, and overwhelmed the Ninth Legion as it was advancing from Lincoln to the rescue. Only the commander and the mounted troops escaped. It looked as if the end of the Roman dominion was at hand. Suetonius, however, rose to the emergency. He had at his disposal the Fourteenth Legion, a portion of the Twentieth, and some auxiliaries —probably the better part of twenty thousand men. Hurrying on ahead of the main body, he reached London, already a populous and flourishing commercial centre. Finding that he could not hope to hold the town with practically no troops, he abandoned it to its fate. Along with the *municipium* at St. Albans it was given over to fire and sword. Seventy or eighty thousand Romans and Romanized provincials are said to have been massacred. Meanwhile the Roman commander had fallen back on his main body. The Britons followed him. In a fierce battle, fought on ground of his own choosing, perhaps in the southern midlands, certainly on or near the line of Watling Street,[1] he crushed them utterly and took a terrible revenge. The fugitives were mercilessly hunted down. Their lands became a desolation. Multitudes died of hunger. So deeply scarred were the Icenian districts that generations did not suffice for their recovery. The infrequency of the traces of Romano-British life in Norfolk during the succeeding centuries may well be the outcome of the devastation.[2] It is a strange harvest to have been sown in the notorious *quinquennium Neronis*.[3]

The conquest of the uplands, to which we now turn, required not four years but forty, and the forty were followed by a whole century of intermittent struggles. The tale is one of slow advance chequered by individual disaster. Ostorius had made a beginning. But his defeat and capture of Caractacus or, rather, Caratācus involved no real flagging of the Silurian resistance. And further north the Ordovices remained defiant. Suetonius was engaged with them at the moment when the peace of the province was violently broken by Boudicca's insurrection. Had his term of office been prolonged, he might have resumed his interrupted task. His own countrymen, however, were shocked by the stern savagery of his measures of repression. He was recalled, and his successor Petronius Turpilianus did nothing. Of the latter Tacitus characteristically says:[4] '*non inritato hoste neque lacessitus honestum pacis nomen segni otio imposuit*'. But another explanation is possible. The Roman Government may have taken the rising as a warning and preferred to consolidate.

However that may be, ten years elapsed before the advance was resumed. Vespasian, who succeeded in A.D. 69, is not generally called a '*Mehrer des Reichs*'. He is usually described as—what he certainly was—

[1] See F. H. in *The Antiquary* l (1914), pp. 439 f.
[2] *Vict. Hist. Norfolk* i, p. 286.
[3] See J. G. C. Anderson in *J.R.S.* i, pp. 173 ff., with 'Note' by F. H.
[4] *Annals* xiv. 39.

a ruler of coarse, practical, efficient common-sense. Such men rarely strike out new lines. But Vespasian added much to the Empire in many lands. In Britain he added Wales and part of North England. '*Magni duces*', says Tacitus,[1] '*egregii exercitus, minuta hostium spes*.' Between 71 and 74 Petilius Cerialis vanquished the Brigantes in a series of bloody encounters and overran much of Lancashire and Yorkshire. Between 74 and 77 or 78 Julius Frontinus conquered the Silŭres. By this time garrisons had been planted all over Wales, and the subjugation of the land was fairly complete. Disasters still occurred; the hillmen were still ready to cut off isolated regiments.[2] But the end was near. When Agricola arrived in 77 or 78[3], only the Ordovices still gave trouble, and a single brief campaign brought or restored them to order.[4]

We have reached a great name. Amid the long succession of provincial governors of the Empire, Agricola is one of the very few who come before us with a clear-cut individuality, deliberately recorded. His is a typical figure, significant of the time in which he lived. Like his contemporary Vespasian, his son-in-law Tacitus, and his son-in-law's friend the younger Pliny, he belonged to a new social class which rose to prominence during the later part of the first century and slowly superseded the older senatorial families. It was a class of men born in the remoter parts of Italy or in the provinces, bourgeois in rank and endued with the virtues and defects of a bourgeoisie. Of this class Agricola was a good example. He lacked the characteristic pride of the old senators, the stubbornest aristocracy known to history. Their contempt, half magnificent and half inhuman, alike for the

[1] *Agricola*, 17. 1. [2] *Ibid.* 18. 2.

[3] In one of the last papers which he wrote (*P.S.A. Scot.* lii (1917–18), p. 180, foot-note) F. H. says, "I rather incline to 77". That is quite in accord with the general trend of recent opinion: see Gaheis in Pauly-Wissowa's *Real-Encycl.* x. 129 f., R. Knox McElderry in *J.R.S.* x, pp. 68 ff., and Appendix I in the revised edition of Furneaux's *Agricola*, begun by F. H. and completed by J. G. C. Anderson (Oxford, 1922).

[4] See F. H., *Military Aspects of Roman Wales*, pp. 12 f. (*Cymmrodorion Soc. Trans.* 1908–9, pp. 64 f.).

emperors who ruled them and for the dependants who served them, for personal danger and for the misery of others, their uncompromising obstinacy, their extravagant vices, their colossal wealth and reckless luxury, were all equally foreign to this respectable middle-class official. Instead, a shrewd obsequiousness enabled him easily and even elegantly to adapt himself to the times and during his later years to submit quietly to the insults of Domitian. '*Peritus obsequi eruditusque honestis utilia miscere*'—"quick to obey and trained to combine the honourable and the advantageous"—so his son-in-law describes him,[1] damning him with strange praise, and revealing by an unconscious candour the temper of an age and of a class.

But Agricola had at the same time the qualities of a good provincial. Simple in manner, honest in finance, cheerful and optimistic in all things, he made a sound soldier and probably a sounder administrator. In the field he was an indifferent tactician, and perhaps not much of a strategist. But he was a first-rate commissariat officer and he chose sites for forts and blockhouses with the eye of a singularly capable engineer. The greater side of his achievement, though not that which appealed most forcibly to his son-in-law, was in civil government. Here his provincial origin and sentiment made him sympathize with the native population. Like others among his contemporaries, he wished not only to rule them well—Cicero had done that—but to encourage the diffusion of Roman culture amongst them, and fit them for membership of the Roman State. Probably his own forbears had benefited by that policy in Gaul, and he desired to extend the benefit to others. It may be that modern men, with their theories of governing with the consent of the governed, might not call this policy of Romanization true sympathy. But it bore good fruit in Britain. From the age of Agricola onward we trace the beginnings of orderly civilized life in the island, the growth of towns, the spread of the Roman language.

[1] *Agricola* 8. 1.

Agricola ruled Britain for seven years, and this long, though not unparalleled, term of office allowed him to accomplish much. His biographer and all subsequent historians have emphasized his military successes, and they undeniably demand notice. Acting (we may think) from a base at Chester, he set the seal on the conquest of Wales by subduing the Snowdon district and Anglesey. The work was thoroughly done. Whether it was his own merit or that of his predecessors, or whether it was the fault of the Britons, Wales gave no further trouble to Roman soldiers. This effected, he passed on north. Probably he started from the same base Chester, and moved up the west coast route. Vestiges referable to no one but him occur in Cumberland and Dumfriesshire, though it must be confessed that they are few and faint. We trace him, or some Romans of his age, building a post at Carlisle.[1] We can detect him, as it seems, besieging the great hill fortress of Burnswark, which looks over all the Solway plain and half of Cumberland.[2] But the traces of his operations which have quite recently emerged near Melrose suggest that his main advance was by the east. Here on a flat hill-top, 150 feet above the Tweed, are the remains of a fort of unusual area, occupied more than once by Romans, but first, as is plain, by the troops of Agricola.[3] It is not impossible that it was he, rather than Petilius Cerialis, who made York a Roman place of arms. It is virtually certain that he was the builder of the Roman road which under various names (Leeming Lane, Dere Street, and the like) can still be followed northwards from York to Corbridge-on-Tyne [4] and thence to Newstead on Tweed and Inveresk outside

[1] *C. and W. Trans.* (n.s.) xvii, 235 ff. For 'vestiges' elsewhere in Cumberland see R. G. Collingwood in *Archaeologia* lxxi, p. 14.

[2] *Trans. Dumfries and Galloway Ant. Soc.* 1920–1, pp. 96 ff.

[3] The excavation was in progress when these Lectures were delivered. For a full account of the results see Curle, *A Roman Frontier Post and its People* (1911).

[4] On Corbridge as a link in the chain, see *Northumberland County History* x (1914), p. 478, and *P.S.A.L.* (2nd. ser.) xxiii, p. 485.

of Edinburgh. Geographically, it will be remembered, this was the line of least resistance.

Of what Agricola did or did not do when he reached the Tyne and Solway isthmus, we know nothing definite.

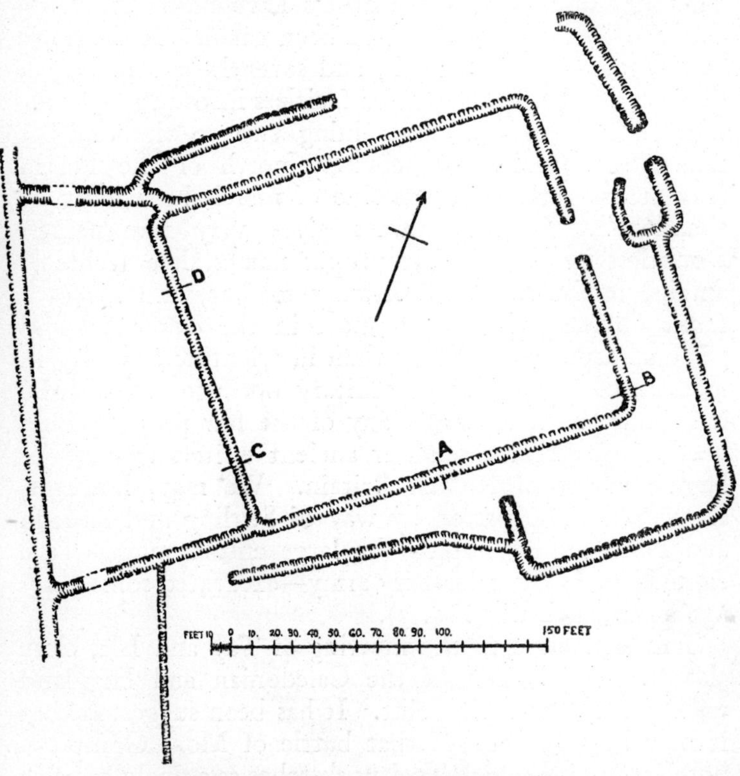


Fig. 2. AGRICOLAN FORT ON THE BAR HILL

The elaborate character of the defences is noteworthy, also the fact that, small as the fort was, it was provided with the usual annexe for traders and camp-followers.

The pen is silent, and up till now the spade has helped but little. It is otherwise with the neck of land that separates the firths of Forth and Clyde. Here we are at once on firm ground. In his fourth campaign (A. D. 80 or 81), as his son-in-law tells us, he was able to fortify the northern isthmus by a chain of forts. One of these, a tiny stronghold whose garrison can have been barely 150 men, was identified in 1903 on the Bar Hill, a few miles west of Glasgow, buried under a fort of the time of Pius (FIG. 2). The sites of two or three others have been discovered since. All alike seem to have been small. Three more campaigns—the fifth, sixth, and seventh—are recorded, the first devoted perhaps to a fruitless inroad into south-western Scotland, the remaining two to the difficult task of conquering the country north of the Forth. Any attempt to trace the line of march here must be abandoned. Tacitus always gives very few names. Doubtless he feared that proper names, like technical details, might shock his literary readers, and his own tastes obviously lay much more in the emotional and personal aspects of history than in scientific accuracy in matters of geography or military operations. Besides, it so happens that hardly any of the few proper names he does give recur in other ancient writers among the known names of Roman Britain. We may, however, suppose that he passed by way of Stirling and Ardoch and Perth, and occupied the large encampment—large enough for an expeditionary army—excavated some years ago at Inchtuthil [1] (FIG. 3).

This site, close to the meeting of Tay and Isla, close also to the junction of the Caledonian and Highland railways, is a strategic point. It has been suggested that it may be the scene of that battle of Mons Graupius—not Grampius—which Tacitus sketches as a final dramatic close to the governorship of Agricola. Certainly, it is the most northerly instance of Roman encampment attributable to Agricola's time which the critical instinct of a southern or Saxon inquirer can at present accept. '*Cetera iam fabulosa*', says Tacitus in another context,[2] '*quod ego ut incompertum in medium relinquam.*' We

[1] See *P. S. A. Scot.* xxxvi (1901–2), 182 ff., from which FIG. 3 is taken. For an interpretation of the plan, and particularly of the 'Villa', the 'Stone Buildings', and the 'Wooden Buildings', see *J. R. S.* ix, pp. 113 ff.

[2] *Germania* 46.

must, however, remember that Roman 'camps' have been noted west and north of Inchtuthil—one at Comrie in Strathearn, others near Forfar in Strathmore. and one or two yet further north beyond Aberdeen. They are camps, not of permanent occupation, but of armies on campaign. They are as yet wholly unexplored; till the

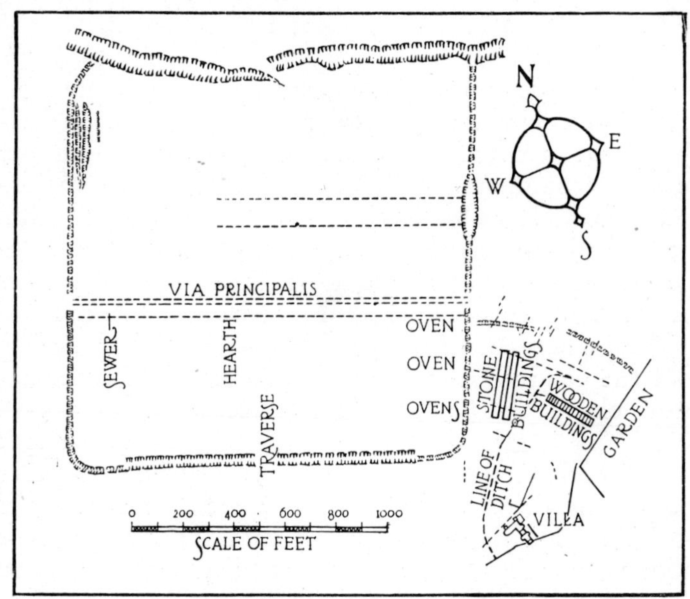


Fig. 3. AGRICOLAN CAMP AT INCHTUTHIL

spade has unmasked their secrets, it will be rash to stop Agricola at Inchtuthil on the Tay.[1]

Almost immediately after the great battle he was recalled. Perhaps he had now reached the natural term

[1] Two of the Aberdeenshire camps were examined in 1913 and following years, but it remains doubtful whether they should be associated with Agricola's campaigns or with some later advance. See 'The Roman Camps at Raedykes and Glenmailen' in *P. S. A. Scot.* l (1915–16), pp. 317 ff., and F. H.'s 'Roman Britain in 1913', *British Academy Supplem. Papers* ii, pp. 7 ff. At Comrie there is also a 'fort'.

of his governorship. Perhaps the home Government judged his enterprise to be fruitless. Perhaps troops were needed to join in more serious wars on the Rhine and Danube. No positive evidence is available as to this—save that troops were now beyond all doubt withdrawn from Britain to serve on the northern continental frontier.[1] But we may fairly ask, What was the result of Agricola's work, of the long and toilsome campaigns? To judge by what we really know, it was very little. Tacitus, whose reticence often speaks more plainly than his aptest epigrams, seems to say as much, and recently discovered archaeological evidence indicates that his Scottish conquests could not be maintained by his successors.[2] It seems plain, too, that he did not realize the difficulty of his task. He had forced his way up to the Highlands. But it was not without reverses, and it really accomplished nothing. Rome had not the number of troops needed to conquer and—a harder thing—to hold the conquered country for the length of time that must elapse before the natives accepted a foreign dominion. Agricola made the mistake in actual fact about Scotland that Tacitus tells us he made on paper about Ireland, on which island it is clear that he never set foot.[3] He judged (we read) that Ireland could be subdued by one legion and some auxiliaries or, say, 7,000

[1] See Ritterling, *Jahreshefte des österr. archäol. Instituts* 1904, vol. 7, Beiblatt, 37 f. and *infra*, p. 264, footnote 2.

[2] The allusion here is to the inferences originally suggested by the excavation of the Agricolan fort on the Bar Hill: see Macdonald and Park, *The Roman Forts on the Bar Hill* (1906), pp. 14 f. A different complexion has, however, been put upon the facts by the excavation of Newstead and by a critical examination of the evidence from Ardoch, Camelon, and Inchtuthil. It is now clear that it was only the tenure of the isthmus forts that was short-lived. Central and south-eastern Scotland were in all probability held for many years after the recall of Agricola: see *J.R.S.* ix, pp. 111 ff. Had the new facts been available when the lecture was written, it is probable that not only this sentence but the whole estimate of Agricola's achievement might have been considerably modified.

[3] *Class. Rev.* xiii, pp. 302 f. and xiv, p. 53.

or 8,000 men. It is only the first of many pleasing dreams of how to deal with that difficult land. But it was utterly astray. It was not in his military successes that the true ability of the man came out. It was, as I have already said, in the other aspect of his governorship. Under his régime, and just before and after, the Romanization of Britain took its first great step forward. But with that we are not concerned in the present lecture.

After the departure of Agricola and a portion of the troops he had commanded, deep obscurity falls on the island. We do not know where the Roman frontier was or how it was guarded.[1] We can discern by doubtful traces the advance of Roman culture in the south and even in some northern districts like Derbyshire.[2] But thirty years pass before the next military event of which we have any record. This occurred late in the reign of Trajan or early in that of Hadrian. A new generation of Britons had grown up, forgetful of their fathers' battles and defeats. The north rose and not in vain. The Ninth Legion, then stationed at York, was annihilated. The rising was, of course, crushed. Hadrian supplied another legion, the VI Victrix Pia Fidelis, and came over in person about A.D. 122. Numismatic memorials of his visit are abundant (FIG. 4). Before departing he established a definite frontier across the isthmus of Newcastle and Carlisle. I shall describe it more fully in the next lecture; now it suffices to say that a wall, continuous from sea to sea, henceforward barred the northern tribes from their southern kinsmen.

Hadrian's work was not final. He did, however, secure that after him the Roman frontier was never south, and sometimes north, of this wall. It was carried north twenty years later by the generals of Pius, when the northern isthmus, fortified long ago by Agricola, was reoccupied and a wall built along it from sea to sea. The date was about A. D. 142 (FIG. 4, 3). The object of the step

[1] See, however, *J.R.S.* ix, pp. 133 ff., and *Archaeologia* lxxi, p. 15.
[2] See *Vict. Hist. Derbyshire* i, pp. 199 ff.

was possibly to provide a breakwater outside the still-occupied Wall of Hadrian and to increase the difficulty of barbarian invasion by a double line. For a while it succeeded. But, twelve or fifteen years later, the natives retaliated fiercely. Provoked, it may be, by some harshness of Roman officials—perhaps interference with their local autonomy—the whole of north Britain took up

FIG. 4. COINS OF HADRIAN AND OF PIUS

1. Coin of Hadrian. The Emperor addressing the army of Britain.
2. Coin of Hadrian, with type of 'Britain subdued'.
3. Coin of Pius, celebrating the imperial *acclamatio* for victories won in Britain (A.D. 142–3).

arms. The governor, Julius Verus, suppressed the rebellion, with the aid of special reinforcements from Germany. We can trace the signs of his activity in various parts of the territory of the Brigantes—from Brough in Derbyshire to Birrens in Dumfriesshire and Newcastle in Northumberland.[1] Our knowledge of the governor's name and of the facts as to the German

[1] *P.S.A.Scot.* xxxviii, pp. 454 ff., and *Ephem. Epigr.* ix, 1163 and 1230.

reinforcements we owe to a slab recovered from the bed of the river Tyne in 1903 (Fig. 5). A fragmentary tablet from the fort at Birrens has supplied the date (Fig. 6). Of the details of the war we hear nothing. Beyond a chance reference in Pausanias,[1] it is unknown to history, like so much else of real importance in the second century. But the Roman again triumphed, though not without

Fig. 5. SLAB FROM THE TYNE

'In honour of the Emperor Antoninus Pius, erected by a draft for the Legion II Augusta and the Legion VI Victrix and the Legion XX Valeria Victrix, specially sent over from the two provinces of Germany,[2] under Julius Verus, Governor of Britain.'

difficulty; from 161 to 165 there was still unrest in northern Britain.

The end of the story approaches. Twenty years later,

[1] viii. 43. 4.

[2] On the phrase '*contributi ex Germaniis*' see *Arch. Ael.* xxv, p. 143, and *Ephem. Epigr.* ix, 1163. Cf. the steps taken by Nero to reinforce the army in Britain after the Ninth Legion had been cut to pieces in Boudicca's rebellion (Tac. *Ann.* xiv. 38).

with the coming of yet another generation, fresh trouble broke out. The Roman historians tell us that Ulpius Marcellus crushed it. At the same time, however, the Romans lost the country north of Cheviot, including the Wall of Pius. Mommsen, it is true, has maintained that this wall and the land behind it was continuously held by Rome into the third century.[1] But the evidence of the Roman coins found in Scotland—evidence unknown

FIG. 6. INSCRIPTION OF A.D. 158 FOUND AT BIRRENS

The text can be completed and restored as follows:

**IMP(ERATORI) CAES(ARI) T(ITO) AEL(IO) HADR(IANO) ANTONINO AVG(VSTO) PIO P(ATRI) P(ATRIAE) PONT(IFICI) MAX(IMO) TR(IBVNICIA) POT(ESTATE) XXI CO(N)S(VLI) IV COH(ORS) II TVNGR(ORVM) MIL(IARIA) EQ(VITATA) C(IVIVM) L(ATINORVM), SVB IVLIO VERO LEG(ATO) AVG(VSTI) PR(O) PR(AETORE).**

That is: 'In honour of the Emperor Caesar Titus Aelius Hadrianus Antoninus Augustus Pius, Father of his Country, Pontifex Maximus, invested for the twenty-first time with the tribunician power, consul for the fourth time, the second cohort of Tungrians, Latin citizens, a thousand strong, including a contingent of horsemen, [erected this] under Julius Verus, governor of Britain.'

[1] *Rom. Prov.* i, p. 187.

to Mommsen when he wrote, since it was only published in 1899[1]—proves conclusively that the whole was lost in or before A. D. 185. We may well believe that the success of Marcellus was limited to maintaining the southern barrier. Thenceforward the Roman frontier remained on that southern barrier, with a few forts north of it but on the south of Cheviot. Indeed, we may well call Cheviot then (as now) the dividing line between north and south. The great raid of Severus apparently carried the Roman arms beyond the Forth in A. D. 208. Possible vestiges of his presence have been detected on the site of the fort at Cramond, hard by Edinburgh, and there have been found on chance spots in the counties of Fife, Kinross, and Kincardine Roman coins which might be connected with his campaign. On the other hand, Newstead and the forts on the Wall of Pius seem never to have been trodden in by Roman feet after they were abandoned in the reign of Commodus. If a guess must be made, we might ask whether Severus sailed round to the Firth of Forth,[2] marched thence across Kinross and followed the east coast northwards, there entrenching some of those encampments which have been already mentioned as existing in and beyond Forfarshire. In any event the raider did not march to annex. His reconstruction of Hadrian's Wall proves conclusively that the day of Roman annexation was over. The tale of the conquest of Britain is complete.

Perhaps it is not so much the conclusion that is significant as the century which preceded it. The second century is famed as being the Golden Age in the history of the Empire or, indeed, of any state. But there were exceptions to this prosperity, and one of those exceptions was Britain. Even in the second century the north of England—the region from Derbyshire to Cheviot—was

[1] *The Antonine Wall Report* of the Glasgow Arch. Soc., pp. 159 ff. For a later and fuller list see *P. S. A. Scot.* lii, pp. 203 ff.

[2] This suggestion is strengthened by the evidence of the coin-finds: see *P. S. A. Scot.* lii, p. 252.

still unquiet and disordered. When we come to discuss the growth of Roman civilization in the south of the island, the importance of this prevailing unrest, this opposition to Mediterranean fashions, will again concern us. To-day we have only to note the long resistance. Perhaps we may praise the Britons for their stubborn fight; it is doubtful whether we ought to blame the Romans. Britain was distant; war in Britain was costly and difficult; it may have been thought best to be inefficient. That is the attitude of many great empires. They are too vast for human rulers to secure efficiency in every corner, too vast also for little faults to seem to matter. Like the larger animals of the natural world, they are slow to see little things and slow to suffer from them. Yet the development of nature is towards the increase of the smaller animals and the extinction of mammoth and mastodon.

PLATE IV HADRIAN'S WALL ON HOTBANK, LOOKING EAST TO SEWINGSHIELDS

# LECTURE III

## PERMANENT MILITARY OCCUPATION OF BRITAIN

From the Roman conquest of Britain, which formed the subject of the last lecture, we pass naturally to the permanent military occupation by which Rome held the conquered province. The theme has a twofold interest. It brings before us, in an excellent instance, the military system of the Roman Empire. And it involves, less directly but still quite definitely, the ultimate problem of the effect of Rome upon Britain, more particularly with respect to the areas garrisoned by the troops and to the nationalities of the soldiers. Parts of my material will be perfectly familiar to some of my audience. But that is inevitable in lectures which aim at connecting ancient and modern history, and which cannot presuppose a knowledge of either. It will be convenient to consider, in the first place, the general Roman military system and, in the second place, its local application in Britain.

The 'regular' army of the Roman Empire developed out of that of the Republic. But it differed more widely from its forerunner than is always realized. Let me emphasize its more notable features. To begin with, it did not consist—as did the army of the later Republic, from the time of Marius and Sulla onwards—entirely, or almost entirely, of legions. A second class of troops, the auxiliaries, made their appearance. These had existed, indeed, under the later Republic. But they had counted for little, although by Caesar's day some value had come to be set upon the cavalry.[1] They now became as important as the legions, and ultimately they became far more important. The Imperial army thus consisted of two classes of troops.

[1] *Bell. Afric.* c. 78.

The legion was a brigade of from five thousand to six thousand heavy infantry, with a handful of mounted men serving as dispatch-riders and the like. Its general was a senator of high rank. Its chief officers were six tribunes—mainly young men of good birth and total inexperience [1]—and sixty centurions, often promoted from the ranks,[2] who did the real work of command. In theory, its common soldiers were recruited from free-born Roman citizens and represented the old citizen-army of Republican Rome. In practice, they were either Romanized provincials [3] or the sons of legionaries on service, the so-called ‘ children of the camp ’ ; and, if not already citizens, they were given the franchise on enlistment. After a term of nominally twenty years they received their discharge and a bounty in money or in land. Sometimes they returned to their original homes ; sometimes they were planted by the Government in provincial municipalities ; not a few remained quietly in the places where their active life had been spent. Until the third century the legionaries were, after the Praetorian Guard, the best troops in the regular army, at once the most trustworthy in battle and the most fully rewarded and recompensed.

The auxiliaries, on the other hand, were an inferior grade, inferior alike in birth and education, in pay and conditions of service, and (under the early Emperors) in morale and fighting power. They included both horse and foot, the regiment of auxiliary infantry forming

[1] The equestrian tribune, however, was a man who had already served as a *praefectus cohortis* of auxiliaries.

[2] Such promotion was the rule under the Republic. Under the Empire direct appointment was not infrequent. Those so appointed were either men of equestrian rank who voluntarily resigned their privileges in order to become centurions, or, more commonly, men below equestrian rank, drawn from decent families in the (chiefly Italian) *municipia* : see Ruggiero, *Dizionario Epigrafico* ii, p. 196, and Karbe in *Diss. phil. Halenses* iv, p. 424.

[3] F. H. is here speaking of the second century and later. Down at any rate to Flavian times the Western legions were largely recruited from Italy : see *infra*, pp. 156 and 168.

Fig. 7. TOMBSTONE FROM CIRENCESTER

See note 1 on next page for transliteration of the inscription.

a cohort, that of cavalry an *ala*, and they were organized on a very different basis from the legions. Their unit was five hundred or often one thousand men. Their chief officers were Roman, but of lower than senatorial standing. Their rank and file was levied, not always voluntarily, from those who were subjects but not citizens of Rome, and from the more unquiet districts of the Empire—not least from Britain—or, as these districts became civilized, from beyond the frontiers. Many auxiliary regiments bore territorial names. But, except in the earliest Empire, recruiting rarely followed strictly territorial lines. FIG. 7, for instance, is the tombstone of a Frisian[1] who was a trooper in a 'Thracian' *ala*, which helped to garrison Britain about the end of the first century of our era. The men served, in theory, twenty-five years. On discharge they gained the Roman franchise, and probably settled down much as did the legionaries.[2] Their internal organization offers one curious characteristic. Infantry and cavalry—true cavalry, not merely mounted men[3]—were sometimes combined in one and the same regiment, so that (to quote the commonest case) an infantry cohort might consist of approximately 750 foot and 250 horse. To this arrangement I know no close parallel in any other army.

Legions and *auxilia* are supposed to have existed in

[1] SEXTVS VALERIVS GENIALIS EQ(V)ES ALAE THRAEC(VM) CIVIS FRISIAVS TVR(MA) GENIALIS AN(NORVM) XXXX ST(IPENDIORVM) XX H(IC) S(ITVS) E(ST) (H)E(RES) F(ACIENDVM) C(VRAVIT).

That is: 'Here lies Sextus Valerius Genialis, soldier in the Thracian horse, in the troop of Genialis; born in Frisia; aged forty; served for twenty years. His heir had this set up.'

[2] Our knowledge of the auxiliaries is relatively very incomplete. By far the most satisfactory account of them available in English is G. L. Cheesman's *Auxilia of the Roman Army* (Oxford, 1914).

[3] Yet not quite equal to the regular auxiliary cavalry, the *equites alares*: see Hadrian's speech to his troops in Africa—'*Difficile est cohortales equites etiam per se placere, difficilius post alarem exercitationem non displicere*' (*CIL*. viii. 2532 = Dessau, *Inscr. Sel.* 2487).

about equal numbers, although in all likelihood the auxiliaries were, or soon became, the more numerous. Together, they may have constituted a force of from 300,000 to 400,000 men which, whatever its original size, probably grew larger as time went on. This force was predominantly an infantry army. Not only were the legions foot; no attempt was made to redress the balance by the auxiliaries, the bulk of whom were also footmen. But perhaps the most remarkable features of the Roman army arise from its distribution. Except, of course, for the Praetorian or Imperial Guard, it was confined to the provinces. More than that, it was organized by provinces. The garrison of any one province was independent of all other garrisons, and we may more truly speak of a number of provincial armies than of one Imperial army. Further, it was not posted in all provinces, but only in those provinces where frontiers needed protection or hill-tribes were restless. And in the provinces which were thus garrisoned, the troops were not scattered all over the country. They were concentrated strictly where they were wanted, somewhat on the system that Lord Kitchener introduced into India. The result was striking. A province with an army reproduced, in a curious and informal but significant fashion, the old Roman distinction between *domi* and *militiae*. Part of it was a military region and, very likely, contained practically nothing suggestive of civil life. The other part had its towns and villages and farm-houses, and was free from the (doubtless vexatious) presence of soldiers.

One more feature, and perhaps the most important, has still to be mentioned. These long-service infantry armies, whose duty was to protect, were garrison armies. Each legion or auxiliary regiment occupied a definite fortress or fort, and in general (as we shall see presently) one military unit occupied one fortified post. We might almost say that the motto of the Imperial army was: 'One regiment, one fort'. Our modern system is to keep troops quartered in barracks, ready for use in the field. The Empire knew nothing of such an arrangement until its later days. Indeed, the very theory of the Empire excluded a field army. The advice which its founder bequeathed to his successors was: '*coercendum intra terminos imperium*', "to keep the Empire within its existing frontiers". Wars of aggression were not contemplated. Individual crises might no doubt require field forces. An advance might be necessary beyond the Channel or the Euphrates. A punitive raid might be thought wholesome for vexatious Germans east of the Rhine. A revolt in Gaul or in Judaea might call for repression. But such troubles occurred seldom, and they could always be met by denuding garrisons in untroubled provinces until the disturbance was over. Thus, an insurrection in eastern Gaul was crushed by troops from the Rhine frontier, and a rising in Armorica by reinforcements from the legions and auxiliaries in Britain. Similarly, as we learned in the last lecture, when the army in Britain was hard pressed by the revolting Brigantes, its depleted ranks were filled by drafts of trained men from the other side of the North Sea. So long as disorder was confined to one province or one district at a time, this opportunism was efficient and inexpensive. And it was the good fortune of the Empire, as it had been of the Republic, to meet its enemies one by one. It is not surprising that the garrison system should have remained so long in use.

This connexion of men and forts was strengthened by the Roman policy as regards reliefs. According to our modern custom, a regiment spends a few years in a station, perhaps in Africa or in India, and is then relieved by another regiment. Such changes were rare in the Roman army. Legions and cohorts and *alae* remained in their stations for scores of years and sometimes for centuries. Changes were commoner among the auxiliaries than among their companions in arms. But even for an auxiliary soldier it must have been the rule to live all his military life, say from his twentieth to perhaps his fiftieth year, in one and the same spot. Small wonder that on his discharge he often settled down there, and did not seek a new home or care to return to his birthplace. In the Roman army, therefore, the most important element for us to consider is not the soldiers themselves so much as the places within which they dwelt while they were with the colours. We have somewhat obscured the character of this fact by our persistent habit of using the word ‘ camp ’ to denote such places. A camp to us is something comparatively unfortified and probably temporary : it connotes tents and an army on the march. This is not what we have to do with in considering the Roman army. The posts which we should associate with it were permanent, and the true English equivalents for them are ‘ fortresses ’ or ‘ forts ’.

These posts were of two kinds, matching the two classes of soldiery. The legions occupied fortresses (*castra stativa* or *hiberna*) of some fifty or sixty acres—about the size of the Christ Church Meadow—and one legion went to one fortress. In the early Empire two legions were sometimes quartered together, but in A.D. 89 the rule as to separation was made absolute by Domitian, who realized that combination involved a serious danger once it had been discovered that emperors could be made elsewhere than in Rome. The *auxilia* occupied forts (*castella*) ranging in size from three to eight or nine acres—from the area of Gloucester Green to that of Balliol Cricket Ground or Merton Meadow—and here again one regiment usually held one fort. The variations in size are to be explained by the fact that the auxiliary regiments varied in strength and in composition : the largest possible unit, a cavalry *ala* of one thousand men, needed much more space than the smallest, a cohort of only five hundred infantry. Between the two main kinds of fortified places there was a marked contrast in point of number and of geographical distribution. The *hiberna* were few, and they were placed in central positions as befitted the head-quarters of provincial defence. The *castella* were many, and they were scattered about the military area according to need—along main roads, along frontiers, or in the heart of troublesome hills.

Despite this contrast, fortresses and forts were laid out on one model. Their internal arrangements were determined, not by the whims of individual officers or the peculiarities of special sites, but by a single common and preconceived plan. The origin of this rigid plan was the scheme used by the Romans for troops on the march, and described for us by Polybius and Hyginus. The scheme is, however, only the prototype; we must not adopt it wholesale for our forts and fortresses, though this has often been done by antiquaries and by professed scholars. Permanent quarters for from five hundred to five thousand men could not possibly be the same as a marching encampment designed to accommodate from ten thousand to twenty thousand for two or three nights or weeks. As we actually see it in excavated remains, the plan of the fort or fortress shows a general resemblance to the scheme of the camp. But it exhibits considerable variations in various instances. Even a cavalry *ala* of one thousand men did not require nearly so much room as a permanent garrison of five thousand infantry with important officers. Again, there exist between province and province differences of arrangement, which may be due either to differences of date or to the prevalence of different fashions in different countries. Nevertheless, all examples, whether of forts or of fortresses, are marked by a strong family likeness. It can be traced in the following details.

The general type was a square or oblong enclosure, with rounded corners, girt with rampart and ditch, entered by four symmetrically placed gates, and traversed by four main streets running from the gates to the centre. At the centre, where the streets met, stood the Headquarters with the regimental offices and the shrine for the worship of the soldiers. Near by were the commander's residence, the other officers' quarters, and the stores and so on, while the ends of the enclosure were filled with barracks or tents for the rank and file, stables for their horses and the like. To this general type all known forts and fortresses conform, at least as rigidly as medieval monasteries conform to their special types, and more rigidly than do Oxford colleges. The chief elements of which it is composed deserve a closer examination. We know them best from the smaller *castella*, many of which have been explored in many lands. From these the great majority of our illustrations must necessarily be taken.

The ramparts of the forts were either banks of earth or of regularly laid sods, or walls of stone. In regard to this, different periods had apparently different preferences. In the first century earth or sods were much employed, and sometimes a skin or facing of stone was added to ensure strength and a steeper slope to the rampart. During the second century the superior advantages of stone became gradually recognized. By the opening of the third century it was universally used, and the older earthen ramparts were sometimes altered to suit the newer fashion. In front of the ramparts were V-shaped ditches, often two in number, and usually separated from the ramparts by level intervening berms. As a whole, these defences admitted of considerable elaboration. In some provinces they appear to have been more elaborate than in others. In north Britain, for example, we meet with numerous ditches, massive ramparts, and substantial ravelins.[1] Such occur hardly anywhere else in the Roman Empire, and we may be tempted to think that even in Roman days the Highland charge was uniquely fierce and irresistible. The remains of the fort at Ardoch in Perthshire (Figs. 8 and 9) furnish an excellent illustration of the precautions it was deemed

[1] The reference is to certain features of the defences of Ardoch (*P.S.A. Scot.* xxxii, pp. 413 ff.). Whether the excavators were right in calling them 'ravelins' is doubtful.

desirable to take when the foe to be reckoned with was more than usually formidable.

Fig. 10 represents the ground-plan of the fort at Borcovicium or Housesteads on Hadrian's Wall, as ascertained in 1898 through the excavations directed by Professor Bosanquet. It will give a good idea of the general character of the internal buildings and arrange-

Fig. 8. NE. CORNER OF ARDOCH FORT

ments of Roman *castella*. Entrance was had to the interior by four gates, disposed symmetrically, one on each side. Six gates are not unknown, but they occur much more rarely; Birdoswald or Amboglanna,[1] another of the forts on Hadrian's Wall, may be cited as an example. From each of the gates a street ran straight towards the centre of the fort, and other smaller lanes and passages

[1] Possibly the true Roman name was Camboglanna: see F. H. in *C. and W. Trans.* (n.s.) xviii, pp. 224 ff.

divided the various buildings. These streets and lanes were all parallel to one or other side of the enclosure, and the internal laying out of the whole thus preserved the same rectangular character as its outline.

In the centre was the so-called Praetorium—perhaps more correctly styled Principia—or Head-quarters Building. This was a square or oblong structure, varying in

Fig. 9. ARDOCH FORT: APPROACH TO N. GATE

size in various forts; a small specimen might measure 70 by 80 feet, and a large one 140 by 180 feet. The largest so far uncovered in Britain is at Newstead, where the dimensions are 104 by 131 feet. As an important edifice, the Principia was almost invariably built of stone.[1]

[1] A noteworthy exception is Ardoch, where all the buildings of the earlier fort (or rather forts), including the Principia, were of wood: see *J.R.S.* ix, p. 126. So, too, apparently, the Agricolan fort at Ambleside (*C. and W. Trans.* (n.s.) xxi, pp. 6 ff.). There are other examples, and these may be expected to become more numerous as excavation proceeds.

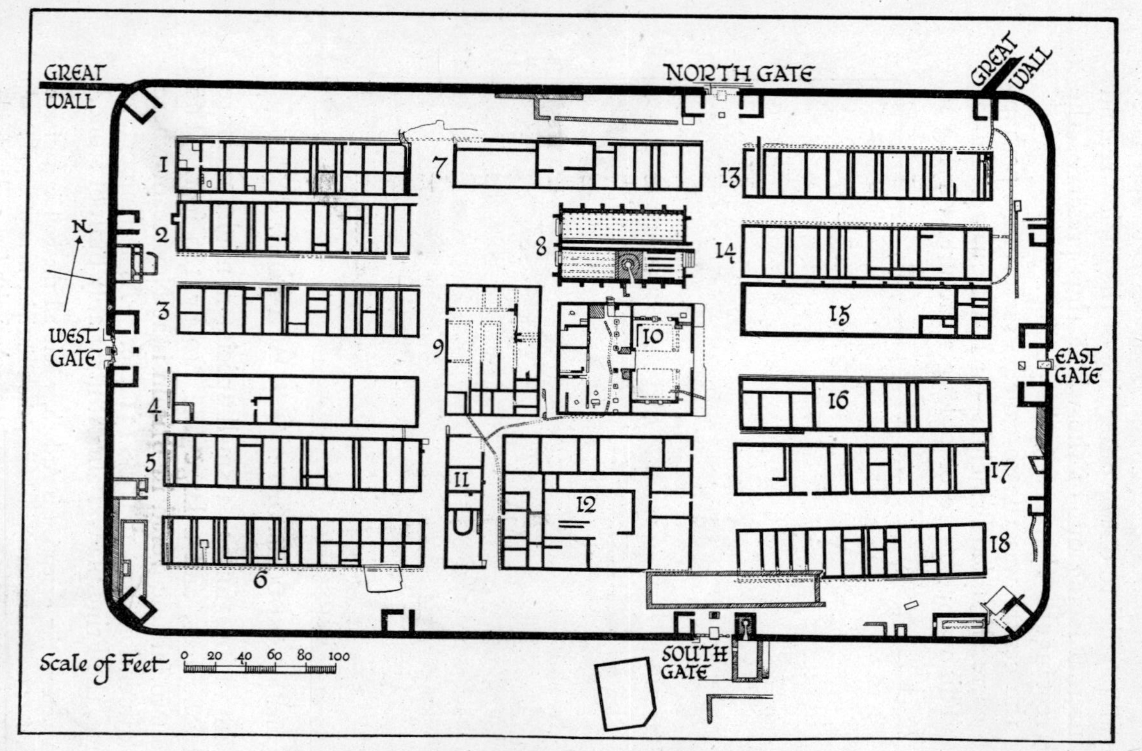


FIG. 10. PLAN OF FORT AT HOUSESTEADS

The more important buildings can be readily identified. 10 is the Principia; 12, probably the commander's house; 8, the storehouses; 1, 2, 3, 5, 6, 13, 14, 16, 17 and 18, barracks. The purpose of the

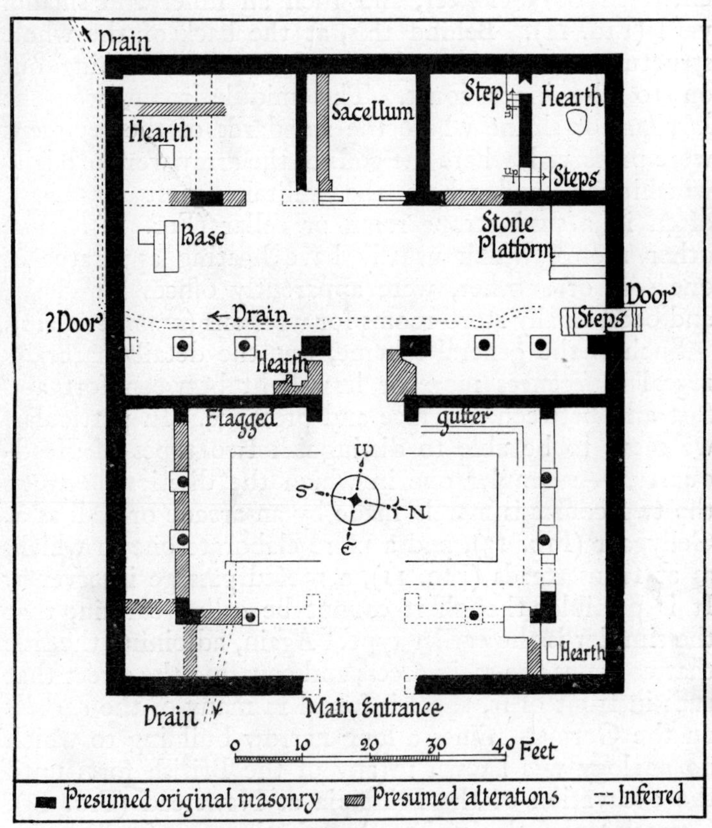


FIG. 11. HEAD-QUARTERS BUILDING, HOUSESTEADS

Its entrance, or at least its chief entrance, was in the middle of one side, usually one of the shorter sides. Through it the visitor reached first an open yard encircled by a cloister, and then an inner and smaller yard (FIG. 11). Behind this, at the back of the whole structure, was a row of some five rooms, looking out on to the inner court. The middle room was the *sacellum* or shrine where the standards of the regiment were preserved, where the gods of the army were officially worshipped, and where the military chest was kept, often in a sunk strong-room or cellar (FIG. 12). The other rooms, which usually have heating apparatus of one sort or another, were apparently offices for clerks, and occasionally store-rooms for weapons (*armamentaria*).

Such is the general scheme, but the details naturally reveal differences more or less slight between fort and fort and between province and province. In particular, we seem to be able to distinguish two types of Head-quarters—a simpler one in which the division between the two courts is merely made by an arcade or wall as at Gellygaer (FIG. 13), and a more elaborate one in which, as at Housesteads (FIG. 11), a roofed passage intervenes. It is possible, though it cannot be called certain, that the simpler is the earlier type. Again, adjoining the side that contains the main access and covering the street that runs in front of it, there is found in many of the *castella* on the German Limes a long narrow building to which no analogy was known in any of the British forts until the excavation of the Principia at Newstead (FIG. 14). German archaeologists have been in the way of calling this an '*Exercier-Halle*' or drill-hall. But the name is purely conjectural, and has been suggested merely by the spaciousness of the structure to which it is applied. The term 'entrance hall' is perhaps preferable. A crowd waiting for admission to the Head-quarters on special occasions could take convenient shelter here if the weather were inclement. At the same time there may have been an intention of lending a certain dignity to

Fig. 12. SUNK STRONG-ROOM IN THE HEAD-QUARTERS BUILDING OF THE FORT AT BROUGH, DERBYSHIRE

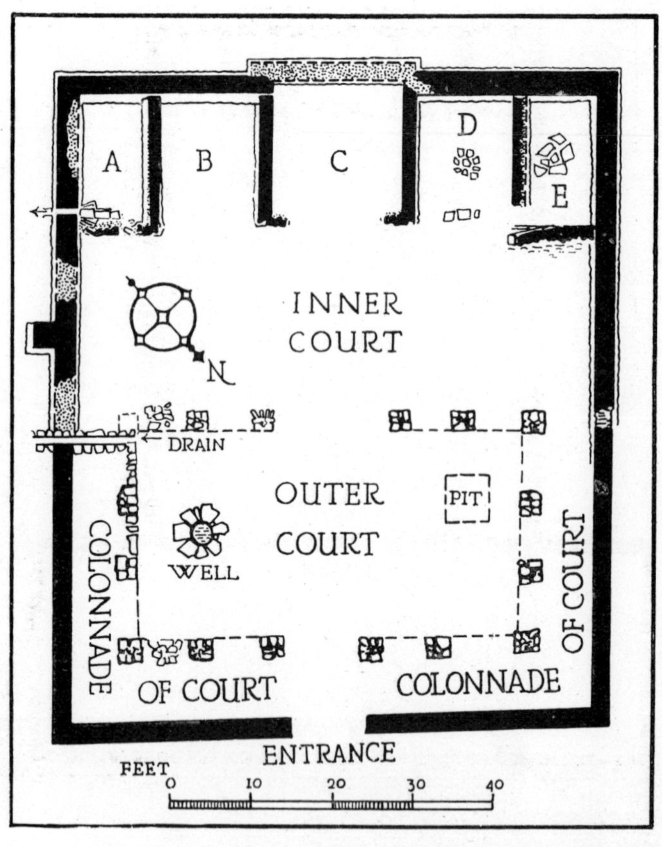


FIG. 13. THE PRINCIPIA, GELLYGAER

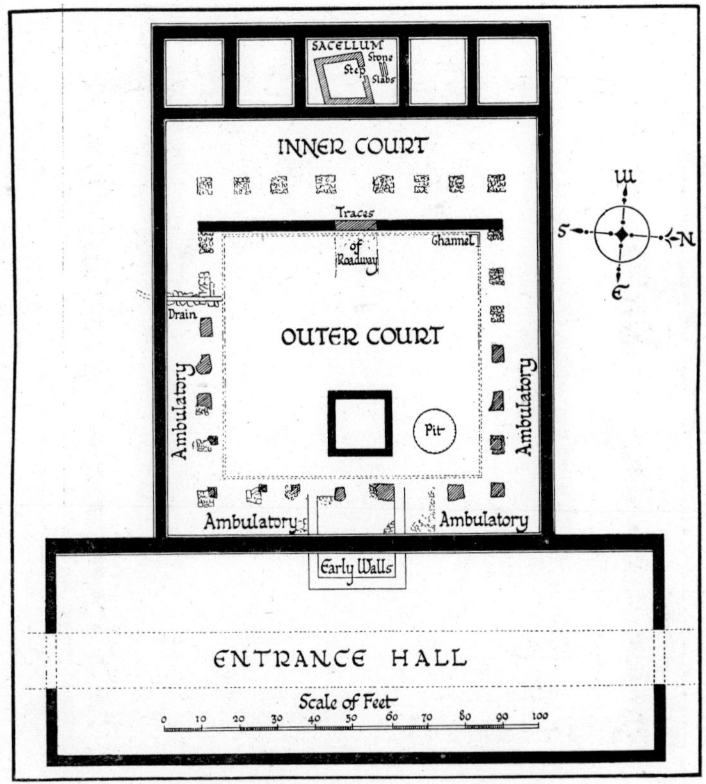


FIG. 14. THE PRINCIPIA, NEWSTEAD

The 'Early Walls', which are seen projecting into the Entrance Hall, represent the remains of the *sacellum* of an older Principia which faced in the opposite direction. The nature and purpose of the square building in the outer court are uncertain.

Fig. 15. ENTRANCE HALL OF THE 'PRAETORIUM' AT LAMBAESIS

the approach. The building, in fact, would seem to be the counterpart in miniature of the imposing pile that still stands fairly complete at the entrance to the Head-quarters of the great legionary fortress of Lambaesis in North Africa (FIG. 15).

Close to the Head-quarters stood other important buildings, usually of stone. Two of these are constant features — the commander's house, which perhaps accommodated other officers as well, and the granaries or storehouses. The former was a residential structure, comfortably fitted with hypocausts and sometimes with baths. The latter, of which there might be one or more, were long buttressed buildings with damp-proof basements, in which traces of wheat have occasionally been discovered. Some typical examples from forts in Britain are shown in FIG. 16.[1] Their architectural peculiarities were so marked that their remains are easily recognizable. The floors were regularly raised two or three feet above the adjacent surface-level, and were supported by dwarf sleeper-walls, or by low stone pillars, so that each granary had beneath it a shallow basement. This basement was, as a rule, ventilated by small openings between the buttresses, which ensured a through draught, keeping the granary itself free from damp or from dry-rot. The floors were constructed sometimes of very solid stone flags, sometimes of wood-planking. Nowhere is there any trace of hypocausts or of heating. The structure above the floor was a large open hall; sometimes two halls stood side by side, a device which ensured abundant room, without requiring unduly wide spans of roof; sometimes a row of columns down the middle of the hall supported the roof. The original heights of the walls and roofs are naturally unknown, but abundance of débris often shows that the walls must once have been high, while heaps of fallen roof-tiles not seldom point to

[1] In Germany a rather simpler style of construction seems generally to have been adopted. See E. Ritterling, *Das frührömische Lager bei Hofheim im Taunus*, pp. 52 ff.

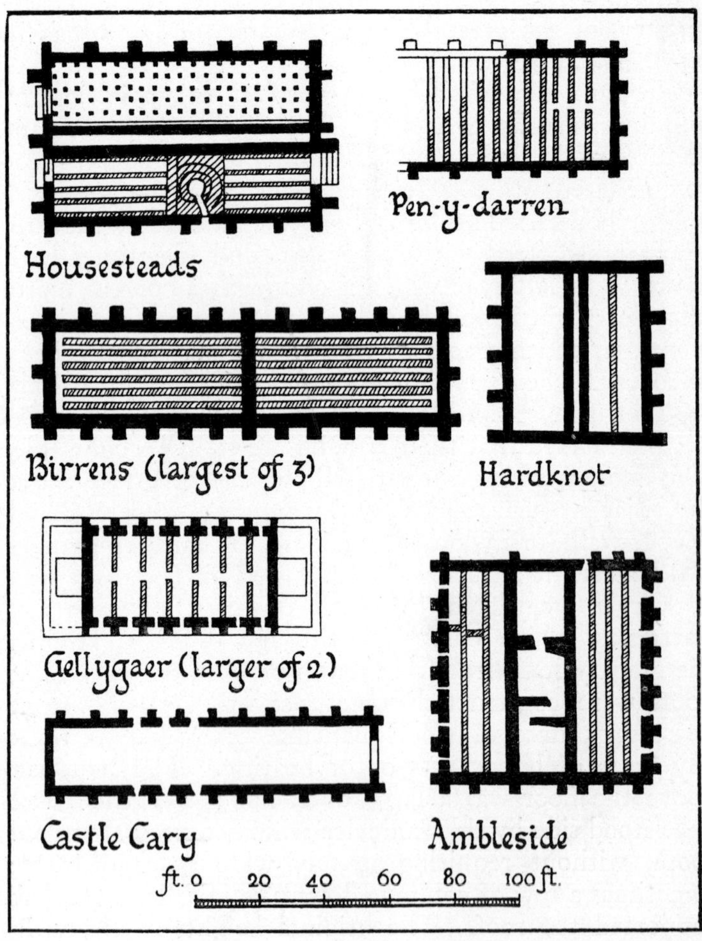


FIG. 16. GRANARIES

solid roofage, so confirming the inference which the buttresses suggest. If the roofs were tiled, they would have been free from any danger of being set on fire by red-hot sling-bolts or fire-arrows from besieging barbarians. Thus the garrison's food-supply was safe both against fire and against damp.[1]

The remainder of the fort was occupied by barracks and other apartments for the use of the soldiers. The barracks, when built in stone, were usually long, narrow edifices divided up into numerous rooms by transverse walls. At Newstead the rooms were separate huts. The individual blocks not infrequently assume an L-shaped appearance on the plan, being fronted by a colonnade and terminated at one end by a piece of building as broad as the other rooms and the colonnade together. The employment of stone for these barracks is, however, not at all universal. We find it in the *castella* on Hadrian's Wall and in many British forts, in which the whole interior, except the streets and one or two open spaces, is covered by stone buildings. But in other British forts—the Antonine fort on the Bar Hill is a case in point—wood was freely used. And on the German frontier stone-built barracks seem hardly ever to occur. Here again, therefore, we seem to have two types of forts, one simpler than the other.[2]

The interior of the fort accommodated only the fighting men with their weapons, stores, and horses. Other elements of the soldier's life found their place outside the ramparts. One feature that was never wanting was the bath-house, often mis-described as a 'villa'.

[1] For a fuller discussion of the granaries and their capacity, see 'The Provisioning of Roman Forts' in *C. and W. Trans.* (n.s.) xx, pp. 127 ff., with appendix by R. G. Collingwood, who, however, has underestimated the floor-area of several of the granaries in question. The article is reprinted, in a somewhat different form, as Appendix III to J. G. C. Anderson's revision of Furneaux's ed. of the *Agricola* (1922).

[2] Allowance must, however, be made for the different extent to which the different materials might be conveniently available. The German forests, for instance, would yield abundance of timber.

It was a detached building, generally some 50 or 100 yards beyond the gates, but sometimes inside the fort, perhaps 40 or 50 by 90 or more feet in extent, fitted with the usual arrangements of the Roman bath—a furnace to heat the air, hot rooms providing vapour baths, a small tank for the cold-water dip which completed the bathing process, dressing-rooms, and offices.

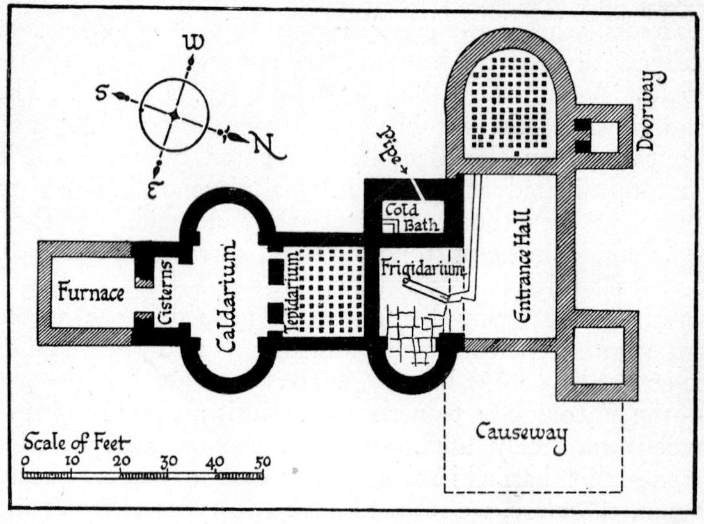


Fig. 17. PLAN OF BATH AT INCHTUTHIL

No excavated example is more typical than that discovered in 1901 at Inchtuthil on the Tay (Fig. 17). There is good ground for believing that the baths served other purposes than merely that of ablution. They would seem, indeed, to have been, in a secondary degree of course, places of recreation—club-houses, in short. The fact that altars to Fortune are occasionally dug out of their ruins may indicate that games of chance were indulged in.[1] Not seldom two or three shrines to other

[1] For an excellent account of these bath-houses see G. Wolff's article on 'Kastelle und Bäder im Limesgebiet' in *XI. Bericht der röm.-germ. Kommission 1918–19*, pp. 71 ff.

deities, Mercury for instance, stood hard by, and sometimes there was a cave of Mithras. Outside the ramparts, too, was the civil settlement of camp-followers, women, and traders, with perhaps an old soldier or two and a few slaves and natives.

I have described this fort system as being that of the Empire. But changes naturally occurred during four centuries. They were not indeed many. War Offices distrust innovations and, like the soldiers whom they control, they never know when they are beaten. The Roman War Office was, I think, even more soldierly than the average. A cynic might find significance in the fact that one of its emblems went back to early Republican days and depicted Mars beside a goose. Still, it advanced. We have seen that during the late second century it learned to use stone instead of earth for the ramparts of its forts—a change analogous to, though less important than, the change from wooden ships to ironclads. During the third century it devised, or revived, the projecting bastions or rampart-towers which enabled a flanking fire to be brought to bear upon assailants. During the fourth century it adopted narrower and crooked gateways and higher and stouter walls, and it often abandoned the old strictly quadrilateral enceinte for an outline which followed the natural aptitudes of the ground. Taught by the Two Hundred Years' War, by the repeated impact of barbarian multitudes, unflinching and innumerable, it thus strengthened its arts of defence. At the same time cavalry, archers, and the like were introduced more freely into the army-list, fresh tribes were found to supply recruits, and fresh units of auxiliaries were adopted to suit the new soldiers.

Extant remains bring the process of development vividly before us. During these centuries many an earth-built rampart of the earlier age arose afresh in stone; many a fort was fitted with bastions, or had its gates half walled-up to present a narrower or more difficult entrance. Pevensey in Sussex, between Eastbourne and St. Leonard's, may serve as an illustration of the latest form of construction. It belongs to the fourth century, and its thick, high walls of concrete with their bonding courses of brick, its hollow semicircular projecting bastions (FIG. 18) present an instructive contrast

FIG. 18. BASTION FLANKING A GATEWAY OF THE ROMAN FORT AT PEVENSEY

to the simpler and more dignified masonry of, say, the *castella* on Hadrian's Wall, originally designed a couple of centuries earlier (FIG. 19). Yet even on these *castella* the change of attitude towards the enemy has left its mark. The gateway shown in Fig. 19 is wider than it was when the Romans finally left it. It has been cleared of the fourth-century additions which are so noticeable elsewhere along the line of the Wall and which tell exactly the same tale as does the blocked-up town-gate of Caerwent (PLATE VIII).

So far, I have been trying to sketch some material features of the Roman military organization under the Empire, without particular reference to Britain; and I have done so of set purpose, because the garrisoning of Roman Britain was part of a system and cannot be understood unless it is so regarded. We may now leave the whole and turn to the part.

FIG. 19. WESTERN GATEWAY OF THE ROMAN FORT AT BIRDOSWALD

Roman Britain is a singularly good example of the Roman system. Its military and civil areas, its *domi* and *militiae*, were divided with peculiar plainness. They agree precisely with those upland and lowland areas on which I insisted (with seeming needlessness) in the last lecture. The lowland area (FIG. 20) contained no troops, at all events until in the latest years the coast defence against pirates brought with it nine or ten forts along our south-eastern shores. Here and there in these lowlands we meet traces of military men, but they are very

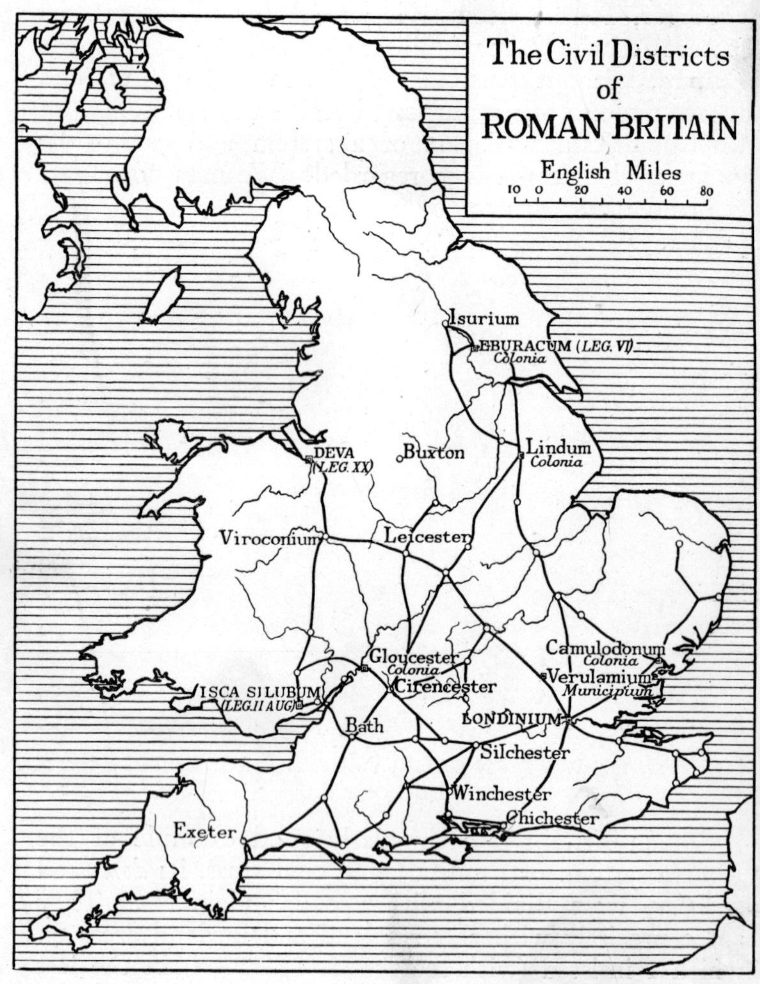
The Civil Districts
of
ROMAN BRITAIN
English Miles
10 0 20 40 60 80
Isurium
EBURACUM (LEG. VI)
Colonia
Lindum
Colonia
DEVA
(LEG. XX)
Buxton
Viroconium
Leicester
Gloucester
Colonia
Cirencester
Camulodonum
Colonia
Verulamium
Municipium
ISCA SILURUM
(LEG. II AUG)
LONDINIUM
Bath
Silchester
Winchester
Chichester
Exeter

Fig. 20.

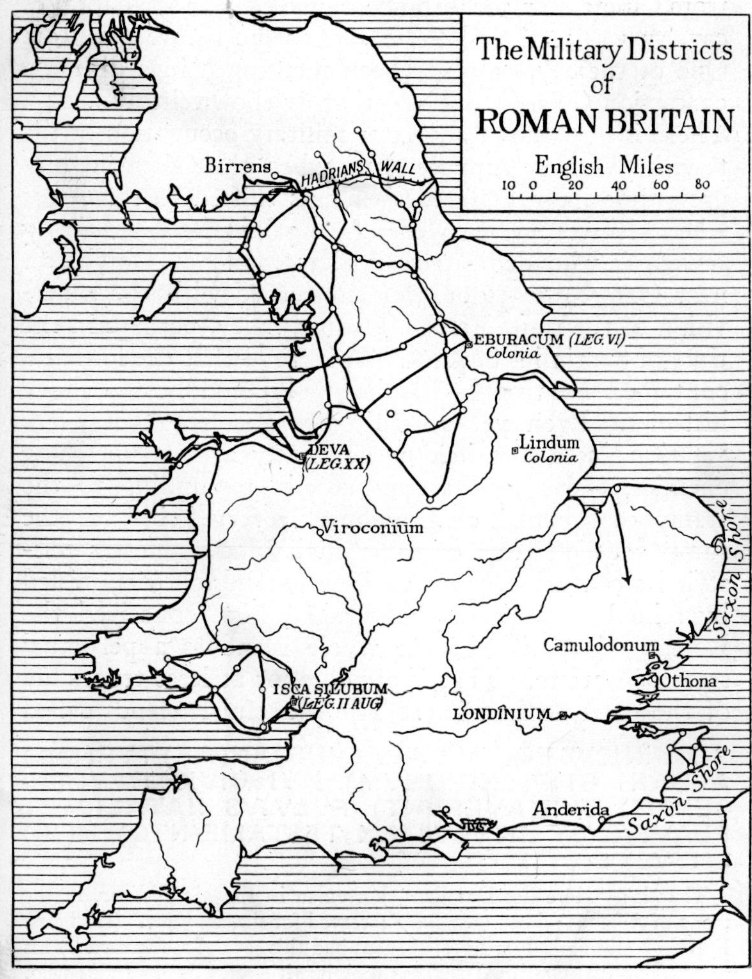
The Military Districts
of
ROMAN BRITAIN
English Miles
10 0 20 40 60 80
Birrens
HADRIANS WALL
EBURACUM (LEG. VI)
Colonia
Lindum
Colonia
DEVA
(LEG. XX)
Viroconium
Saxon Shore
Camulodonum
Othona
ISCA SILUBUM
(LEG. II AUG)
LONDINIUM
Saxon Shore
Anderida

FIG. 21.

few, and they either date from the earlier conquest or are matters of commissariat or roads. Two tombstones from Cirencester, for instance, suggest that a small force of cavalry was stationed there some time before A.D. 100. One of them has already been mentioned in a different connexion (FIG. 7). The other is shown in FIG. 22[1]. There is no trace of any later military occupation of the town. We may suppose that, when the Cotswold hills grew quiet, the little garrison was shifted to some fort where it was more needed.[2] Again, the *beneficiarius consularis* who dedicated an altar found at Dorchester near Oxford,[3] was doubtless concerned with the supervision of the route up the Thames valley, perhaps in the time of Septimius Severus. This fact—that the lowlands contained no troops—has been obscured in too many histories. Even yet accredited writers speak of every 'station' as a fort held permanently against unceasing enemies, every road as perpetually resounding to the tramp of the mail-clad legionary, every 'villa' as the sumptuous quarters of some high officer, mostly misstyled a centurion. Our antiquaries and scholars, misled by school reminiscences of Caesar, have conceived the Roman occupation of the whole island as a perpetual state of warfare. That is credible, or at least true, only of the extreme frontiers. The peaceful lowlands called

[1] DANNICVS EQ(V)ES ALAE INDIAN(AE) TVR(MA) ALBANI STIP(ENDIORVM) XVI CIVIS RAVR(ACENSIS) CVR(AVERVNT) FVLVIVS NATALIS ET FLAVIVS (?) BITVCVS EX TESTAME(NTO) H(IC) S(ITVS) E(ST).

That is: 'Here lies Dannicus, horseman in the *ala Indiana*, in the troop of Albanus; born near Basle; served for sixteen years. (His heirs) Fulvius Natalis and Flavius (?) Bitucus had this set up, as directed by his will.' The *ala* (*Gallorum*) *Indiana* took its title from Julius Indus who, if he did not raise it, was certainly its commander when it won great distinction *c.* A.D. 21 (Tac. *Ann.* iii. 42, 46). From the second century onwards it was in Upper Germany.

[2] See *Archaeologia* lxix, p. 195.

[3] *CIL.* vii. 83, and *Ephem. Epigr.* ix, pp. 520 f. The somewhat similar altar at Elsfield Manor is probably a forgery: see *Ephem. Epigr.* ix, p. 681.

FIG. 22. TOMBSTONE FROM CIRENCESTER

See foot-note 1 on preceding page.

for armed control by legions and fortifications no more in Roman times than they do to-day.

The upland area then (FIG. 21) is the sole military region. Here we find troops enough—three legions and numerous auxiliaries, in all perhaps 35,000 to 40,000 men, one-tenth or one-twelfth of the whole Imperial forces. The three legions were posted, one each in a fortress, at York, Chester, and Caerleon. All three fortresses have left traces at least of their enceinte. At Caerleon the ruins of the Roman walls can still be seen for a good part of their course—work apparently of the third or fourth century — little disturbed by the houses of a modern village. At Chester and at York, cathedral cities stand above the débris of the Roman fortresses. Here the medieval walls mark in part the line of the Roman defences. The towns have grown out south and west, as towns love to grow (except Oxford), and on these sides the Roman ramparts have been obliterated. But on the north and east Roman and medieval fortifications coincide, and Roman work can yet be seen—at Chester (FIG. 23) courses of masonry massive beyond the powers of any medieval builder and reared probably by Septimius Severus in lieu of an earthen mound; at York the well-known Multangular Tower (FIG. 24), plainly a creation

FIG. 23. FACE OF THE NORTH WALL OF THE ROMAN FORTRESS AT CHESTER, SHOWING PLINTH

of the later Roman age. Inscriptions also tell us something of the men who garrisoned here (Fig. 25). But of the interior of these fortresses we know practically nothing. We can only fill in the details from legionary fortresses elsewhere, like Novaesium (Neuss) or Lambaesis or Carnuntum. Still, the historical position is plain. From Caerleon, Chester, and York legionaries could be sent out to guard small forts in the vicinity, to build new forts or frontier walls, to combine into field armies for open war.

Fig. 24. THE MULTANGULAR TOWER, YORK

The auxiliaries were used in a different way. But the strategic relation between fortresses and forts was simple. The forts stood along main roads in the north or in Wales, or in disturbed regions, or along the frontiers. They formed, as it were, the first line of defence. This position, in advance of the legions, is assigned them elsewhere than in Britain. It suits well the needs of the case. But it may have another reason. Tacitus, in one of the very few descriptions of battle-tactics that we possess from this age, tells us how at Mons Graupius Agricola posted his legionaries in the rear as a reserve, while the auxiliaries formed the fighting line. It would be (he adds) a great glory to win without losing a legionary : '*ingens victoriae decus citra Romanum sanguinem bellandi*'.[1] No doubt the legionary was too precious and too expensive to be

FIG. 25. TOMBSTONE FROM CHESTER

**D M P RVSTIO FABIA CRESCEN(TI) BRIX(IA) MIL(ITI) LEG(IONIS) XX V(ALERIAE) V(ICTRICIS) AN(NORVM) XXX STIP(ENDIORVM) X GROMA HERES FAC(IENDVM) CVR(AVIT).**

That is: 'Sacred to the memory of P. Rustius Crescens, of the Fabian tribe; born at Brescia; soldier in the Legion XX Valeria Victrix; aged thirty; served for ten years; Groma, his heir, had this set up.'

After about A.D. 70 recruiting for the legions almost ceased in Italy. Very probably, therefore, Crescens enlisted before then. This helps to date the stone.

[1] *Agricola* 35.

unnecessarily exposed. The policy of the battle was also the policy of the garrisons.

The auxiliary forts in Britain—so far as our knowledge goes, and inclusive of some doubtful cases—numbered seventeen or more[1] in Wales, some sixty or seventy in north England (reckoning in Hadrian's Wall), and some thirty-three or thirty-four north of that line (reckoning in the Wall of Pius). This total of well over a hundred forts did not, however, all exist at once. Some, as for example a certain proportion of those in Wales, were evacuated in the course of the second century, perhaps under Hadrian or Pius when the northern frontier was reorganized.[2] Again, the Caledonian *castella* were finally lost about A.D. 180 at latest. Others were not established at all until later. What number was actually held at any one time cannot now be determined, and very possibly will never be known, for date-revealing discoveries have been too systematically neglected by our local antiquaries. Even during the occupation of Caledonia, however, the full tale must have fallen well below the hundred. It is significant that an ancient list, the *Notitia Dignitatum*—imperfect probably, but yet not seriously imperfect—records thirty-eight forts in northern Britain as occupied at a date just before or during the fourth century.[3]

Two groups of our British forts claim special notice, those which strengthened the Walls of Hadrian and of

[1] It is now known for certain that there were more: see, for instance, J. P. Hall's *Caer Llugwy* (Manchester, 1923).

[2] *Roman Wales*, pp. 89 and 118, and *Arch. Cambr.* lxxvi, pp. 17 and 196. For similar indications from Yorkshire see *Yorks. Journ.* xxiii, pp. 395 ff., xxiv, pp. 102 ff., and xxvi, pp. 83 ff.

[3] The underlying assumption here is that, as Mommsen argued, the British section of the *Notitia* is a survival of pre-Constantinian date. This view has hitherto found practically universal acceptance. Quite recently, however, it has been challenged by Professor Bury as 'certainly erroneous' (*J.R.S.* x, pp. 131 ff.). He assigns the British section to A.D. 428–37, and consequently infers that, instead of abandoning the island in 407, as is usually supposed, the Romans continued to hold it until about 442. This conclusion conflicts with the general trend of the literary tradition, and is unsupported by archaeological evidence (see R. G. Collingwood in *J.R.S.* xii).

Pius. Here we reach a noteworthy characteristic of Roman frontier defence. The artificial frontier meets us in Roman history over a period of nine centuries, from Domitian to Anastasius I and, indeed, to Nicephorus Phokas, and it occurs in all frontier provinces where nature furnished no river boundary. Its form varies. In Africa and Arabia, as now seems likely, the *limes* was marked by a road with forts along it, and was emphasized (at least in Africa) by a ditch. This was apparently sufficient throughout the four centuries for which the Western Empire lasted. In Europe—in the Dobrudja, in Dacia, and in the interval between Rhine and Danube—we meet with the more elaborate device of a ditch and a mound or wall, too weak to resist a serious assault and intended rather as an obstacle to passage than as a fortification. In some places, however, for instance in the Dobrudja during the Constantinian period, this was sooner or later strengthened into a real military work.

In Britain the first demarcation of frontier with which we have any acquaintance shows the military stage full-grown. This frontier was drawn by the Emperor Hadrian, in consequence (as we can gather) of grave disasters to the Roman garrison. We do not know much of his work. The fact of it is well attested by literature and by inscriptions. The line of it is certain—from Tyne to Solway. Its character is less clear. The most recent evidence[1] suggests that it consisted of a substantial rampart of sods, built up as if they were bricks, fronted by a formidable ditch, and defended at intervals by forts. Hadrian's Wall lasted ninety years. Then, like other earth-works elsewhere, it was rebuilt in stone by

[1] The reference is to the wall of turf discovered in 1895 at Appletree near Birdoswald (*C. and W. Trans.* xiv (o.s.), pp. 185 ff.). It seemed best to let this passage stand as it was originally written. But it is only right to say that, two or three years later, the simple solution here indicated as probable was ruled out by the results of further excavation, the significance of which F. H. was prompt to recognize. For details see next foot-note.

Septimius Severus. This is the wall we see to-day, with its sixteen forts, its numerous mile-castles—so called from being a mile apart—and its turrets separated by lesser distances. Outlying forts were held for a while north of the Wall, and at no time did it mark the final limit of Roman occupation. But its purpose was plain. It was a barrier to cut off the southern lands from the free barbarians. That purpose it served till the end of the Roman dominion. Its forts were occupied in some form or other till about A.D. 400.

We need not now enter into the many problems which surround the details of the Wall. They have provoked disputes of theological intensity and stubbornness. But they cannot be profitably discussed except on the spot, nor can they be solved until our antiquaries excavate and record the results of their excavation. Indeed, so much mischief has already been effected by unscientific exploration, and so much evidence destroyed, that certainty has perhaps been made unattainable. Thus, it has been questioned whether the mile-castles on the Wall belong to Hadrian or to Severus or to a supposed later builder about the end of the fourth century. Several of these little posts have been uncovered, and coins and pottery found in them. But hardly any record has been kept of such finds or heed taken of the evidence of dates which they might provide.[1] The truth is that, valuable as the

[1] This criticism is no longer of general application. The series of excavations initiated in 1909 by the late Mr. J. P. Gibson and Mr. F. G. Simpson was carried to completion by the latter with a care and thoroughness which won F. H.'s warmest approval. The result was a most important contribution to the discussion of the problems of the Wall (*C. and W. Trans.* xiii (n.s.), pp. 297 ff.). It showed conclusively (1) that the mile-castles and turrets were coeval with the wall of stone, and (2) that they had been occupied by Roman soldiers long before the reign of Septimius Severus. This proved that the stone wall was much older than Severus, but it left the turf wall at Appletree as much of a mystery as before. F. H. remained convinced that the latter, whatever its precise significance, must be Hadrianic (*Arch. Anz.*, 1912, 489 ff., and *Roman Britain in* 1913, p. 41). For the rest, he was more strongly impressed than ever with the need for systematic and properly directed excavation

stimulus of curiosity may be, it is seldom (if ever) equal, unaided, to research as research is now understood. It must be reinforced by the habit of trained observation and by the familiarity with Roman antiquities and institutions, which would guide the enthusiast to note or to interpret the remains with which he is dealing. Local archaeological societies may do most useful work, and the maintenance of local interest is a matter of first-rate importance. But to plan and carry through an extensive and coherent excavation, such as is required to solve the mural problems, calls for a combination of all the available forces. Lack of money and public indifference are not the only obstacles to be overcome. It would be well if the Universities were to remember that they too have their part to play.

The actual ruins of the Wall, in its central mountainous region, are among the stateliest monuments of Roman power that time and man have spared (PLATE IV), and at any rate preserve their own historical lesson. Here the Wall passes along a marvellous line of natural defence, a range of sheer basalt cliffs that face the north. Here, as a traveller wrote a century ago, the remains of ancient splendour abide in bold characters. Forts stand visible on the hillsides, lifting above the grass the masses of their stubborn masonry; the Wall itself still rises shoulder high for hundreds of yards together; nature and man combine in a unique landscape. As you look east and west and trace the long line of wall winding for miles from end to end of perilous ledges and climbing from hill to hill, as you turn south to the Tyne and the dark fells beyond it or north to long flat wastes and pathless mosses, the vision of

on a scale not hitherto attempted. Since his death substantial progress has been made. For a general account of this, see R. G. Collingwood's *Hadrian's Wall: A History of the Problem* in *J.R.S.* xi, pp. 37–66, and for details *The Purpose and Date of the Vallum and its Crossings*, by F. G. Simpson and R. C. Shaw in *C. and W. Trans.* (n.s.) xxii, pp. 353–433. Mr. Simpson's next enterprise, which may be expected to throw light on the Turf Wall, is to receive financial support from the Haverfield Bequest Committee.

a great Empire rises. Here, on the uttermost limit of the Roman world, the desolate land has been stamped for ever with the sign of its former lords. On these high moors we can realize, almost more clearly than in the Forum of Rome, the secret of that defence by which Rome guarded the fabric of civilization through the long menace of darkness and dissolution.

FIG. 26. THE WALL OF PIUS, ON FERGUSTON MUIR, NEW KILPATRICK

The Wall that Pius drew across the northern isthmus had a far briefer life. It was occupied (as we now know conclusively) for hardly forty years and during some part, at least, of that time a few forts were also held beyond it—at Camelon, just north of Falkirk, and at Ardoch and probably elsewhere along the line of approach to the Highlands. But the movements of this act of the drama go on in twilight. Neither the cause for the advance that culminated in the erection of the Wall, nor the fortunes of the Wall itself during the four decades for which it was garrisoned, nor the circumstances of its abandonment, nor the meaning of its northern outposts, are more than matter for guessing. The facts have not yet been dug up which will lighten these dark problems. But there the Wall stood for forty years, beaten upon by shocks of violent wars, once (at least) taken and recovered, and lost in the end by Caledonian assault. And there it stands to this day, where the later Caledonian has spared it (FIG. 26), to teach us, like other remains elsewhere in Great Britain, that neither religious nor national hatred hurts antiquities quite so deeply as the plain emotionless farmer or the builder of modern houses or even the too ardent restorer of the past.

Enough of the barrier is left [1] to enable us to form a fairly clear idea of its original character and appearance. On a carefully laid stone base, some 14 feet broad, sods have been piled up methodically so as to form a solid rampart.[2] This rampart may have been as much as 10 feet high, with a width of 6 feet at the top. It stretched continuously from the shores of the Firth of Forth near Bo'ness to the banks of the River Clyde at Old Kilpatrick, a distance of some 36 or 37 miles in all. On its northern or outer side there ran a great ditch, of an average depth of perhaps 12 feet and an average breadth of about 40. Protection was ensured by a series of forts, probably nineteen in all, planted at intervals of two miles apart and linked together by a well-made road. The forts were almost all rather small, if compared with Roman forts of the same type in north England or in Wales. Some, indeed, such as Rough Castle, were very small. Even Castlecary, which is one of the best built and has been

[1] For a detailed account of the remains see Macdonald, *The Roman Wall in Scotland* (Glasgow, 1911).

[2] There is reason to believe that towards the eastern end the Wall was built not of sods but of earth, though the stone foundation was uniform throughout (*P. S. A. Scot.* xlix, pp. 120 ff.).

judged the most important, did not exceed 4 acres in area. Not less remarkable is the variation in the methods of construction. Bar Hill and Rough Castle had ramparts of turf. Castlecary and Balmuildy were walled with stone.[1]

Tactically the new line was strong. The isthmus from Forth to Clyde is barely half the length of that from Tyne to Solway. Add to this that it is crossed by one continuous valley, along whose southern side low hills form an unbroken scarp, seldom disturbed by rivers cutting through from the south, but defended almost everywhere by rivers running parallel to it and in front. Here was a position well suited for defence. If the basalt cliffs, the tall hills, the wild lakes of the Wall of Hadrian move our admiration, if the wanderer will always seek for choice its stately scenery and its spacious prospects, the soldier turns with warmer praise to the less interesting Wall of Pius. It is mostly so. Great battle-fields are, as a rule, dull things to see; the better they were chosen, the worse (it may well be) their present scenic merits. Where could you find so prosaic a stretch of country as at Waterloo?

But, if the Wall of Pius was tactically strong, we must admit that its strategic weakness was pronounced. At more than one critical point the northern hills rise dangerously near and threatening. On the west its defences could be easily outflanked from Renfrewshire and Clydesdale. On the east, though it was virtually prolonged for 15 or 20 miles by a road and forts along the south shore of the Forth as far as Inveresk, its right could readily be turned by troops in Haddingtonshire. The rearward was weaker still. The whole position is in a sense askew. The natural retreat from the isthmus ought to lie southwards; actually it runs sharp south-east. This is the secret of the failure of the Romans, and indeed of many later conquerors. Every enemy who

[1] For the latter, see S. N. Miller, *The Roman Fort at Balmuildy* (Glasgow, 1922).

advances from the Tyne and Solway base, has on his left flank an ever-increasing expanse of moss and mountain, too large and difficult to conquer and yet too dangerous to leave untouched. The English in the Middle Ages made some effort to control this land: witness the many 'motes' which dot its southern half. The Romans left it alone. Their neglect of the south-west was a fatal flaw in their defensive scheme. Even if the barrier be regarded as only an outwork to intercept the fury of the

Fig. 27. RUINED WALL OF THE FORT AT RICHBOROUGH, NEAR SANDWICH

tempests sweeping down from the Highlands and as a breakwater to protect Hadrian's fortifications between Tyne and Solway, that does not in the least excuse the fault. Perhaps it is more surprising that the Wall of Pius was held so long than that it was lost so soon.

We have still to consider a third piece of Roman frontier defence, which Rome devised for Britain on the verge of the third and fourth centuries. There had been during the previous period a *classis Britannica* with its head-quarters not in Britain but at Boulogne, and with smaller ports at Dover and at Lymne. But about 284 its admiral, Carausius—Stukeley's hero—used it to make himself Emperor of Britain; and when the central Government recovered the province, thirteen years later, the fleet was apparently suppressed.[1] Instead, we find nine or perhaps ten forts planted round the coast from the Wash to Southampton Water.[2] Some occupied sites already in active use. Such, for example, was that of which the lonely ruins rise above the marshes of Sandwich, breaking the sky-line for miles around (FIG. 27).

FIG. 28. BURGH CASTLE, NEAR YARMOUTH, IN SUFFOLK

It guarded the harbour of Rutupiae, the combined Dover and Folkestone of Roman Britain—a landing-place so famous that, when Roman poets wished an alternative for the adjective 'British', they used the word 'Rutupine'[3] and, by giving the place a perhaps false reputation

[1] There is no reference to the *classis Britannica* in the *Notitia Dignitatum*. It is last heard of in A.D. 287 (Eumenius, *Panegyr. Constantio Caes.* 12).

[2] The *Not. Dign. Occ.* (xxviii) enumerates nine. But the ruins of ten appear to be identifiable—Brancaster (Norfolk), Burgh Castle (Suffolk), Walton Castle (Suffolk), Bradwell (Essex), Reculver (Kent), Richborough (Kent), Dover (Kent), Stutfall Castle (Kent), Pevensey (Sussex), Porchester (Hants). See F. H.'s article '*Saxonicum litus*' in Pauly-Wissowa's *Real-Encyclopädie* ii A, 327–34.

[3] See F. H. on '*Rutupinus*' in *Class. Rev.* xxi, p. 105.

for oysters, obscured its true eminence as a harbour. Others were placed on sites hitherto wholly or practically uninhabited—Brancaster on one of the lagoons of north Norfolk, or Pevensey (Fig. 18) on an islet in the marsh between Eastbourne and Hastings.

All these forts have certain features in common. They are large, with a tendency to be irregular in shape, and

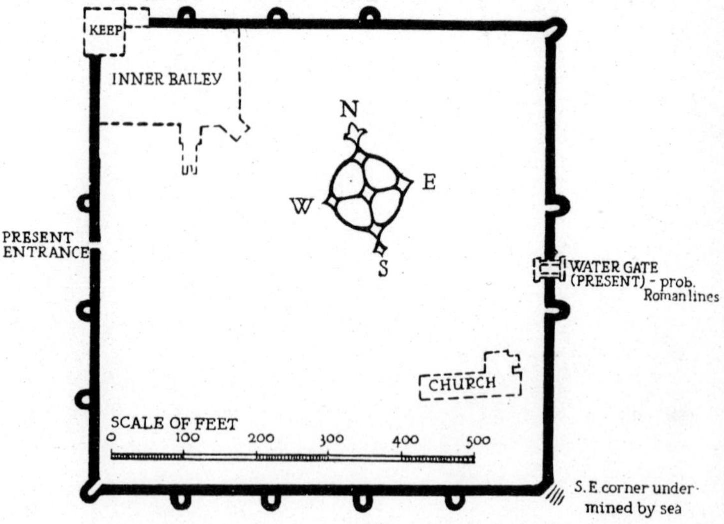


Fig. 29. PLAN OF PORCHESTER

are built in what we have already noted as the fourth-century style, with high thick walls (Fig. 28) and frequent bastions (Fig. 29). According to the *Notitia Dignitatum*, the normal garrison of each was a regiment of auxiliaries, but the most important, Rutupiae, was held by a legion, probably by this time little more than one thousand strong. Each stands, lastly, on a harbour slightly withdrawn from the sea and now in most cases silted up like so many harbours of Kent and Sussex. Each was probably, therefore, not only a point of refuge for merchant vessels or fishers, but a station for a few ships under the orders of the commander of the garrison, though we possess no definite references to such squadrons. The whole was but a little scheme for a province threatened by swarms of pillaging English and Irish. But it seems to have succeeded. Certainly till A.D. 350 the sea-robbers made small impression upon Britain. As in all ages of pirate incursions from the north, the opposite continental coast suffered worse and its defences availed it little.

We have reached the end of the Roman military occupation of our island. We have traced its progress in the conquest, its system, its permanent character in Britain, and its notable features of frontier guard by land and sea. One question remains: What effect had this military occupation on the general history of the island? Two points immediately suggest themselves, both of very real importance. In the first place it is plain that the military occupation made possible the peaceful civilization of the inner country, the midlands and the south-east. What this means must be left to the fourth and fifth lectures. Here it is enough to note the fact. The second point is no less plain. The military area was not itself a civilized region. We know, indeed, very little about its population outside the forts. But we do know that, with scanty exceptions, it contained neither towns nor villas. In the north no town can be traced beyond Aldborough, and no villa beyond Well, near Ripon. Only a couple of military centres close behind Hadrian's Wall, Carlisle and Corbridge, appear to have formed 'bazaars' (as it were) for the soldiers on the Wall itself, and these were dependent on the presence of troops, and cannot be counted as part of the civilized life of Britain. Similarly in the west, no villa or town has been discovered within the limits of Wales, save a fine house overlooking the Severn Sea, at Llantwit Major in Glamorgan, and one or two other isolated exceptions—just enough to prove the rule.[1] The whole of the north and west was military and not civilized.

[1] See *Cymmrodorion Soc. Trans.* 1920–1, pp. 81 ff., and also *infra*, p. 182.

When we attempt to go further, we are met with serious difficulties. Our knowledge is defective, our statistics untrustworthy to an extent that would have satisfied Lord Beaconsfield. Our best conclusions can only be inductions from single instances or calculations of slender possibilities. At the same time, it is worth inquiry how far the soldiery may have left its mark on the population of the island. We are at once met by the difficulty that we do not know the numbers of either soldiers or native population. We may, however, assume the accuracy of the usual estimate that the army counted some 40,000 men, and hence—since the normal service lasted from twenty to twenty-five years and many must have died before its completion—we can reckon the recruits required annually at rather more than 2,000. In that case the time-expired men would run to a total of perhaps 1,000 to 1,500 a year. But these would not all remain in the province. Some, indeed, settled outside their old quarters, and their tombstones as veterans occur there.[1] Others were incorporated in the municipalities of the province, such as Camulodūnum (Colchester), and their tombstones, too, remain in evidence. But there were others who went elsewhere across the seas. We can trace them, for instance, in towns of southern Gaul, whence they probably sprang.[2] Taken altogether, the addition to the British population by discharged soldiers would not be very large. Whatever infusion of foreign blood it brought would be relatively small, and coming gradually would be easily absorbed.

It is not, however, likely that all these veterans were foreigners. During the early years of the conquest, the bulk of the legionaries in Britain came apparently from towns in the north of Italy,[3] but after about A.D. 70

[1] So at Caerleon (*CIL.* vii. 122 f.), York (*Ephem. Epigr.* iii. 79), and Chester (*Ibid.* ix. 1051, 1062, 1079).

[2] Thus, inscriptions mentioning veterans who had served in the legions in Britain occur at Arles (*CIL.* xii. 677 ff.) and at Nîmes (*Ibid.* 3175 f.).

[3] See, for instance, Figs. 1 and 25, and cf. *supra*, p. 126, foot-note 3.

Italians became very few. Spain and Gaul were also laid under requisition during the first century, and some men hailed from the Danubian provinces. In the second century under Hadrian—that is from A.D. 120 onwards —the legions were to some extent filled up by British

FIG. 30. TOMBSTONE FROM MUMRILLS, STIRLINGSHIRE.

**DIS M(ANIBVS) NECTOVELIVS F(ILIVS) VINDICIS AN(NORVM) XXX STIP(ENDIORVM) VIIII NATIONIS BRIGANS MILITAVIT IN COH II THR(ACVM)**

That is: 'Sacred to the memory of Nectovelius, son of Vindex, aged thirty, a Brigantian by birth. He served for nine years in the Second Cohort of Thracians.'

levies, and to some extent supplied from the Rhine and the Danube. The auxiliaries were drawn from a greater variety of sources; most came from the valley of the Lower Rhine or from Gaul, some from Spain, some from the Danubian provinces, a few from even further east, such as the Syrian bowmen who helped to garrison the Walls.[1] It is probable that, at least during the earlier part of the occupation, hardly any of those who served in Britain were of British birth. From time to time generals like Agricola may have employed local levies. Occasionally, too, a Briton found his way into one of the ordinary auxiliary regiments. About A.D. 145, for example, a Brigantian from northern England served in a 'Thracian' cohort on the Forth and Clyde isthmus (FIG. 30). But as a rule Britain was too restless to admit of the employment of British auxiliaries there.[2] We may infer, therefore, in this respect an infusion of Germans, who might be either of Teutonic stock or of Celtic. And we can add occasional contributions from other races, such as a wholesale deportation of Sarmatians who were apparently settled in Lancashire.[3]

But, after all, the most noteworthy effect of the military occupation in Britain was doubtless to accelerate its Romanization. The mere presence of the troops might count for little, since only a few served in regions where civil life ever developed. Still, York and its vale, for instance, must have learnt much of Roman ways from the legion quartered where the cathedral now stands. The discharged veterans must have contributed still more. By long service they acquired Roman speech —if they did not know it from childhood—and in a manner Roman culture. So far as they stayed in the island, they brought it not Gaulish or Teutonic blood so much as the pattern of Roman citizenship. Here, however, we are trespassing on the fringe of another subject, the civilized life of the province. That must be reserved for the next two lectures.

[1] Cf. *CIL*. vii. 748, etc. (Carvoran) and 1110 (Bar Hill).

[2] During the later period of the occupation, however, Pons Aelii (Newcastle) was garrisoned by the *Cohors I Cornoviorum*, a regiment whose name would indicate that it was a British levy: see *Not. Dign. Occ*. xl. 34.

[3] Dio, lxxi. 16. *CIL*. vii. 229, 230.

PLATE V CORINTHIAN CAPITAL AND PART OF COLUMN FROM BATH

# LECTURE IV

## THE CIVILIZATION OF THE PROVINCE

### I

In the two preceding lectures I have tried to give an outline of the Roman military occupation of Britain, the size and character of its garrison, the number and distribution of its forts, the extent and massiveness of its frontier-lines. This is, indeed, the side of the subject which imperatively demands first notice. If we study the province by itself, we find the garrison its dominant feature. If we study the Empire as a whole, the British garrison meets us as a chief element in the imperial armies. Even the traces of its former presence, where they still survive, possess a singular interest. Not only walls and ditches, but small inscribed stones deserve attention, broken and barely legible though they often are. I remember Mommsen once, long ago, talking about recent finds on Hadrian's Wall. "Ah," he said, "you have such wonderful inscriptions in your north country; no land tells us more about the Roman army."

But there is another aspect of the matter. However disinclined a soldier may be to admit it, armies are after all only a means to an end. Like the dark rows of cypresses that guard the fields of Provence from the Mistral, they protect a nation's life against the chill winds or wild hurricanes of external enemies. It was the peculiar glory of the Roman army that it saved, not a single nation, but civilization itself, that behind its encircling shelter the culture of the old world took firm root in western Europe, and that the final triumph of the barbarian involved a corresponding triumph of civilization over the worst evils of barbarism. The organization which effected this must always claim the attention of educated men. But, none the less, the real interest attaches to the end and not to the means, to the civilization that was protected and not to the sheltering army. That civilization is the thing that counts in the history of mankind, and it must be our main concern, even in the poor province of Britain.

If, however, we are leaving the garrison behind, we must not allow ourselves to forget it. As I have endeavoured to make clear, it was a definite institution with precise and well-marked features. Any one who fails to grasp these features will probably misunderstand also the true character of the civilization of the province. Let me give one small instance on which I chanced the other day. In a very recent history of Wales there is a paragraph which sketches the civilization of the district in Roman times, and at its outset comes the statement that there were towns, such as Chester and Caerleon. Neither place, of course, is in Wales, but for the purposes of Roman history that may not matter. The important points for us to note are that both places were fortresses, and that fortresses, in the Roman sense of the term, were not fortified towns, like Plymouth or Metz or Antwerp, but purely military strongholds. Civic life—all that the word 'town' implies—was wholly wanting. To call Chester and Caerleon towns is to introduce spurious elements into our picture of Romano-British civilization. As well might one describe Oxford as a home of learning, and illustrate the description by a reference to the Parks or the Boathouse or the Running-ground or the Mitre.

For a sketch of this civilization we have two kinds of material. The first (which usually receives but scant consideration from English writers) is provided by the general civilization of the rest of western Europe in Roman times. Britain, as was explained in the second lecture, belongs geographically to northern Gaul. What occurs in the one area may therefore be expected to occur, to some degree, in the other. Moreover, in two respects the initial conditions prevailing through all the provinces of the western Empire were marked by a virtual identity, from which similar results might naturally follow. In the first place, all these regions were devoid of advanced civilization at the time of the Roman conquest. And, secondly, they were inhabited by races of European stock. In great part, indeed, they were inhabited by Celts, who can be traced not only in Britain and Gaul but in Spain, in north Italy, in the Alpine lands and (as the art and the names of places and of persons recorded on inscriptions show) even in Austria and Bosnia. Such races were akin to their Italian conquerors. They were, therefore, inherently fitted to pick up Italian civilization. In these two respects the western Empire presents a marked contrast to Greece and the East. Greece and much of Asia and Syria and Egypt were occupied by a race kindred to the Italian, but it was a race that had already an ancient and elaborate civilization of its own. The country districts of Syria and Egypt had indeed remained uncivilized, but their inhabitants were racially incapable of accepting a higher culture in any better form than that of a thin varnish. In this regard, Roman Africa, with its partly Phoenician people and culture, held the same intermediate position as it did geographically. There, however, the non-indigenous elements had been so far reduced by the Republic that there was room for a new civilization to enter and to impose itself on a renascent population during the Empire.

What, then, was the general civilization of the western Empire, the conditions of which were so similar in all its districts? The general answer is easily given. The whole area, in varying degrees, became Romanized. In speech and literature, in fashions, in art and architecture—in short, in the whole fabric of the habits of life—it adopted Roman ways. Put thus broadly, the statement is almost too familiar to convey any definite impression. To give it reality, we must enter into particulars more fully.

In the first place, we know the method by which the Italian civilization overflowed Celtic and other lands. It was not the method by which civilizations usually enter fresh countries. As a rule, a movement of civilization means a movement of race—as when prehistoric Celts brought a new art, a new metal and new burial-fashions with them into Britain, or when English emigrants carried English life to Australia and America. No such multitudinous emigration took place to diffuse Roman life. No doubt the last century of the Roman Republic and the first century of the Empire saw many Italians rush to newly conquered provinces. But such rushes were not the wholesale inroads of population which attend the opening of some Oklahoma in the Indian reserves of the United States. Despite the epigram of Seneca [1]—'*ubicunque vicit Romanus, habitat,*' "wherever the Roman conquers, he settles"—emigration from Italy seems substantially to have been limited to two classes. Traders and moneylenders, especially moneylenders, flocked abroad and frequently formed tiny settlements in important provincial centres. Or soldiers recruited in north Italy, for legionary service in the provincial garrisons, were often planted in provincial municipalities when their time with the colours had expired, and occasionally some of the Roman proletariat were sent to join them. But the emigrant traders can never have formed more than a drop in the population of a province, and the recruiting of Italians for the legions practically ceased (as we have already learned) before the end of the first century of our era.

The Roman provinces must not therefore be thought of as containing any large infusion of Italians who had come to make their homes there. It is in fact likely that most of them at most times contained very few Italian-born inhabitants even of the temporary class who came on duty or on business and stayed only for a half-dozen or a dozen years. Rome did not send forth her sons to

[1] *Dial.* xii. 7. 7.

replenish waste places in western Europe or drive out the aborigines. The spread of Roman civilization was not the spread of a race. It was the adoption of an external civilization by other races, kindred indeed, but hitherto distinct in blood and speech and customs. It follows from this that we must not admit the idea, which India or Algiers suggests to us, of a native population contrasted with a body of immigrants. Such a phrase as 'the Romans in Gaul' may have contained truth at the moment of the conquest, while a foreign army of soldiers or a foreign crowd of traders was in occupation. But Roman Gaul in general did not consist of an antithesis of Romans and Gauls. So far as it consisted of two classes, it consisted—at least in the early period—of Romanized Gauls, Gallo-Romans as they are often styled, and un-Romanized Gauls, and the latter became gradually assimilated to the former. Similarly, we should not expect to find in Britain a sharply marked distinction between Britons and Romans. If we do find such a distinction, it will constitute a difference between Britain and provinces that are otherwise like it, and we shall require reasons to explain its existence.

The growth, then, of Roman civilization in the western provinces was not due to the movement of a race. It is an instance, and perhaps the best instance in all history, of the influence of a higher civilization on lower races fitted to assimilate it. It represented on a gigantic scale the change which we can see proceeding to-day in any country district, where the peasantry desert their native and picturesque costumes for the stamped calicoes of town fashions. It was in the main a voluntary movement. Doubtless some official measures encouraged it by accident or intention. But it was the entire absence of any coercion that contributed most powerfully to the destruction of the old national sentiment—a sentiment which, like Nature herself, recurs obstinately whenever attempts are made to eject it with a pitchfork.

Within the area in question the movement affected all

branches of life. Latin became the predominant tongue, and remains so to-day. Even in Bosnia a species of Roman dialect lingered on far into the Middle Ages. A copy of the Graeco-Roman art of the capital spread everywhere, hardly deserving the name of art but possessing its own character—neat, imitative, uniform, with certain local varieties, but throughout plainly the same art. Politically the framework of the Empire embraced all the provincials. Their loyalty was centred on Rome, and even their disloyalty assumed Roman forms. In religion, however, the Roman victory was less complete. The Roman gods, it is true, penetrated all temples. There is no region in which they lacked worshippers or were not identified with the native deities. But the religious beliefs of men especially defy eradication. Just as paganism has lived on in the corners of Christianity, so German or Celtic religion survived among the Romans. Hence we meet religious calendars in the Gaulish language—such strange Gaulish that one wonders if the writers themselves understood it.[1] So, too, the Celtic cult of the Three Mothers lingered on with the Roman title of Matres or Matronae ; indeed, it finally perished as a piece of superstitious folk-lore under the ban of Christianity in the advanced Middle Ages.[2]

We may illustrate what has been said, more fully, from individual districts. Thus in Gaul the Gaulish language persisted in many curious written evidences. As late as the second century the potters of the Auvergne manufactories stamped their pots or moulds with such labels as **SACRILLOS AVOT** or **VALENS AVOTI**, 'Sacrillus potter' or 'Valens potter', perhaps only a survival (like the '*pinxit*' of our painters) but a significant survival.[3] Rather earlier a Gaul of Alesia, whose

[1] See, for example, Rhys on 'The Coligny Calendar' in *Proc. Brit. Acad.* 1909–10, pp. 207 ff.

[2] *Arch. Ael.* (2nd ser.), xv (1892), p. 319, and *infra* p. 249.

[3] The precise meaning of *avot* or *avoti* is not quite certain; on the arch of Orange it seems to mean 'sculptor'. Some even doubt whether it is Gaulish at all.

name declares him of the Roman period, one Martialis, son of Dannotalus, records some work or dedication in a text of Celtic words (Fig. 31). We have, further, literary testimony that Celtic was still spoken near Trier, perhaps among the forests of the Hunsrück, during the fourth century.[1] Basque, too, which still survives in its little valleys beneath the shadows of the Pyrenees, does

Fig. 31. CELTIC INSCRIPTION FROM MONT-AUXOIS[2]

not seem to be, like Hungarian, a barbarian import of the Migration Age, and must have been to some extent in use throughout the Roman period. On the other hand, Latin spread rapidly through most of the land. The four thousand Roman inscriptions discovered in Gaul north of the Cevennes, excluding the German frontier, are no doubt comparatively few, if put beside the yield of Africa or southern Gaul. But they are considerable in themselves and they are matched by singularly few Celtic inscriptions.[3]

[1] Jerome, *Comment. in Ep. ad Galat.* (Migne, *Pat. Lat.* xxvi. 357).

[2] *CIL.* xiii. 2880. For a suggested interpretation see Rhys, *Proc. Brit. Acad.* 1911–12, pp. 290 ff.

[3] See Jullian, *Histoire de la Gaule* vi, pp. 104 ff.

So it was also in politics. Even when two movements for separation from Rome occurred, in A.D. 70 and 258, they took Roman forms. Indeed, the Gaulish Empire set up in the middle of the third century was a copy of the Roman, with consuls and *tribunicia potestas* and all proper details complete.[1] Nor was it otherwise in local government. North Gaul was granted a liberal measure

FIG. 32. SOUTH GAULISH 'SAMIAN' BOWL FROM NEWSTEAD

This bowl is of the Flavian period. In the centre, beneath the boar, is a fowler throwing a net over a bird. On the left is a figure of Victory; on the right, Diana with a hind.

of local autonomy by the Romans. The native cantons formed the units; the native nobles were the magistrates. This liberality was rewarded. Neither canton nor noble became a centre of sedition. Instead, much eagerness was shown to follow Roman patterns, and titles

[1] See Jullian, *Histoire de la Gaule* iv, pp. 570 ff.

borrowed from the Roman municipal system—duumvir, aedile, quaestor, and the like—were adopted to describe the native magistracies and adopted, as it seems, quite voluntarily.

The case of Gaulish literature is even plainer, so plain indeed as scarcely to call for special notice. As early as

FIG. 33. ARRETINE BOWL FROM HALTERN

The bowl is decorated with groups of girls playing with astragali. The fort of Haltern, where it was found, lies in the valley of the Lippe and was occupied from *c.* 13 B.C. till the defeat of Varus in A.D. 9.

the Flavian age it was a Gaul whom Tacitus chose as a representative and defender of the most modern school of contemporary oratory.[1] Two or three centuries later we have names like Eumenius of Autun, Hilary of Poitiers, Ausonius of Bordeaux.

If we turn to the kindred domain of art, the so-called

[1] *Dial. de Orat.* 5–10 and 16–23.

'Samian' pottery adds a no less clear example. This red 'sealing-wax' ware is characteristic of the Romano-provincial art. At its best, it is handsome enough. But it is imitative and conventional. It treats its details in a manner usual to a conventional art, making them often a mere jumble of decorations that do not fit into any

FIG. 34. SOUTH GAULISH BOWL FROM POMPEII

The bowl is one of a group of ninety found together in 1881 at Pompeii.[1] South Gaulish ware must therefore have become fashionable in southern Italy before A.D. 79.

coherent story or sequence, and it derives them directly and without alteration from classical sources (FIG. 32). It very closely resembles a red ware made at Arezzo in Etruria in the Augustan age (FIG. 33), and doubtless represents an attempt to copy that. But there is a limit to its imitativeness. It is not mechanical, like certain modern oriental copies of western products. Its selection of subjects and ornaments is more or less inde-

[1] See D. Atkinson in *J.R.S.* iv, pp. 26 ff.

pendent of Arezzo, and in execution it falls indeed considerably below the Arezzo standard. It forms a distinct class of ware, distinct to the modern student and doubtless equally distinct to the ancient purchaser. Strange as it may sound, its manufacture soon grew vigorous enough to oust its Arretine predecessor and to impose its own fashion on Italian households (FIG. 34).

I might proceed to cite similar evidence from other provinces—Spain, the Danubian lands, Dalmatia. Even Punic Africa with its very different conditions tells the same tale. But enough has been said to justify a general conclusion. Here, as in all historical inquiry, there is an historical framework to which we must fit our views of single districts. We must commence our survey of the civilization of Britain with the statement that, in the western provinces generally, the distinction between Italian and provincial died out. Both were Roman, alike in language, in political and intellectual life, and in material culture. Native sentiments and native fashions did indeed survive. But they survived in harmony with an ever-increasing Romanization. The Roman Empire was one of those periods which naturally and, as it were, automatically set towards uniformity, towards the combination of diverse racial and linguistic and national elements, and the grouping of individuals round one common centre. Much as the Empire resembled our present age—in its Imperialism, its care for administrative efficiency, its neglect of purely imaginative literature and art—in this one respect it differed wholly. Modern Europe is (for the moment) individualist, nationalist, separatist, and it finds some difficulty in conceiving of a world devoid of such tendencies. There is all the more reason why, as we pass on to the civilization of Roman Britain, we should notice the world of which the island formed an outlying part. The glimpse we have had of it will quicken our appreciation of the second kind of material available for our study—the actual remains.

One cardinal feature in the civilization of Britain has

already been referred to in these lectures. I have indicated that it was confined to a definite area in the centre, the east, and the south of the province—to the lowlands south of the Yorkshire hills and east of the Dee and the Usk and the Exe. Outside that area we may search practically in vain for traces of civilized life. Inside it we shall find almost nothing else. Exceptions necessarily occur. But they are few and intelligible. Isolated cases of unarmed civilized life have been observed in the military district. In the last lecture I mentioned two sites in the north, Carlisle and Corbridge near Hexham, which may possibly have served as centres of civil life, as playgrounds during a happy holiday, for soldiers garrisoning Hadrian's Wall. In the west a lonely country mansion at Llantwit in the lowland of Glamorgan, of which I also spoke, may be connected as much with the opposite coast of Somerset as with Wales, while the appearance of another at Llanfrynach near Brecon merely proves the adjacent country to have become peaceful and in a measure civilized.[1] Similarly, a few military stations occur here and there in the civilized area. But they all belong either, like Lincoln, to the first years of the conquest or, like Pevensey and its companions, to the later days when the Saxon Shore needed defence.[2] For practical purposes we have to deal now with one region, the lowlands, and with one form of occupation, that of civilized life.

Even within the lowland region, however, further distinctions must be drawn. The local distribution of the civilization was uneven. No such differences, of course, existed as are visible to-day between modern great industrial centres and agricultural or pastoral

[1] See *Roman Wales*, p. 73, note 60, and *Cymmrodorion Soc. Trans.* 1920–1, pp. 81 ff.

[2] The resulting insecurity caused London and other towns to surround themselves with walls, probably towards the end of the third century or in the course of the fourth. But these were not, in any sense, military stations, any more than the occasional 'villas' which we find protected in similar fashion by a rampart. As to the latter, see *infra*, p. 266.

districts. But both population and civilization varied widely in various places. North Kent and the Maidstone basin, the Colne valley in Essex, south-west Sussex, the slopes of the Cotswolds overlooking the Severn Sea, and parts of Somerset—to give a few instances only—were then occupied by a population both numerous and wealthy and (as we may think) well educated. It is interesting to note, in passing, that most of these areas are still thickly peopled by other than urban inhabitants. The Thames valley from Oxford to Goring was probably the home of an abundant riverside population much less advanced in culture. You may see their traces, in any dry summer, in cornfields between Oxford and Radley or round Dorchester and Wallingford. The mud walls and ditches of their meagre farms have indeed vanished, but they have left damper soil along the lines they followed. Here in scorching heat the grain grows taller than around, and the circles and squares that thus arise raggedly above the general level are plain to any moderately observant eye.[1]

On the other hand, though several of them have now large rural populations, the North and South Downs and the Weald, the greater part of Norfolk[2] and Suffolk, the fertile vale of Taunton[3], the eastern coast of south Devon are instances of districts where Romano-British civilization took little hold and Romano-British inhabitants were few. In particular, the midlands were thinly and poorly peopled.[4] Great roads, the work probably of the earliest conquest, ran direct across them. But these roads passed through no important towns or villages, and the country on either side of them was tenanted neither by well-to-do farmers nor by struggling peasants. Leamington claims to-day to be the very heart of England, and its cabmen point out an aged oak as the precise middle of the land. But to the mere student of Roman

[1] *P.S.A.L.* (2nd Ser.) xviii, pp. 10 ff.
[2] See *Vict. Hist. Norfolk* i, p. 284.
[3] See *Vict. Hist. Somerset* i, p. 216, and *Somerset Proc.* lxiv, pp. xxix f.
[4] Cf. *Vict. Hist. Warwick* i, pp. 228 ff.

Britain it is probably the least interesting site and the least convenient centre within the four seas. The reason for this emptiness of the midland area is clear enough. Amidst its great woodlands, and on its damp and chilly soil, agriculture can expand only under the exceptional conditions of a Napoleonic war. Pigs, sheep, and cattle may flourish better, but the absence of good waterways and of natural communications of all sorts, combined with the distance of markets, renders their pasturage comparatively unprofitable in ordinary times. Therefore the midlands of the Roman period were what, but for certain industrial intrusions, they still are—a sparsely populated, unimportant tract, traversed but not affected by trunk lines carrying through-traffic to the circumference. If a map of the population and the chief centres of the Roman province could be constructed, it would show the midlands as a relatively blank space ringed round by a row of towns and a belt of inhabited country.

From this sketch of the geographical limits and distribution of Roman civilization in Britain, we may proceed to describe its character. And first the system of government. The Roman practice provided for each

---

. . . PAVLINO LEG(ATO) LEG(IONIS) I[I] AVG(VSTAE), PROCONSVL(I) PROVINC(IAE) NARBONENSIS, LEG(ATO) AVG(VSTI) PR(O) PR(AETORE) PROVI(NCIAE) LVGVDVNEN(SIS), EX DECRETO ORDINIS RESPVBL(ICA) CIVIT(ATIS) SILVRVM.

That is: 'Pursuant to a decree of the cantonal council, the Canton of Silures set this up in honour of . . . Paulinus, commander of the Legion II Augusta, formerly Senatorial Governor of Gallia Narbonensis and Imperial Governor of Gallia Lugdunensis.' The inscription was discovered during the excavations of 1903.[1] The reading '*Paulino*' is hardly doubtful, and the individual meant is almost certainly Ti. Claudius Paulinus, who is known to have been governor of Gallia Lugdunensis in the reign of Alexander Severus (A.D. 222–35). The identification is confirmed by an inscription from High Rochester (*CIL.* vii. 1045), which mentions him as governor of Britain. The command of one of the British legions was, from Flavian times, a normal prelude to the governorship of the island.

[1] See *Archaeologia* lix, p. 120, and *Ephem. Epigr.* ix. 1012.

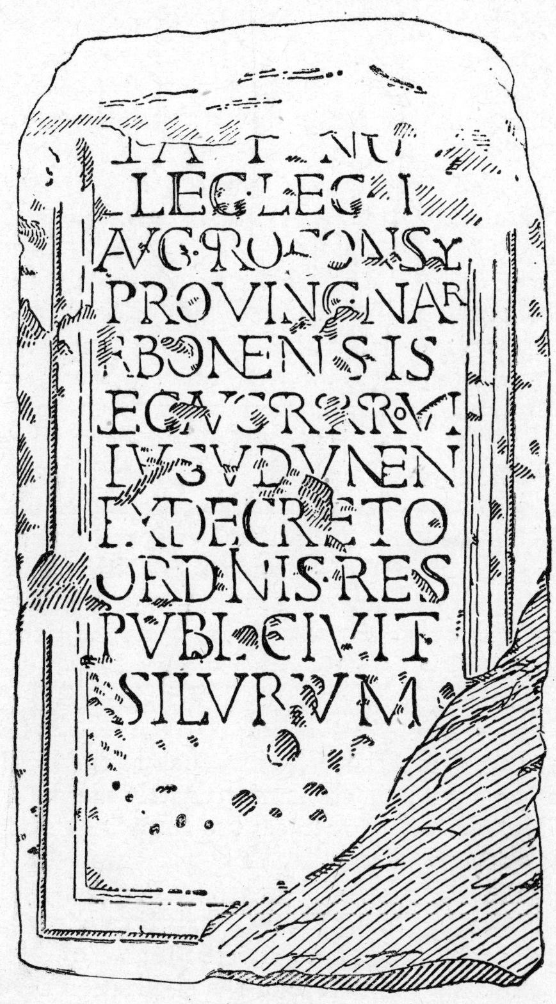


Fig. 35. INSCRIPTION FROM CAERWENT

See foot of preceding page.

province a governor who might (in the case of an Imperial province like Britain) remain at his post for several years together. But, as a rule, the governor interfered only to ensure peace and order, the payment of taxes, and the administration of justice to Roman citizens. The whole management of local affairs was left to the local officials. Of these in Britain we can discern two classes. The Roman 'municipalities'—to be noticed below—had their own magistrates, and through them ruled the surrounding territory. Most of the rest of the country seems to have been left, as it was in northern Gaul, to the chiefs of the native cantons—not, of course, as chiefs but as magistrates of districts in the Empire. Thus we find at Caerwent a monument raised to a high Roman officer, commanding the garrison at Caerleon, fifteen miles away (FIG. 35). It is erected by decree of the *ordo reipublicae civitatis Silurum*, the county council of the Canton of Silŭres. It would therefore seem that here, as in Gaul, the cantonal authorities were organized on the Roman municipal system and adopted its terminology; the local administration of the canton was municipalized, just as, under the county council system, the local administration of our English counties has lately been municipalized. Nearly all civil Britain was probably under either municipal or cantonal rule. What was exempted was Imperial property, such as the lead mines in Somerset,[1] and of this unfortunately we have little knowledge. In most provinces the Imperial estates grew steadily during the Empire. But they were smaller in Gaul and Britain than elsewhere; they only reached their full size in Gaul about A.D. 200, and in our own island they may never have covered such large areas.

In considering the nature of the civilization of Roman Britain, it will obviously be best to begin with the towns. Among our numerous debts to Rome, not the least is that connected with its legacy of town life. Long before the beginning of the Roman Empire, before the Roman conquest of central and western Europe, Italian civiliza-

[1] *Vict. Hist. Somerset* i, pp. 334 ff., and *infra*, pp. 255 ff.

tion was already based on towns. In part this was due to the geographical features of the Italian peninsula. Its many hills, steep, isolated, strong for defence, rising high above the malaria-haunted lowlands, yet not too high to be habitable here and there in winter, drew men up to the heights, wherever these gave room. And there were fertile little plains and valleys, which could each support a whole town of its own. Thus Italy became the land of towns which Vergil praised:

> '*adde tot egregias urbes operumque laborem,*
> *tot congesta manu praeruptis oppida saxis*
> *fluminaque antiquos subterlabentia muros*'.[1]

The Italian civilization, then, was essentially based on towns. That was the dominant feature of Italy; the town was the unit of local government. All the soil, except the Imperial properties, was divided up among towns and under the rule of the town magistrates. This was natural in that land of sharp physical contrasts. It was not natural in northern Europe. There no spot fulfils the Italian poet's boast, '*bis gravidae pecudes, bis pomis utilis arbos*'[2]; there no soil yields two crops in a year, no herds two sets of offspring. But there, on the other hand, the fertility is distributed more evenly. Towns are fewer, or at least smaller, save for the industrial developments. But wholly barren hillsides and wholly uninhabited uplands are also rarer, and accordingly the early races of central Europe did not generally live in towns. They dwelt scattered up and down the land. The Germans and English occupied villages. The Celts preferred the hamlets and lonely homesteads that we can still see in Cornwall and north Cumberland.[3] The

[1] *Georg.* ii. 155 ff. The second line might refer to towns in middle Italy, the third to towns in Cisalpine Gaul beside the Po and other streams, as Byron saw.

[2] *Georg.* ii. 150.

[3] The contrast between the Germanic and the Celtic systems is well brought out in the maps printed in the illustrated edition of Traill's *Social England* (1901) i, pp. 164 f.

appearance of town-life among any of them is a sign from the south.

In Britain town-life sprang up in the Roman period and under Roman influence. At this point, therefore, it may be convenient to glance at the terms which the Romans actually used for towns. *Urbs* was simply the most general word for a fair-sized town, and was often applied to the largest of all Roman towns, Rome itself. It need hardly concern us here. *Civitas*, from which our word 'city' is derived, may also be set aside. It denoted in good Latin of the first century of our era a body of citizens rather than a complex of buildings. In late Latin it came to mean a town simply, without regard to size or legal status. *Colonia* and *municipium* call for fuller notice. They were technical terms, indicating towns to which the state had granted formal charters, and which lived under definite constitutions, set forth in such charters. These constitutions, all more or less similar, resembled that which was used in the old Italian towns generally, and it is not inaccurate to speak of *coloniae* and *municipia* as 'towns on the Italian model'. The two—*coloniae* and *municipia*—had much the same form of government; in both the citizens were *cives Romani*. The main distinction between them was in the matter of origin. The *coloniae* of the earlier Empire were either new towns, founded full-grown on sites hitherto unoccupied, and peopled by drafts of time-expired legionaries, or pre-existing native towns whose character had been transformed by a similar plantation of Roman veterans (*deductio*); the *municipia* were rather pre-existing native towns which had reached by natural progress some size and some civilization of a Roman (or Italian) kind, and which seemed to merit from the central government the grant of a definite charter and of an urban constitution. Collectively, we may speak of *coloniae* and *municipia* as 'Roman municipalities'. But the real Roman element was naturally stronger in the *colonia*, originally a settlement of Roman soldiers, than in the *municipium*, which was more definitely of native provincial origin, as unfriendly critics of it sometimes observed. *Oppidum*, a vaguer, weaker word than almost any of those yet mentioned, was applied to towns of all sorts, from Rome down to the rude 'camps' of the Britons. Of itself it hardly implied any real town-life, though it was used of many unquestionable towns.

I have said that in Britain town-life sprang up in the Roman period and under Roman influence. But, just as in northern Gaul, it did not spring up in definitely Roman fashion. The Roman municipality, the town of Roman citizens established under government charter and administered on a definite Italian model, was rare in Britain. The fact has been obscured by the eighteenth-century forger, Bertram of Copenhagen, masquerading as Richard of Cirencester. He credited Britain with two *municipia*, nine *coloniae*, and ten '*civitates Latio iure donatae*'[1]—this last a high-sounding title which he probably did not understand. In reality the municipalities numbered five. One was established at Camulodūnum (Colchester) by Claudius and peopled with time-expired soldiers. It seems to have been known as Colonia Victricensis,[2] and was for a while the capital of the province. Another, almost as early in date, was at Verulamium (St. Albans), and deserves notice because it included no veterans, but was more probably a native town which had become Romanized. The remaining three were connected with the army. Lindum (Lincoln)—still declaring its colonial rank by its name—was probably founded when the Ninth Legion was pushed forward to York, some time between A.D. 70 and 80[3]. Glevum (Gloucester), one of whose magistrates—a *decurio*—left an inscription at Bath,[4] was planted under Nerva (A.D. 96–

[1] *De Situ Britanniae*, i. 7.
[2] *CIL*. xiv. 3955 (Dessau, *Inscr. Sel.* 2740).
[3] Cf. R. Knox McElderry in *Class. Rev.* xviii, pp. 398 f.
[4] *CIL*. vii. 54. See *Vict. Hist. Somerset* i, p. 277.

98)[1] and in all likelihood contained as its first inhabitants time-expired men from the Second Legion at Caerleon. Lastly, York saw grow up under the walls of the legionary fortress, though across the Ouse, a settlement which earned in later days municipal rank.[2]

This may be regarded as a fair provision of 'towns on the Italian model'. It is a longer list than that of northern Gaul. But the value of the fact may be easily overrated. Narbonese Gaul, that part of southern Gaul which lay along the Rhone valley and the Mediterranean coast, and the several parts of Roman Africa—Tunis, Algeria, and so on—had far more. The forms of policy adopted by the Empire in its various provinces differed as much as did the circumstances of the provinces themselves. It will be observed that all the British municipalities save one owed their birth to the army. Verulamium excepted, Britain can show none of those grants of municipal status to Romanized provincial centres of non-military character, which were common elsewhere in the late first, the second, and the early third centuries. Nor did the five British towns flourish greatly. Of all there are remains left, and there is no doubt as to sites or titles. But the remains vary in extent, and the inscriptions of the five barely total six dozen, while those of any ordinary continental municipality often run into hundreds. We need not reckon very high the contribution of these towns to our picture of Romano-British civilization.

More characteristic of Roman Britain, more numerous, and at least as prosperous were other towns of lesser legal status. The existence of these is attested mainly by archaeological finds. But we have also written evidence. A collection of lists of names of towns, rivers, and sites

[1] *CIL.* vi. 3346 (Dessau, *Inscr. Sel.* 2365). Cf. *Ephem. Epigr.* ix, p. 519, and Mommsen in *CIL.* x, p. 12 (Scolacium).

[2] It had become a *colonia* before A.D. 237, as is proved by the Bordeaux inscription already referred to (*supra*, p. 90, foot-note 1). Cf. *CIL.* vii. 248 and *Ephem. Epigr.* iii. 80.

in the Roman world was drawn up in the seventh century of our era at Ravenna by a geographer of unknown name, who is usually styled '*Anonymus Ravennas*' or 'the Ravenna Geographer', or, simply, 'Ravennas'. The collection is a schedule of names, grouped more or less locally by countries, and arranged under such headings as *flumina* or *civitates*, with as little comment or description as one looks for in Bradshaw. Throughout, the lists are full of errors. Italy must have been fairly familiar to the compiler, if he worked in Ravenna. Yet even in his Italian section misspellings abound; seldom do half a dozen consecutive names appear in their proper forms. The British section is naturally worse. Neither the original seventh-century author nor the later scribes who copied his work after him can have been familiar with Romano-British place-names except on some map; they certainly present them in wonderfully corrupt forms and in confused order. Still, like other scraps that have come down to us from the last days of the Empire, the lists of Ravennas are based on earlier authorities and, like them, preserve occasional vestiges of truth not known through other extant sources. For one instance, the town or village of Wall, near Lichfield, is called in most of our authorities Etocetum. Ravennas[1] has the spelling 'Lectoceto', and philology shows that this is correct, at least in respect of the initial 'L'.[2] The ancient name of Wall was apparently Letocetum, and that is the origin of the early English forms of the name, like 'Lyccidfeld', which occur in Bede and elsewhere, and also of the modern 'Lichfield', which does not derive from any 'field of corpses', but from a Celtic name, meaning 'grey wood'. Other details could be quoted in which the Ravenna Geographer has preserved facts better than have other sources; it would seem that his authorities here and there enshrined a true

[1] *Rav.* p. 429, 8.

[2] See Holder, *Altceltischer Sprachschatz*, s.v. 'Letoceton', and Bradley in *Essays and Studies by Members of English Assoc.* i (1910), pp. 20 f.

tradition which is otherwise lost.[1] Sometimes this makes him more valuable than even the generally more correct *Antonine Itinerary*.

Now the Ravenna lists of British sites name certain items in a special way; they add to various town-names a tribe-name in the genitive plural. For example, a section which mainly relates to East Kent contains a short sequence of names, in which to one, the name of Canterbury, is appended the tribe-name *Cantiacorum*, 'of the men of Kent': [2]

*Lemanis* (Stutfall Castle near Lymne).
*Dubris* (Dover).
*Duroaverno Cantiacorum* (Canterbury).
*Rutupis* (Richborough).
*Durobrabis* (Rochester).

In all, ten such nomenclatures occur:

*Isca Dumnaniorum* [3] = *Isca Dumnoniorum* (Exeter).
*Venta Velgarom* [4] = *Venta Belgarum* (Winchester).
*Ventaslurum* [5] = *Venta Silurum* (Caerwent).
*Navimago Regentium* [6]

[1] Thus nearly all our authorities on the geography of the Empire give 'Vindolana' as the name of a Roman fort in Northumberland, now known as Chesterholm, close to the Wall of Hadrian. All three MSS. of the Ravenna lists (p. 431, 11) spell it 'Vindolande', and an altar found on the spot in July 1914 confirms the 'd' spelling, which indeed agrees better with the requirements of Celtic philology. See F. H., 'Roman Britain in 1914' in *British Academy Supplem. Papers* iii, pp. 31 f., and *C. and W. Trans.* (n.s.) xviii, pp. 223 ff., where other names are also discussed.

[2] *Rav.* p. 428, 2–6. It should be noted that, besides being frequently misspelt, the names in Ravennas are often in the locative.

[3] *Ibid.* p. 425, 1. In p. 425, 9, the name is repeated as '*Scadoniorum*'. The citations from Rav. are from Parthey and Pinder's text.

[4] *Ibid.* p. 426, 10.

[5] *Ibid.* p. 426, 18.

[6] *Ibid.* p. 426, 13 f. The ordinary text of Rav. treats '*Navimago*' and '*Regentium*' as two separate names. F. H.'s suggestion is that the two are really one. If so, '*Navimago Regentium*' would stand for '*Noviomagus Regnensium*', i.e. 'of the Regnenses or Regni', Chichester being meant; see *Vict. Hist. Surrey* iv, pp. 347 ff.

| | |
|---|---|
| *Cironium Dobunorum* [1] | = *Corinium Dobunorum* (Cirencester). |
| *Caleba Arbatium* [2] | = *Calleva Atrebatum* (Silchester). |
| *Duroaverno Cantiacorum* | = *Durovernum Canti(ac)orum* (Canterbury). |
| *Utriconion Cornoviorum* [3] | = *Viroconium Cornoviorum* (Wroxeter). |
| *Rate Corion* [4] | = *Ratae Coritanorum* (Leicester). |
| *Venta Cenomum* [5] | = *Venta Icenorum* (Caister-by-Norwich). |

All of the ten sites to which Ravennas adds tribal names have yielded archaeological remains indicating town-life. They are the sites of towns and, so far as one can judge from their remains, of more or less considerable towns. We may take it, then, that in effect Ravennas gives a list of the towns of Roman Britain. We may even go further and conjecture that those which he selected, or rather which his sources selected, for special tribal nomenclature were tribal or cantonal capitals. The Caerwent inscription, as we have seen,[6] affords evidence that in Britain, as in northern and central Gaul, the old tribal system lived on, within certain limits. It suggests pretty plainly that Venta Silŭrum was the *chef-lieu* of the Silures—if one may adopt a convenient French expression, which has for English ears no administrative associations and therefore conveys no false impressions. Equally reasonably one might assume, as many have actually done, that Venta Belgarum or Winchester was the *chef-lieu* of the Belgae. The exact sense of 'Venta' is unfortunately obscure. Perhaps the best explanation is that it means a market-centre or gathering-place for the adjacent country; that sense would certainly suit its various usages for Caerwent, Winchester, and Caister-

[1] *Rav.* p. 427, 16.
[2] *Ibid.* p. 427, 17.
[3] *Ibid.* p. 428, 11.
[4] *Ibid.* p. 429, 6.
[5] *Ibid.* p. 430, 1.
[6] *Supra*, p. 186.

by-Norwich.[1] No doubt there were other capitals besides those which Ravennas enumerates.[2] It would be too much to hope that his list is exhaustive. But the ten examples he provides us with do help towards a better understanding of various remains known by excavations or otherwise.

It would seem that, as the province became Romanized, the old tribal *oppida* grew naturally into towns and, though they did not win the technical rank of municipalities, possessed some sort of municipal organization. Of their origins we know nothing, but can guess a little. In Caesar's day the nearest approach to a town in Britain was a military place of refuge, hidden in forests.[3] But Caesar wrote nearly a hundred years before the Claudian conquest, and during that long interval continental and Roman influences were steadily crossing the Channel. Things may have been very different in A.D. 43 from what they were in 48 B.C. The continental Gauls in Caesar's time had 'towns' which served not only as fortresses but as market-centres, and which were defended by strong walls constructed after a definite and elaborate method. Thus Bibracte, now Mont Beuvray, stood high on a hill, but it was essentially a town, if not a town of very complex organization; there the tribe of the Aedui, or the Gauls in general, met to select a leader;[4] there, too, Caesar once wintered in comfort.[5] If such was the case in central Gaul about 50 B.C., we might expect a knowledge of urban life to have penetrated to Britain by A.D. 40.

No one need, therefore, feel sceptical if he is con-

[1] The current derivation from a supposed Celtic word *gwent*, meaning 'a clearing', is untenable. It was the late Dr. Whitley Stokes who suggested to F. H. that the name might possibly be connected with the Latin *vendere*, and mean a market-town or business centre; he compared the Spanish *venta*, 'a wayside inn'. Cf. *Vict. Hist. Hants* i, p. 285.

[2] See Appendix to Mommsen's *Rom. Prov.* (1909) ii, p. 353.

[3] '*Oppidum autem Britanni vocant, cum silvas impeditas vallo atque fossa munierunt*' (*De Bell. Gall.* v. 21).

[4] *De Bell. Gall.* vii. 63.

[5] *Ibid.* viii. 4.

fronted with evidences which suggest a beginning of town-life in our island during the period between the invasion of Caesar and the advent of Claudius. Traces of such life in pre-Roman Britain are no doubt rare. But they occur at Silchester, where Arretine ware was well known and freely used, a sure sign of early date; they can be inferred at Verulam; and they appear on one or two other sites.[1] None have come to light in Wroxeter, Leicester, or Lincoln, hardly any even in London. Most of the finds which indicate an approach to civilized life of pre-Roman date are from chance spots like Foxton in Cambridgeshire.[2] The late Professor Freeman, it appears, was fairly within the mark when he said that few Romano-British towns stood on British sites.[3] Colchester, for example, has yielded much pre-Roman pottery, of a kind often called 'Late Celtic'. But the Curator of its Museum, Mr. Wright, says that almost none of this ware was actually found on the site occupied in Roman times by the Roman Camulodūnum, and I should infer that pre-Roman or Celtic Colchester probably stood a mile or two away at the Lexden earthworks.[4]

Here, perhaps, we touch a point of Roman state-craft. In order to break national traditions and to cut across memories of freedom, the natives were not left to live exactly where their forefathers had lived, to occupy the same houses or worship in the same shrines. Nor were they allowed to hold the high places—the hill-camps within which, in case of insurrection, they could make obstinate resistance. We may think that the dwellers in the hill-camps were brought down from their upland *oppida*, to dwell in pleasant places, and in peaceful

[1] See *Romanization of Roman Britain*, p. 74.

[2] *Cambridge Antiq. Soc. Proc. and Communic.* xx (1917), pp. 53 ff.

[3] *Historical Essays*, Fourth Series (1892), p. 45, and *English Towns and Districts* (1883), pp. 51 f. and pp. 157 f.

[4] Cf. Wheeler and Laver in *J.R.S.* ix, pp. 139 f., and *Royal Commission on Hist. Mon., Essex Inventory*, iii, pp. xxv f.

civilized fashion among fat meadows by the water-side. Thus, it may be that 'Hills' which overlooks Winchester, and the Wrekin close to Wroxeter, and Maiden Castle near Dorchester in Dorset, and Sinodun Hill which overhangs the Oxfordshire Dorchester, and Bigbury near Canterbury were emptied, and their inhabitants planted in new valley towns beside the Itchen, the Severn, the Frome, the Thames, and the Stour.

This is not mere theory. Gaul supplies definite evidence that, in the early Empire, the Roman Government now and again followed such a policy of provincial denationalization. The native Gaulish town or *oppidum* on Mont Beuvray has been mentioned above.[1] Before our era began, it was dismantled by the Romans. About 5 B.C. Augustus moved its inhabitants from the old native centre on the hill, and planted them sixteen or seventeen miles off in a new town, on a hitherto unoccupied site, beside the river Arroux.[2] Nor is this all. The new town, covering within its walls the ample area of nearly 334 acres, was no mere repetition of Bibracte. It was laid out in Roman fashion; it had, indeed, an irregular outline, but that was determined by the nature of the ground; within it the skill of French archaeologists has discovered a regular chessboard of quadrangular street-planning, such as characterized Roman towns in Italy and in Mediterranean lands.[3] To this town Augustus gave his own name, with a Celtic suffix, Augustodunum, now Autun. His object is clear. Bibracte was a native stronghold, *oppidum apud Haeduos maximae auctoritatis*, as Caesar calls it;[4] it was an old town when Caesar attacked it; round it must have clustered innumerable recollections associated with Celtic independence. Not

[1] *Supra*, p. 194.

[2] See Déchelette, *Les fouilles du mont Beuvray* (1904), pp. 118 f., and *Manuel d'Archéologie préhistorique, celtique et gallo-romaine* ii, pp. 951 ff. The date is fixed by numismatic evidence; see *Rev. Num.* 1899, p. 129.

[3] See *Ancient Town-Planning*, pp. 121 ff. and Fig. 29.

[4] *De Bell. Gall.* vii. 55.

merely because the place was a strong hill-fortress, but also because it was full of such associations, did Augustus clear the hilltop and form a new settlement on lower ground and a considerable distance away. The similar summit of Gergovia seems to have been similarly cleared, also by Augustus, and its inhabitants removed to a new town a few miles off at Clermont-Ferrand (Augustonemetum).[1]

It is reasonable to believe that what happened in Roman Gaul may have happened also in Roman Britain. But the British records are too scanty, and British excavations have been too limited, for much definite evidence to be as yet forthcoming. What is known, however, points in the direction indicated. That is, Roman Britain appears to have been, to some extent, Romanized by the introduction of town-life on certain lines. It is of little use to ask for dates. One might think that the Emperor Claudius was active in helping on the movement. He, at any rate, was interested in the island of which he had begun the conquest; he was not averse in principle to the diffusion of Roman town-life through the provinces of the Empire generally. Indeed, we can confidently ascribe to him the establishment of two of the five British municipalities—the *colonia* at Colchester and the *municipium* at Verulamium (St. Albans).[2] His successor Nero apparently did little to encourage the new development. Probably the succeeding Flavian age did much. It was under Vespasian and his sons that town-life began really to spread abroad over the Empire.[3] It is noticeable that on many Romano-British town-sites, such as Wroxeter, Colchester, London, Cirencester,[4] and Leicester[5], the bulk of the earlier datable remains—coins,

[1] Déchelette, *op. cit.*, pp. 952, 957 ff.

[2] Colchester, of course, is quite certain (Tac. *Agric.* 14, and *Ann.* xiv. 31). Verulamium is hardly less so; it was a *municipium* by A.D. 61 (Tac. *Ann.* xiv. 33).

[3] For Britain see Tacitus, *Agricola*, c. 21.

[4] *Archaeologia* lxix, p. 194.

[5] *Arch. Journ.* lxxv, p. 28.

pottery, or inscriptions—are Flavian. Possibly we should connect the quadrangular town-plans of Silchester (Fig. 36) and of Caerwent (Fig. 37) with Agricola or with his influence.[1] On both sites the remains suggest that town-life grew fast (if it did not begin) during the years when he governed Britain. At Bath the earliest dated inscription is

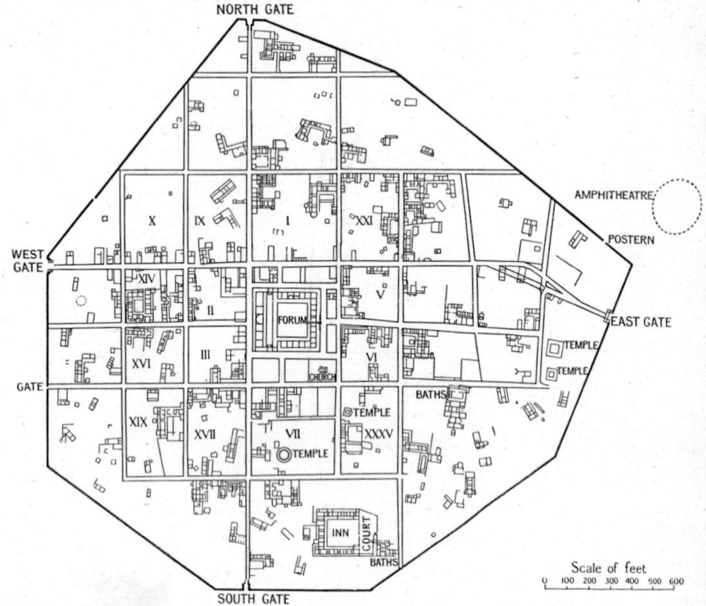


Fig. 36. PLAN OF SILCHESTER

a monument of A.D. 76,[2] and the date shows that the rise of this spa or watering-place was already in progress a year or two before he came out. Of other towns we cannot speak so confidently. But one may assert thus much—that before A. D. 70 town-life was a frail plant in Britain and imperfectly developed, but that by the end of the first century of our era it was well rooted and established.

If the history of the Romano-British towns is obscure,

[1] *Vict. Hist. Hants* i, p. 276.

[2] *Ephem. Epigr.* ix. 996. *Vict. Hist. Somerset* i, p. 269, No. 10.

the archaeological evidence, disjointed and imperfect as it is, enables us to form a rough idea of what they were like. In size they were mostly small. London was the largest—as, indeed, it was one of the larger towns of the western Empire. It grew to cover about 325 acres within its walls, irrespective of any suburb south of the

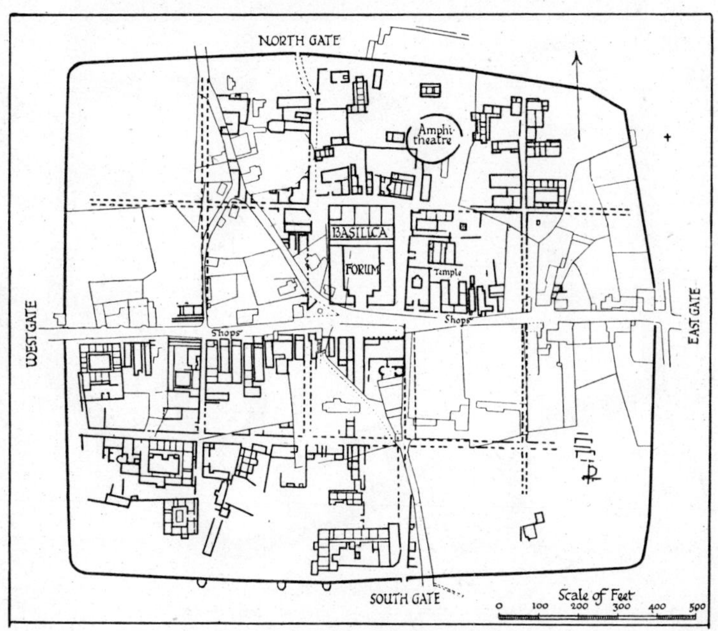


FIG. 37. PLAN OF CAERWENT

Thames. Cirencester, the next largest town in Britain (so far as we know), contained within its walls about 240 acres, Verulam about 200, Wroxeter 170, Colchester and Leicester about 105, and Silchester 100 acres. No other towns in the British province were so large as these. Caerwent, for instance, shut in between the Bristol Channel and the Welsh hills, and remote from the centres of Romano-British trade and traffic, remained small and hardly more than a village. Though it had features characteristic of a town—walls, a street-plan, shops, a town hall, and the like—it never covered much more than 40 acres. To modern ears such figures may sound inconsiderable; modern man reckons towns by square miles rather than by acres. But, compared with the areas of other towns in the ancient world, the Romano-

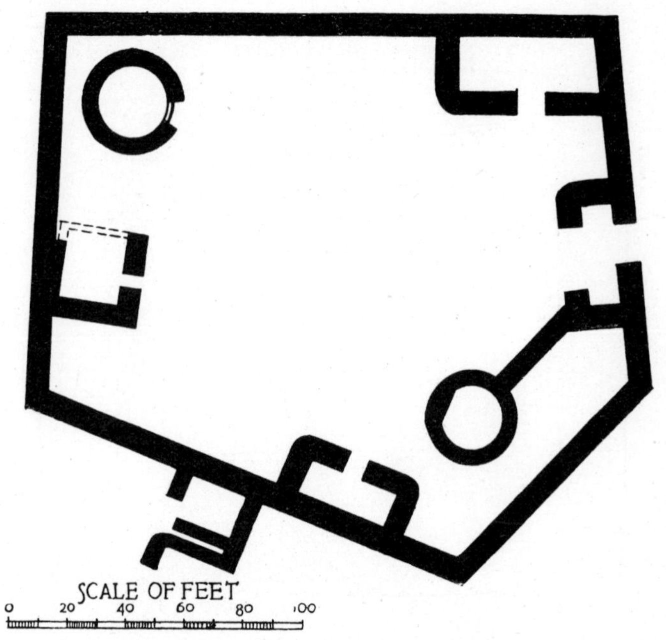


Fig. 38. NATIVE VILLAGE AT DIN LLIGWY, ANGLESEY

British figures are not altogether contemptible. Roman Cologne, one of the chief towns in the West, was smaller than London and about as large as Cirencester.[1] Turin, founded by Augustus about 28 B. C., included within its first walls 127 acres, rather more than half the acreage of Roman Cologne.[2] The Roman *colonia* which Trajan founded at Timgad in Africa in A. D. 100, as first laid

[1] See J. Klinkenburg in Clemen, *Kunstdenkmäler der Rheinprovinz* vi (i), pp. 146, 164 ff.

[2] *Ancient Town-Planning*, pp. 86 ff.

out, was hardly 30 acres in extent, although it quickly spread outside its walls and became much larger.[1]

To judge from Gaulish analogies like Bibracte,[2] as well as from British villages like Glastonbury and the small enclosure at Din Lligwy in Anglesey[3] (Fig. 38), the

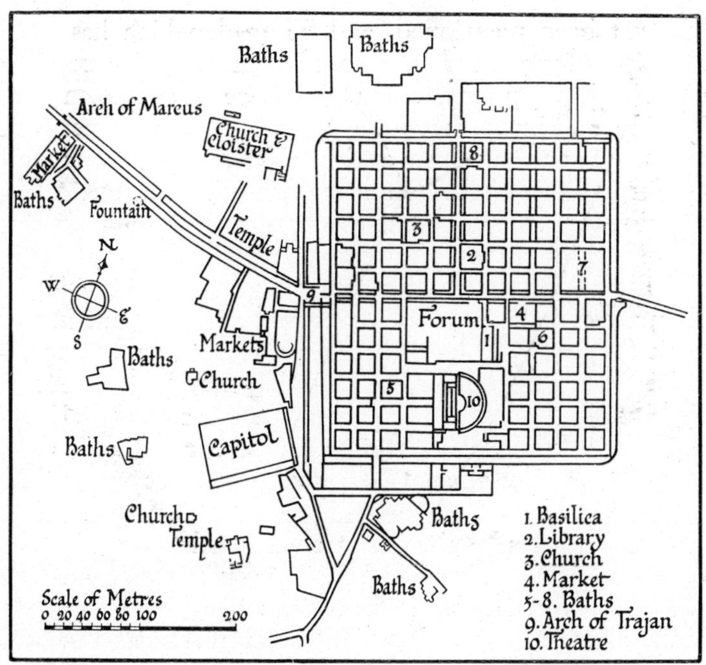


Fig. 39. PLAN OF TIMGAD

original British *oppida* were not plotted out on any definite system. The ancient Greek and Roman world, on the other hand, possessed a very distinct and rigid form of town-planning. Invented perhaps originally in the East—in Babylon, if not further afield—it was adopted and developed by Greek architects, notably in the Macedonian period, one of the greatest ages of town-building in

[1] *Ibid.* pp. 109 ff. [2] Déchelette, *op. cit.*, p. 949.
[3] See *Arch. Cambr.* (6th ser.) viii, pp. 183 ff.

the world's history, and was finally taken over by the Romans. As a result, the towns of the Roman Empire were commonly laid out on a plan resembling a chessboard, with straight streets intersecting at right angles and enclosing rectangular blocks of houses or *insulae*, very much in the manner of modern American cities. Autun has just been mentioned, and Timgad, which has been already referred to, is a most characteristic example (FIG. 39). Under Roman influence the system was introduced into Britain. Silchester and Caerwent (FIGS. 36 and 37) prove this clearly. Wroxeter and Cirencester and Colchester furnish slighter, but fairly certain, indications. Some conjectural plans of Verulam, though they are not very satisfactory,[1] serve to enlarge the list of examples. Roman Lincoln, too, or at least the part of it 'above hill', was probably laid out in the same fashion.[2] So in all likelihood were other Romano-British centres, though the planning may have been less rigorously Roman. But about many we are simply ignorant; various assertions of local antiquaries—for instance, as to Roman Gloucester—are unsupported by evidence.

Rectangular planning on a chessboard pattern would lead one to expect that towns so planned would be square or rectangular in outline. That is the case in Italy and to some extent in Roman Africa, but not universally. Most of the Gaulish towns round which the tracks of the ancient walls can be followed to-day are entirely unsymmetrical enclosures. Nîmes, established as a *colonia* by Augustus, was or became wholly irregular. In Britain, too, the towns of which we can trace the ancient walls seldom exhibit rectangular outlines. The two *coloniae* of Gloucester and Lincoln formed precise rectangles, but the *municipium* of Veru-

[1] See *Vict. Hist. Herts.* i, pp. 130 ff., and *Royal Commission on Hist. Mon., Herts. Inventory*, p. 190.
[2] *Ancient Town-Planning*, pp. 117 f.

lamium had an irregular shape, while many cantonal capitals also—Canterbury, Dorchester, Bath, Wroxeter, Silchester—seem to have presented the same feature.

It has been sometimes assumed that this irregular outline denotes a native or Celtic origin.[1] It is more likely that the irregularity proceeds from another reason. It is probable that the walls of the British, as of the Gaulish,

FIG. 40. SOUTH CITY-WALL OF CAERWENT

towns were in general added somewhat late in the third century, when growing barbarian invasions made walls necessary; their lines were then drawn simply to enclose the necessarily shapeless areas which had come to be occupied by houses. In short, the growth of these towns had been spontaneous and natural. Some started with a regular town-plan such as we see at Silchester. There the area of which the *insulae* numbered X, XXI, XXXV, and XIX form the corners, and the Forum the

[1] So, recently, J. P. B. Karslake, *P.S.A.L.* (2nd ser.) xxxii, pp. 185 ff., and *Antiq. Journal* i, pp. 303 ff.

centre, must have been planned complete from the first.[1] Its presence seems to indicate an initial rectangular outline. When Silchester came to need walling, the houses had spread beyond this, and the line followed by the walls was naturally very irregular. The contrast with Caerwent is instructive. Caerwent, it will be remembered, did not grow. At first, perhaps, it was girt with a rampart of earth. When the still stately stone walls (FIG. 40) were added—in the later third or the fourth century of our era—they followed closely the course of the earlier earthwork, into which they are built[2], and they included nearly the same area—a fairly regular oblong of about 400 × 500 yards (FIG. 37).

As with the laying out of the streets, so with the public buildings. The impress which they bear is unmistakable. This is natural enough. Before the Claudian conquest the Britons can hardly have possessed large structures in stone, and the provision of these necessarily came with the Romans. The *fora*, basilicas, and public baths of the towns followed Roman models and resembled similar buildings in other provinces. The ruins at Wroxeter are still sufficiently imposing (PLATE III), and the ground-plans revealed by the spade at Silchester, Caerwent, and elsewhere show a capacious *forum* or market-place on the Italian plan, with an Italian-looking basilica annexed (FIG. 41). In this basilica or town hall the local *ordo* would meet and transact the business of the canton. Occasionally the temples were of the classical type. That seems to have been the case with the one unearthed at Wroxeter in 1913,[3] as with that at Lydney in Gloucestershire,[4] and nothing could well suggest classical

[1] See FIG. 36, and *Ancient Town-Planning*, p. 129.

[2] See *Archaeologia* lviii, p. 138, lix, pp. 88 f., lx, pp. 115 f., and *Arch. Cambr.* lxxi, pp. 14 f.

[3] See J. P. Bushe-Fox in *Excavations at Wroxeter in 1913*, pp. 2 ff., and F. H. in 'Roman Britain in 1913' (*British Academy Supplem. Papers* ii, 1914), p. 19, and 'Roman Britain in 1914' (*Ibid.* iii, 1915), pp. 52 f.

[4] So also apparently with the temple recently discovered under the Norman castle at Colchester. "The proportions tally exactly and the actual dimensions very closely with those of the Maison Carrée at Nîmes"

architecture more strongly than do some of the fragments which are believed to have belonged to the temple of Sul Minerva at Bath (PLATE V). As a rule, however, in both town and country, the temples are on something more of a local pattern. They consist generally of a small *cella* or shrine, square or nearly square, with a

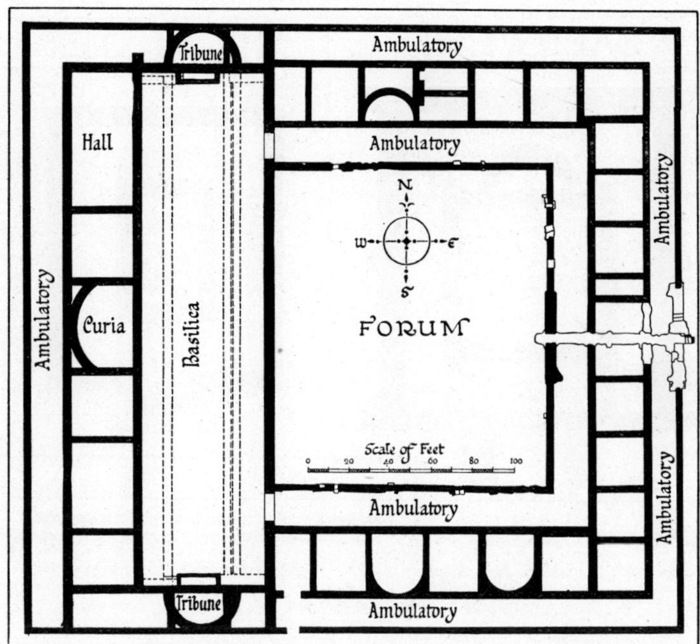


FIG. 41. GROUND-PLAN OF THE FORUM, SILCHESTER

roofed portico or colonnade running round all its four sides, and an entrance usually from the east; the building often stands in a large irregular enclosure. This type of temple occurs at Silchester and Caerwent (FIG. 42) and on many rural sites; it occurs also in northern Gaul and as far east as the Rhine.[1] It differs from the ordinary

(*J.R.S.* x, p. 147, and *Royal Commission on Hist. Mon.*, *Essex Inventory*, iii, p. 25). For Lydney, see *infra*, p. 248, foot-note 5.

[1] For references, see *Romanization of Roman Britain*, p. 37, foot-note 1.

classical type, and is taken by good authorities to be of Celtic origin; it may, however, be a variation from the classical type or even an amalgamation of classical and native.

Besides their temples, the Romano-British towns must often have had Christian churches. The only example so

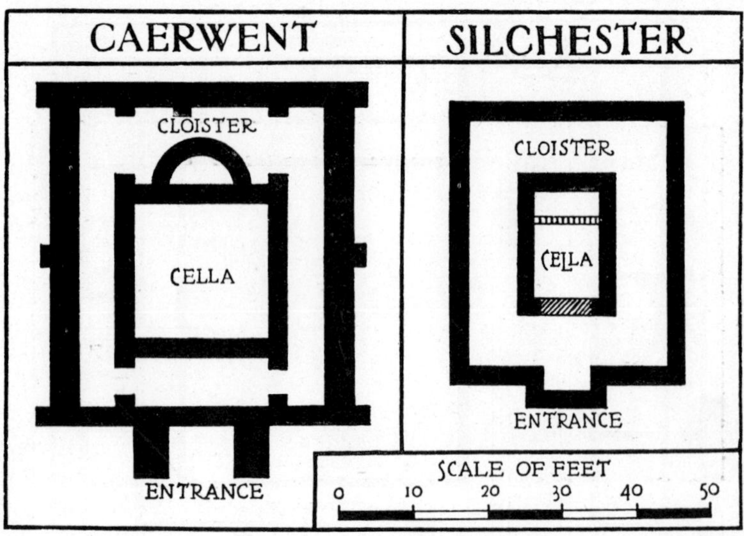


Fig. 42. GROUND-PLANS OF TEMPLES AT CAERWENT AND SILCHESTER

far found is at Silchester, for much the most likely interpretation of the tiny structure uncovered near the Forum (Fig. 43) is that it was a Christian church. Its remains cannot, indeed, be dated; nor was there associated with them any emblem or monogram of a distinctively Christian character. But their ground-plan conforms closely to the ground-plan of the 'basilican' type of Christian church as represented by numerous fourth-century examples in the most widely separated provinces of the Empire. Fig. 44, for instance, is from Roman Africa, where a great many such churches have

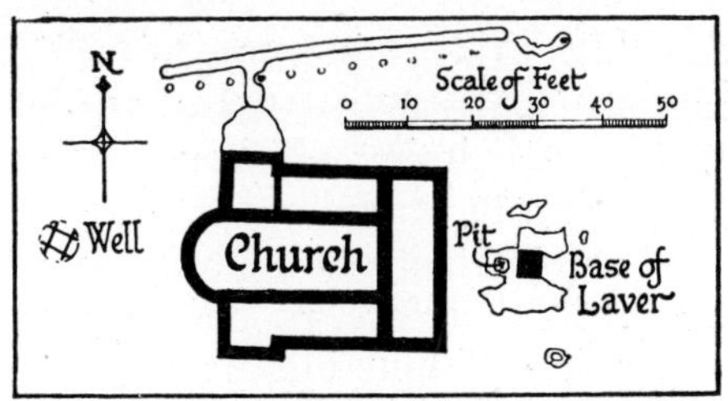


FIG. 43. CHRISTIAN CHURCH AND ITS SURROUNDINGS, SILCHESTER

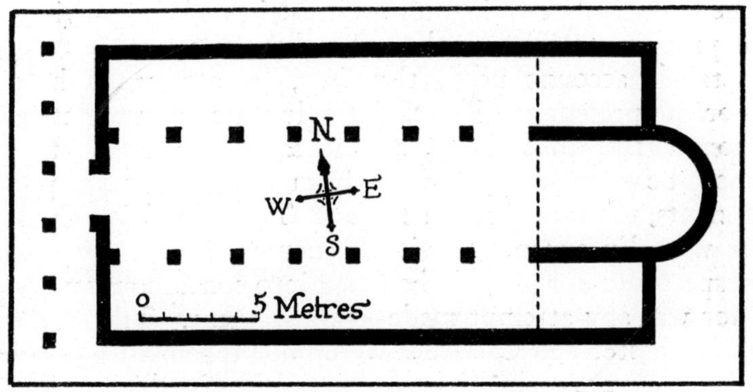


FIG. 44. CHRISTIAN CHURCH OF THE BASILICAN TYPE (AFRICA)

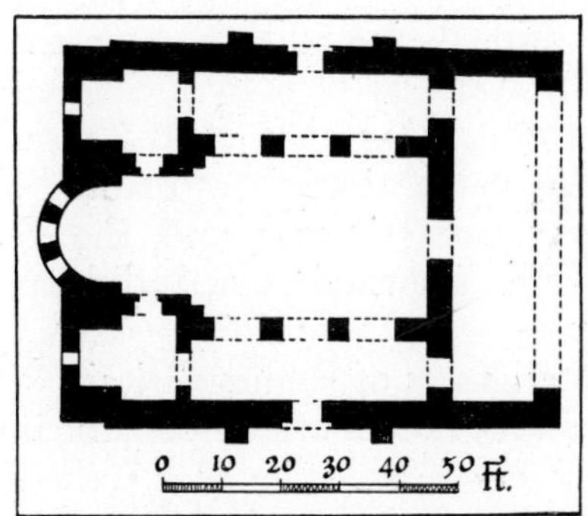


FIG. 45. CHRISTIAN CHURCH OF THE BASILICAN TYPE (ASIA MINOR)

been noted,[1] while Fig. 45 is from Asia Minor. Under the later Empire Christianity spread widely over the civil area of Roman Britain.[2] Bishops of London, York, and (probably) Lincoln attended the Council of Arles in A. D. 314. The appearance of a Christian place of worship at Silchester is, therefore, no matter for surprise.

When we pass from public buildings to private houses, we find less to remind us of Italy. As the excavations of Silchester and Caerwent have proved, the private dwelling-houses in the Romano-British towns resembled the country houses in the rural districts of the province. I propose to discuss these in the next lecture. No detailed account need, therefore, be attempted here. For the present it will suffice to give one or two illustrations (Figs. 46 and 47), and to say that, though they may be ultimately derived from Mediterranean precedents, the types are not Italian. They are rather Celtic or west European. Obviously, houses of such irregular shape could not possibly be fitted into continuous streets. Nor was any attempt made so to fit them. The *insulae* of Silchester and Caerwent were not ' tenement blocks '. They were rectangular spaces, each of which might contain two, three, or even four separate dwelling-houses with ample garden or other open land around them. One house in Silchester deserves particular notice (Fig. 48). Its exceptional size and the fact that it had had a suite of baths attached to it by a covered passage have prompted the suggestion that it was a public hostelry. There were also shops, sometimes planted along parts of the main street, sometimes round the Forum square. These shops were of normal plan, and demand no special remark.

If the private houses of Roman Britain differed a good deal in plan from the houses of Pompeii, the internal fittings were definitely classical. There was the same painted

[1] In Timgad alone at least seven have been catalogued by the French explorers.

[2] See *Eng. Hist. Rev.* xi (1896), pp. 417 ff.

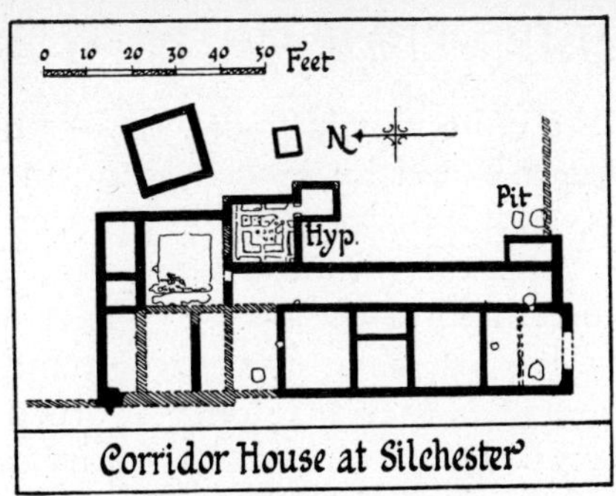


Corridor House at Silchester

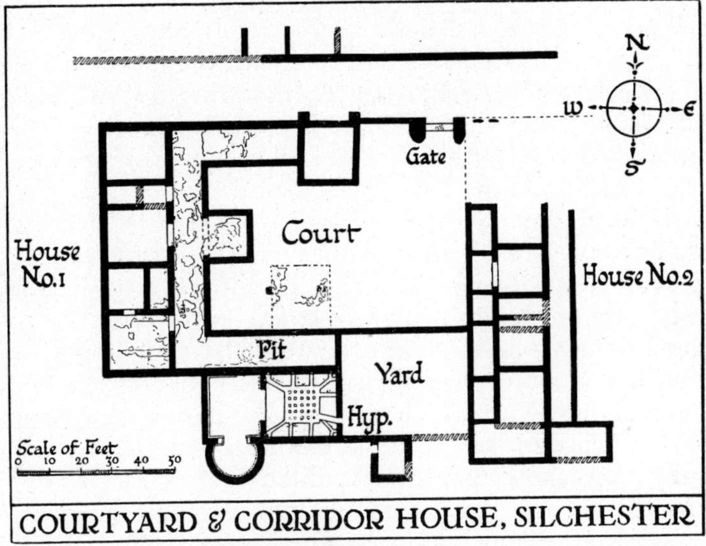


COURTYARD & CORRIDOR HOUSE, SILCHESTER

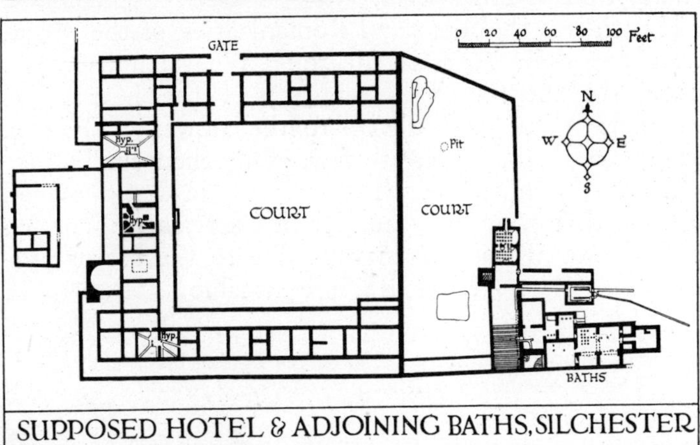


SUPPOSED HOTEL & ADJOINING BATHS, SILCHESTER



Figs. 46–48.

wall-plaster, the same mosaic floors, the same hypocausts and bathrooms as would have been found in Italy. The wall-paintings and mosaics may have been poorer in Britain, the hypocausts more numerous; the things themselves were those of the south. PLATE VI, showing the head of Mercury against a background of red, is a fragment of wall-plaster that once adorned a house in Roman London.[1] Despite a certain crudity of execution, it is a vigorous piece of drawing. But that it should be a Roman and not a Celtic god that is represented, is eminently characteristic. So, too, with the mosaics. No mosaic, I believe, has come to light in the whole of Roman Britain which represents any local subject or contains any unclassical feature. The usual ornamentation consists either of mythological scenes, such as Orpheus charming the animals, or Apollo chasing Daphne, or Bacchus riding on a panther (FIG. 49), or of geometrical designs like the so-called Asiatic shields which are of classical origin.[2] If an Italian had strayed into a Romano-British house, he would have found hardly anything so strange, so alien from his native art, as the Oriental rugs with which modern Europeans deck their floors. Custom has made those rugs familiar to us; really they show how cosmopolitan are our art tastes. The Roman was not cosmopolitan; wherever he went, he was Roman and Italian.

If such was the structural Romanization of the towns, what was their general culture? What language was spoken in them? The evidence of the inscriptions leaves no room for doubt as to the answer. Those of Caerwent, for instance, are few. But their significance is not to be mistaken. They are all in Latin, which suggests that Latin was familiar in Caerwent, but much (though not all) of this may be due to the use of professional 'writers'. It is more notable that some of

[1] Roach Smith, *Illustrations of Roman London*, Plate XIV, 3.
[2] See *Romanization of Roman Britain*, pp. 44 f.

FIG. 49. MOSAIC FLOOR FROM LONDON

This mosaic was found in Leadenhall Street in December 1803. For a coloured reproduction, see Roach Smith, *Illustrations of Roman London*, Plate XII.

their contents indicate real Roman town life. In A.D. 152 M. Nonius Romanus set up a slab at Venta Silŭrum, recording his admission there, free of fee, to a *collegium*, a club or guild, perhaps of worshippers of Mars.[1] That guild could hardly have arisen had there not been in Venta men who knew the ways of Roman city life. Nonius himself was probably not British born but, as his worship of Mars Lenus shows, a stranger from Augusta Treverorum (Trier) in northern Gaul, whence in Roman days men migrated freely into other lands. Again, a bit of wall-plaster, found in 1905, seems, though much broken, to bear part of a message scratched by a girl Domitilla to her lover Victor. The message has disappeared through breaks in the plaster, but it seemingly scandalized some one in Venta, who added to it the unkind wish, '*puniamini*' ("for shame!").[2] Another fragment of plaster bears the letters '*Titi*', plainly the genitive of the name Titus.[3] In Venta, it seems, men and women of the lower classes could read and write, and those who wrote "amorous scrawls on plaster walls", found Latin suited to their uses. The same features recur in Silchester and other Romano-British towns.[4] This does not, of course, mean that only Latin was spoken; doubtless Celtic was often heard, and many were bilingual, as in parts of Wales to-day.

[1] *Ephem. Epigr.* ix. 1009.

[2] *Ibid.*, 1015 *a.* It is fair to say that the whole of the markings are much mutilated, and the reading highly conjectural.

[3] *Ibid.*, 1015 *b.*

[4] See *Romanizaiton of Roman Britain*, pp. 29 ff., and *Arch. Journ.* lxxv, pp. 24 and 27.

PLATE VI. COLOURED WALL-PLASTER, WITH HEAD OF MERCURY, FROM LONDON

# LECTURE V

## THE CIVILIZATION OF THE PROVINCE

### II

The first feature in the civilization of Roman Britain is furnished by its towns. These (as I tried to make clear in the last lecture) belonged for the most part to one definite class. Historically, they were native cantonal centres, developed under Roman influence into towns. Administratively, they formed the capitals of the native cantonal districts, which Rome accepted as the units of local government, and they were ruled by the cantonal authorities. Economically, they differed from the πόλεις and the *coloniae* of the Greek and Roman world, for they grew out of a conglomeration of country elements, and existed because of the country life around them; thus they well deserve the title of country towns. In all these respects they run closely parallel to the towns of northern Gaul, like those cantonal capitals of the Ambiani or Remi or Parisii, which we now call Amiens, Reims, Paris. Only, as Freeman loved to point out, in Gaul such towns came to be called after the cantons, and they bear their names to this day, while nothing of the kind happened in Britain. This was not due solely, as he supposed, to the Saxon conquest, for that conquest has often spared names which were not cantonal. It is rather one of many indications that the British cantons were smaller and weaker than those of Gaul. Thus Venta Belgarum, had it been in Gaul, would probably now be known by some name reminiscent of the Belgae. In Britain it retains the other half of its old appellation, Venta, and is called Winchester.[1] The place-name has survived. The cantonal name has vanished.

[1] The popular idea that 'chester', when it occurs in a place-name, is a sure index to the site of a Roman 'camp' is altogether erroneous. In

Taken altogether, the towns of Roman Britain are numerous, though not so plentiful as to be past enumeration. Let me recall the more important. In Kent, Durovernum or Canterbury was a flourishing little capital of the Cantii, and Durobrivae or Rochester, at the crossing of the Medway, developed sufficiently to deserve walls, though it apparently never attained much size.[1] Of Calleva or Silchester, capital of the Atrebates, I have already spoken in some detail. Chichester, once capital of the Regni, possesses many traces of its Roman period, including inscriptions, the core of its Roman walls, fragments of buildings, and abundance of pottery and other débris of life.[2] Winchester or Venta Belgarum has yielded less evidence and was perhaps a smaller place, but its mosaics prove that it was better than a village.[3] Durnovaria, now Dorchester on the Frome, counted for far more, as its abundant mosaics and well-ordered museum show. Even Exeter, formerly Isca Dumnoniorum, outpost of Romanization in the far west, can boast of mosaics and other vestiges of a town. Bath or Aquae Sulis we may think to have been not so much a town as a temple and a spa, well known in western Europe, with a few comfortable houses round it.[4] Pro-

literary Anglo-Saxon 'chester' was used, without reference to the Romans or to any special people or persons, to denote any enclosed place, inhabited or meant for inhabitation. When the English first learned the word, they apparently used it in this sense in place-names, and, in the Britain which they were conquering, the sites that were inhabited, or meant for inhabitation, were pre-eminently the sites where Romano-British civilization had set its mark. But this civilization stopped at the Roman Wall; north of it the inhabited sites belonged mainly to 'Pict and Scot', and these are the sites which are there called 'chesters'. Thus we get the two uses of 'chester' as a place-name—(*a*) a Roman site, the prevailing sense south of the Tyne, and (*b*) a non-Roman site, the prevailing sense north of the Tyne. See F. H. in *Athenaeum*, 8 Aug. 1896, pp. 201 f.; *Vict. Hist. Shropshire* i, p. 278; *Vict. Hist. Somerset* i, p. 371; *Somerset Proc.* lxiv, pp. xxxix, ff.; etc.

[1] Among the unpublished material belonging to the *Vict. Hist.* are accounts of Roman Canterbury and Roman Rochester by F. H.

[2] For a list see F. H. in *Arch. Rev.* i (1888), p. 436.

[3] See *Vict. Hist. Hants* i, pp. 285 ff.

[4] See *Vict. Hist. Somerset* i, pp. 219 ff.

bably, however, Bath too girt itself with walls at some period in its history. Corinium Dobunorum or Cirencester, the town of the Dobuni, was much more considerable. We can trace its walls. They enclose a space of some 240 acres, and whoever digs within their area finds abundant relics of inscriptions, mosaics, carved stone, and lesser remains.[1] Although Glevum or Gloucester, hard by, was a *colonia*, its extent was nothing like so great, and its prosperity and civilization may well have been actually less. The list of south British towns closes with another tribal capital, the most westerly of the towns of Britain in this neighbourhood, Venta Silŭrum or Caerwent, of which I had a good deal to say in my last lecture.

The land between Thames and Trent was hardly so full of urban life. But it contained Londinium,[2] centre of the Romano-British system, probably the largest of all Romano-British towns, certainly the most important in commerce, and in all likelihood the only mint in the island.[3] Its buried remains, its yields of sculptured stone or artistic ornament declare its pre-eminence no less than does its fourth-century title of 'Augusta'. It may have been a capital of the Trinovantes, but the evidence usually cited for this is bad, and it seems rather to have sprung to size and prosperity owing to the influence of Roman traders and its uniquely convenient position.[4] The towns nearest London, Camulodūnum or Colchester[5] and Verulamium or St. Albans,[6] boasted municipal rank, but neither can vie with it in wealth or in extant remains.

[1] See 'Roman Cirencester' in *Archaeologia* lxix, pp. 161 ff.

[2] See 'Roman London' in *J.R.S.* i, pp. 141 ff.

[3] The London mint dates from the time of Carausius. It was used for bronze during the reigns of Diocletian and Constantine, but was closed by the latter in A.D. 326. For its later history, see Sir Arthur Evans in *Num. Chron.* 1915, pp. 478 ff.

[4] See *supra*, pp. 95 f.

[5] See 'Roman Colchester' in *J.R.S.* ix, pp. 139 ff., and *Royal Commission on Hist. Mon., Essex Inventory*, iii, pp. xxiv f. and 20 f.

[6] See *Royal Commission on Hist. Mon., Herts. Inventory*, pp. 3 f. and 190 f.

Other towns in this midland region were Chesterford in Essex,[1] with its curious late Celtic remains, Venta Icenorum or Caister-by-Norwich, now a huge empty field encircled by massive walls,[2] Chesterton and Castor on the Nen, where the pottery was made,[3] Ratae or Leicester, capital of the Coritani, marked by the stubborn ruin of an ancient gateway or entrance of some kind, and by abundant mosaics and architectural fragments. Though scarcely a single inscription has come to light here, it was plainly, at least in earlier times, a prosperous town.[4]

To the west of Ratae, Viroconium or Wroxeter, five miles east of Shrewsbury, founded first perhaps for military reasons,[5] grew to size and wealth, and served as capital of the Cornovii. To-day it is the shadow of a great name. But its ruins survive (PLATE III), though mostly buried below the earth, and the circuit of its walls can still be made out.[6] Recent excavations, besides providing a plentiful crop of pottery fragments, coins, and miscellaneous relics, have proved that it was much like Silchester and Caerwent in its general character.[7] A good instance of the smaller of the Romano-British towns—they varied much in extent (FIG. 50)—is provided by Magnae or Kenchester on the Wye, near Hereford.[8] Finally, in the far north, a long way beyond the *colonia* of Lindum or Lincoln, and even twelve miles north-west of the fortress of Eburacum or York, the old *oppidum* of the Brigantes at Isurium or Aldborough,

[1] See *Royal Commission on Hist. Mon., Essex Inventory*, i, pp. xxiii and 113.

[2] See *Vict. Hist. Norfolk* i, pp. 288 ff.

[3] See *Vict. Hist. Northants* i, pp. 166 ff. Castor had probably the same name as Rochester—Durobrivae.

[4] See 'Roman Leicester' in *Arch. Journ.* lxxv (1918), pp. 1–46.

[5] See *supra*, p. 105.

[6] See *Vict. Hist. Shropshire* i, pp. 220 ff.

[7] See the Reports of the Research Committee of the Society of Antiquaries of London (1914, 1915 and 1916) by J. P. Bushe-Fox.

[8] See 'Roman Britain in 1913' (*British Academy Supplem. Papers* ii), p. 20, and *Trans. of the Woolhope Naturalists' Field Club*, 1912–13, pp. 157 ff., and 1918–20, pp. 99 ff.

near Boroughbridge, developed into a well-fortified, well-built capital, where it was possible for some one to order (what no one in the place would now understand) a Greek inscription in his mosaic flooring.[1]

Besides the towns, there were villages of some note. In our own neighbourhood of Oxford is Dorchester, a pre-historic site at the junction of Thame and Thames,

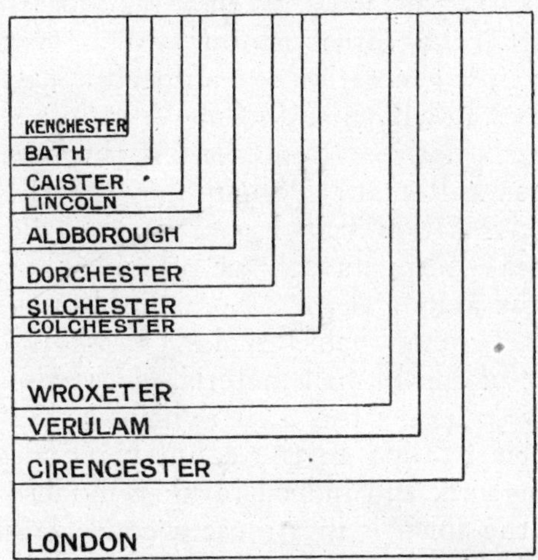


FIG. 50. DIAGRAM SHOWING THE COMPARATIVE SIZE OF TYPICAL ROMANO-BRITISH TOWNS

The extremes are represented by Kenchester (17 acres) and London (325 acres).

just where navigation of the united rivers becomes easy, and where, by Day's Lock, there was ready crossing from east to west bank. Little has been found there—one tessellated floor, one inscription mentioning a Roman officer (*beneficiarius*) often stationed temporarily at a point where routes met, and various coins and trifles.[2] About as far to the north of Oxford, and in the fields near Bicester, is (as it seems) another village. We can

[1] *CIL.* vii, p. 66.

[2] See *supra*, p. 152, and also Manning and Leeds in *Archaeologia* lxxi, pp. 240 f.

trace an enclosure of some 25 acres, more or less square, with one corner abutting on the railway; Roman potsherds and broken bricks lie about; and excavations have proved the existence underneath of walling—perhaps only farm-buildings and cottages—and of an enclosing rampart of earth, rudely faced with stone.[1] Humble settlements of the kind appear to have been not infrequent. Other instances, taken at random, are Ilchester in Somerset,[2] the three or four which General Pitt-Rivers dug up a generation ago a dozen miles south-west of Salisbury,[3] and Baydon also in Wilts.[4] These villages were obviously native. None the less, the material life of the villagers was Roman. Perhaps they knew little enough of Roman civilization in its higher aspects. Perhaps they did not speak Latin fluently or often. They may well have counted among the less Romanized of the southern Britons. Yet round them too clung the heavy inevitable atmosphere of the Roman material civilization.

Before we quit the towns, it remains to say a word or two on their relation to the country round them. In modern England, and indeed in most modern European countries, the town is in a sense a concentration of the activities of the adjacent country. On market or other convenient days farm-produce is brought in from the outside by the dwellers round about. But, partly owing to ancient difficulties of communication, the relation of town and neighbourhood was in the Roman world almost the inverse of what it is now. Labourers did not live in villages or cottages outside and come into the town daily to work. Rather, they lived within the town, and even those who provided food for the town had their homes in the town and came out from thence and walked to their work, perhaps a couple of miles away. This may

[1] See *Vict. Hist. Oxon.* ii, p. 320; F. H. in *P.S.A.L.* (2nd ser.) xxi, pp. 461 f.; and Manning and Leeds *l. c.*, p. 259, *s.v.* 'Wendlebury'.
[2] *Vict. Hist. Somerset* i, pp. 294 f.
[3] A. Pitt-Rivers, *Excavations in Cranborne Chase*, &c., 4 vols., 1887–98.
[4] *Wilts. Mag.* x, pp. 104 ff.

be inferred from the fact that the immediate vicinity of a Romano-British town seldom furnishes remains indicative of rural life. The environs of Silchester have yielded very few Roman relics of this sort, and the same is the case with Wroxeter and with most of the others. The population of the countryside seems to have been no denser close round them than some little way off. Thus, one gets the idea that the allotments or other cultivated gardens and garden-plots round each town must have been tilled by men who slept within the walls and came out of the gates each morning on purpose, not by men who lived just outside, congregated inside on certain pre-arranged days, and sent or brought their wares to shops or to the common markets.

In general the civilization was not urban in the true sense of the word. It was not the full town-life of Italy, dominating the rural district which surrounds it and obeys it. It was rather the life of the country town which depends on its neighbourhood and is, as it were, the nucleus of it—the meeting-place of its farmers, the residence of those who conduct its trade and smaller industries, and even of some of its gentry. In short, Roman Britain rather resembled many parts of England in Elizabethan and post-Elizabethan days. The region east of Exeter with its series of little towns, Ottery, Honiton, Axminster, Seaton, Chard, Crewkerne, or the region west of Oxford with Woodstock, Eynsham, Witney, Charlbury, Burford, Bampton, Abingdon, will serve as illustrations. The towns are thicker than those of Roman Britain, just as the whole population is of course considerably greater. But the economic position appears to be so nearly the same as to justify the parallel.

From the towns it is natural to pass outside to the country which created them. All of our description that concerns the local administration has already been given in dealing with the towns. We may begin with a brief reference to economic matters. The country as a whole was engaged in pasturage and agriculture, and in particular in the production of wool and cloth and corn. The era of peaceful development set in after the opening of the third century. It was then that country-houses and farms became common in all parts of the civilized area. The statistics of datable objects discovered in these buildings seem conclusive on this point. Except in the south-eastern region, coins and pottery of the first century are infrequent, and many sites have yielded nothing earlier than about A. D. 250. Despite the ill name that attaches to the third and fourth centuries, they were perhaps for Britain, as for parts of Gaul,[1] a period of progressive prosperity. Certainly the number of British country-houses and farms inhabited during the years A. D. 280–350 must have been very large. Prosperity culminated, it seems, in the Constantinian age. Then, as Eumenius tells us, skilled artisans abounded in Britain far more than in Gaul, and were fetched from the island to build public and private edifices as far south as Autun.[2] Then also, and indeed as late as 360, British corn was largely exported to the Rhine valley. Julian is said to have given the traffic a new lease of life, greatly augmenting the fleet of vessels engaged in the trade and arranging to have the grain transported inland from the coast by water.[3] In the same period British wool found its way even to eastern Europe, thus anticipating, if feebly, the great wool trade of medieval England; British cloth earned a notice in the eastern Edict of Diocletian,[4] promulgated in A. D. 301.

We know something of the forms under which this pasturage and agriculture were carried on. Traces of dwelling-houses, conventionally called ‘ villas ’, have been detected and excavated in various parts of the civilized

[1] Mommsen, *Rom. Prov.* i, pp. 106 and 116, and Ausonius, *passim.*

[2] *Paneg. Constantio Caesari*, 21.

[3] Ammianus, xviii. 2, 3 ; Zosimus, iii. 5 ; etc.

[4] xix. 36 βίρος Βρετταvικός is the exact expression (*CIL.* iii. Suppl. p. 1943, No. 36). Cf. also the *procurator gynaecii in Britannis Ventensis* (“ administrator of the imperial weaving works at Venta ”), mentioned in *Not. Dign. Occ.* xi. 60, regarding whom see *Vict. Hist. Hants* i, p. 292.

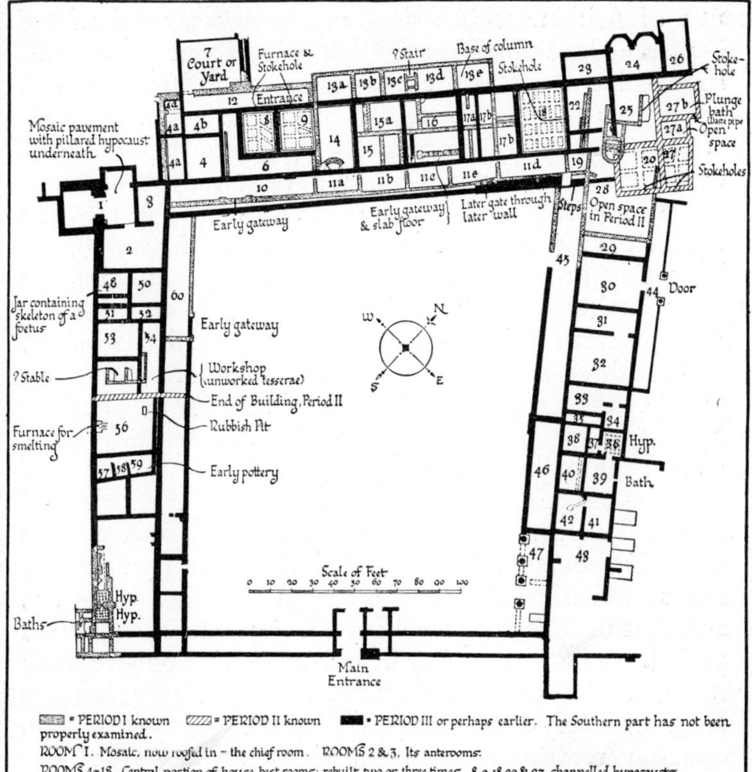


▭ = PERIOD I known ▨ = PERIOD II known ■ = PERIOD III or perhaps earlier. The Southern part has not been properly examined.

ROOM I. Mosaic, now roofed in – the chief room. ROOMS 2 & 3. Its anterooms.

ROOMS 4–18. Central portion of house, best rooms; rebuilt two or three times. 8, 9, 18, 20 & 27 channelled hypocausts.

WEST WING (no numbers): Servants' Quarters, poorish rooms and small bath. Originally outbuildings and separate baths; later probably made into servants' quarters.

The EAST WING was not excavated in 1910.

**Plan of the Roman Villa at NORTHLEIGH, Oxon. as excavated 1813 to 1816 & again 1908 to 1910 when the W. & N. wings were re-measured.**

FIG. 51. The ' villa ' was originally opened up between 1813 and 1816. Thereafter its remains lay exposed till 1908, when F. H. formed a plan of excavating them further and of doing something to preserve them. He secured a liberal lease from the landowner, the Duke of Marlborough, and collected subscriptions which made it possible to roof over the principal mosaic. Some progress was made with the projected excavations, but the scheme was interrupted by the war. The Haverfield Bequest Committee have continued the lease, and have made arrangements for public access to the site.

area of Britain. Some sixty or seventy examples have been noted, for instance, in Somerset, about as many in Hampshire and the Isle of Wight, some fifty in Kent, and thirty in Northamptonshire.[1] The neighbourhood of our own city of Oxford has yielded more than a dozen.[2] One well-known example has been left open and not too well protected near the Evenlode at Northleigh; another, with five mosaics, now covered in, was found in 1711 at Stonesfield, about a mile and a half north, on the opposite bank of the river and actually on a Roman road (Akeman Street), and a third, perhaps less wealthy, two or three miles to the west. Two more have been noted to the north near Ditchley, while a couple of others and a kiln are hardly farther away. The remains of the Northleigh villa itself (FIG. 51) appear to be those of a good-sized country-house; in all likelihood it belonged to some Romanized British noble, who owned land round it. Small objects found in it suggest that the site was occupied as early as the second century of our era, and that it remained inhabited till the end of the Roman period. The house was, in this long time, more than once rebuilt. The best rooms, numbered 4–18 on the plan, probably the apartments of the 'family', were certainly reconstructed several times, as was made clear by the discovery of earlier walls. The southern portion of the west wing, including the unnumbered rooms, seems to have formed the outbuildings and the servants' quarters; the accommodation there is rather poor and the bath small. The east wing cannot be spoken of so definitely: it has been less thoroughly examined. The house was probably one-storied throughout.

Of the remaining Oxford examples, two—both probably small—have been noted near Wheatley, one south-east of the village close to Combe Wood, and one north-west near Holton Stonepits. A third can be made out on the high ground just east of Beckley; there was

[1] See the appropriate volumes of the *Vict. Hist.*

[2] See Manning and Leeds in *Archaeologia* lxxi, pp. 229 f.

a fourth, apparently of no great size, at Woodperry; and there was 'something', either house or shrine of deity, on the low hill between Woodeaton and Islip.[1] Yet another (Fig. 52), a small house systematically excavated more than thirty years ago by Sir Arthur Evans, lay between Frilford and Kingston Bagpuize[2], and vestiges have been suspected at Burcot[3], at Headington[4],

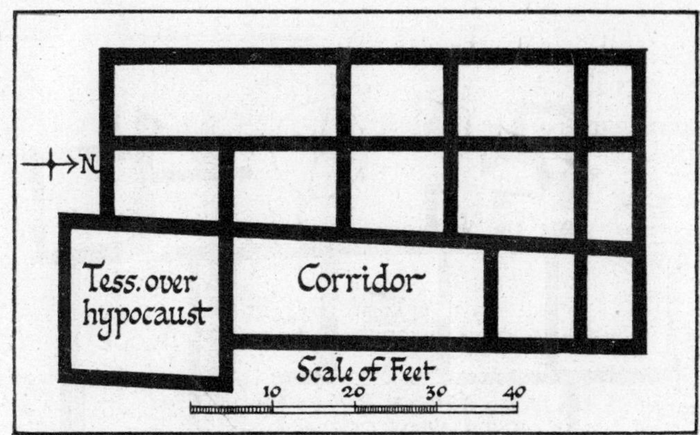


Fig. 52. FARM-HOUSE AT FRILFORD, BERKS

and in Fore Street, Abingdon[5], while only recently unmistakable signs have been detected in the Bishop's garden at Cuddesdon. There is nothing really remarkable in this comparatively frequent occurrence of Roman 'villas' near Oxford. It merely shows that, as I said in the last lecture, the valley of the Thames and its tributaries was well inhabited in Romano-British times. Other 'villas', no doubt, have still to be detected, and reward probably awaits those who care to search for potsherds,

[1] See Miss M. V. Taylor in *J.R.S.* vii, pp. 98 ff., and P. Manning in *Berks., Bucks., and Oxon. Trans.* iv, pp. 42 ff.

[2] See *Oxford Archit. and Hist. Soc. Proc.* (n.s.) iv, p. 233, and *Arch. Journ.* liv, pp. 340 f.

[3] *Archaeologia* lxxi, p. 237.

[4] *Ibid.* p. 245.

[5] *P.S.A.L.* (2nd ser.) iii, pp. 145 and 202 f., and *Vict. Hist. Berks.* i. p. 202.

tiles, or tesserae lying about the fields. These ' villas ', of course, bear no resemblance to their modern namesakes, whether in north Oxford or in any other suburb of to-day. It might, indeed, be better if we refrained from using the word in this connexion. But many persons, and not least antiquaries, are curiously averse to having recourse to an English expression when they can

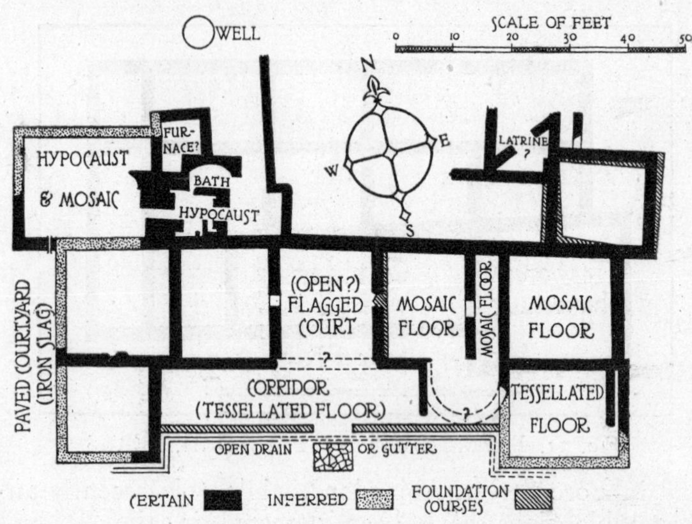


FIG. 53. CORRIDOR HOUSE AT BRISLINGTON, NEAR BRISTOL

find a Latin one and, as the term is quite as much employed abroad as it is in England, the chances are that it will stay. The thing which it means is fortunately clear enough.

It denotes any rural building, whether the residence of a landlord, or the farmhouse and cottages of farmer and labourers, or the barns and sheds required for tillage and pasturage. Any of these structures is liable to be called a ' villa ' by the custom of antiquarian terminology, and all these kinds of buildings can be recognized among our excavated remains. The residential houses fall generally into two classes, exactly parallel to the houses unearthed at Caerwent and Silchester (Figs. 46 and 47). The simplest type is that usually styled the Corridor House. Here the dominant feature is a hall or corridor or veranda, with a row of rooms behind it, and (as a rule) additional rooms at one or both ends. Of this a very simple specimen can be seen in the Frilford farm-house (Fig. 52). It was a one-storied structure of stone—or perhaps of stone foundations with mud or wattled walls—some 70 feet long and 40 feet deep, consisting of a corridor or veranda, a heatable room at one end, and

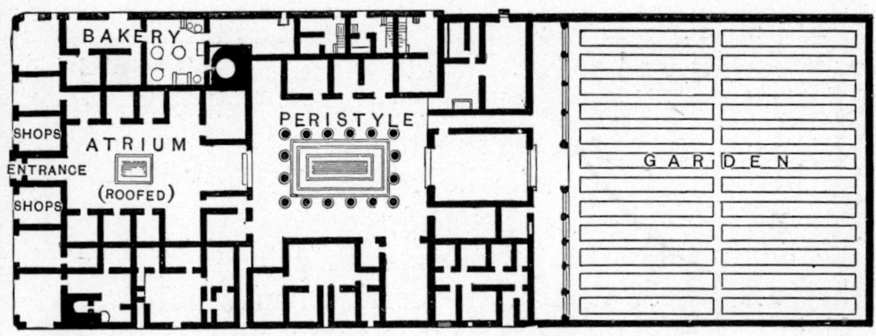


Fig. 54. PLAN OF A POMPEIAN HOUSE

The central features of an Italian house were the *atrium* and the peristyle, into one or other of which practically all the rooms opened. The *atrium* was completely covered in, save for a central aperture through which the rain, running down the sloping sides of the roof, found its way into the *impluvium*. The peristyle, on the other hand, more nearly resembled a cloistered quadrangle, having the part enclosed by the pillars filled with flowers and shrubs in the midst of which a fountain played.

a number of small apartments looking either into the veranda or out at the back of the house. Other examples are much more luxurious (Fig. 53). Sometimes the corridor is more definite, and the enlargement at one end is carried round in an elbow; we can see the development beginning in 'House No. 2' in Fig. 47. This seems to lead up to a second type[1], the Courtyard House, in which three corridors, with three rows of rooms,

[1] Whether the one type really developed out of the other is doubtful. Probably the Courtyard House has more connexion with the south than

enclose a rectangular open court (FIG. 51). The fourth side is often walled or even closed in with buildings. Sometimes considerable elaboration is introduced—in particular, extensive baths, not seldom at a little distance from the main body of the house.

The two types, as I indicated in speaking of the towns, have little direct connexion with the type of house used in Mediterranean lands. The Pompeian house with which we are familiar (FIG. 54), the less-known house of the country districts in Italy and Africa and Spain, are all based on the principle of excluding the sun. They look inwards upon sheltered courts, *atria* or peristyles, and external windows are few.[1] The British houses follow different lines. In our island precautions for excluding the sun are superfluous. The sun does that for himself. Hence the houses of the north naturally face outwards, look over the adjacent country, and catch the light and warmth. The main principle on which they are based, that of the corridor, may be of Celtic origin.[2] Certainly we meet it in the north Gaulish lands between the Channel and the Rhine. No doubt the native model was affected by Roman reminiscences. The architect who put in Italian mosaics and Italian hypocausts might well alter his courtyards with recollections of Italian peristyles. But he never attempted an *atrium*; and in all the smaller examples the characteristic corridor principle holds undisputed sway. The one doubt as yet unsolved concerns the primitive native model and the possibility of a yard among the rooms behind the corridor. On this point inquiry has hardly been started. The few scholars who have hitherto touched upon it

the Corridor House: see *Romanization of Roman Britain*, pp. 42 and 44, with references there.

[1] Recent discoveries at Ostia (see Dr. T. Ashby in *J.R.S.* ii, pp. 177 and 184) have familiarized us with a different type of Italian house with rooms looking on to the street.

[2] The opposite view is maintained by various scholars, notably Cumont, who declares that '*l'origine de ces constructions très perfectionnées est certainement italique*' (*Comment la Belgique fut romanisée*, p. 43).

have not compared sufficiently the remains in various countries.

Other forms of houses also occur. One, in particular, shows an oblong enclosure with rooms at both ends and, as it seems, a yard in the centre. This type, if not peculiarly British, is certainly much more common in Britain than abroad, and even in Britain it has so far

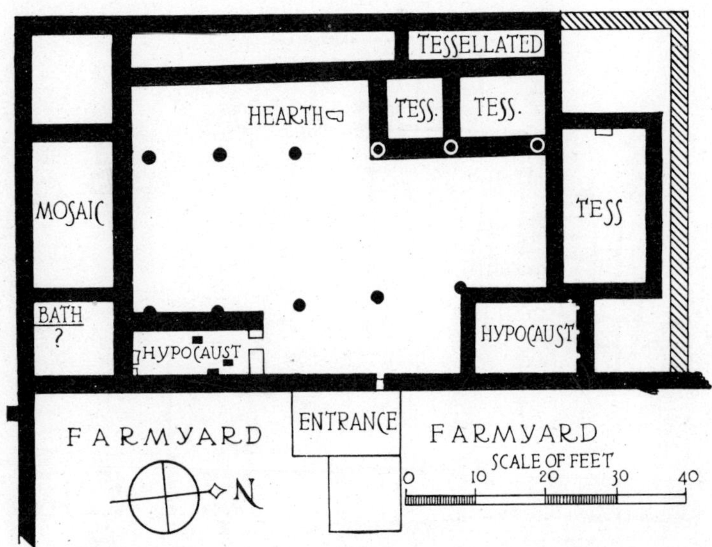


FIG. 55. HOUSE AT CLANVILLE, NEAR ANDOVER

been detected only in the country, never in a town. A good illustration will be described presently (FIG. 57). Another form, which may well be essentially identical, appears to represent a barn with columns and a detached room or two at the end of it. Such apparently was the original scheme of the house shown in FIG. 55, although, at a date which we may suppose to have been subsequent to its first construction, four small rooms have been added by walling off parts of the columned space.[1] Whether the whole was covered over or whether the

[1] *Vict. Hist. Hants* i, pp. 295 f.

central portion was really open to the sky, with sheds or colonnades all round, it is quite impossible to say. In all these cases our explanations are hampered by grave difficulties. We have seldom more than the ground-plan to enable us to read the riddle, and frequently the accidents of time or the carelessness of antiquaries has left even the ground-plan imperfect. It is but rarely,

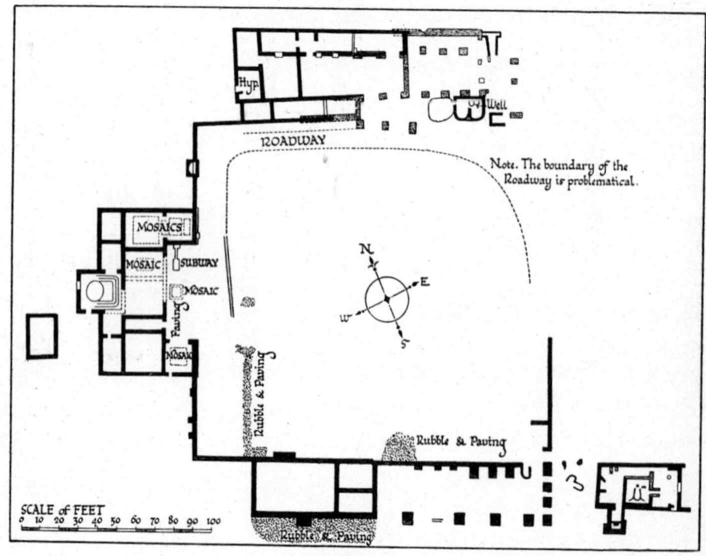


Fig. 56. VILLA AT BRADING, ISLE OF WIGHT

for instance, that we can decide, except by conjecture, where were the doors of the rooms, or which foundations correspond to boundary walls and which to structures. Certainty can only be acquired by a careful scrutiny of many plans from both Britain and Gaul.

Various sorts of buildings frequently occur together. The elaborate courtyard house, indeed, usually stands alone. It is extensive enough to include all needs in itself. But two or three smaller buildings often go to one 'villa'. So at Brading in the Isle of Wight we trace three isolated buildings facing a central courtyard

(FIG. 56).[1] On the west lay the main residence, a corridor house of twelve rooms, covering an area of 55 by 90 feet, and declaring its use by its elaborate mosaics and other details. Obviously this is the dwelling of people who were very well off; it was probably built for some one of the local noblemen. On the north was an oblong block, 55 by 140 feet. Part of the latter was fitted with hypocausts, with glazed windows and painted wall-plaster on its walls, and was plainly meant to be inhabited—though apparently by persons supposed to be indifferent to comfort. Servants and retainers may well have been accommodated here, while two rows of rude column bases in its eastern portion suggest something in the nature of a barn, thus recalling the arrangement at Clanville (FIG. 55). On the south side is a block, 30 by 160 feet, divided into four parts, one of which occupies half of the whole. It is roughly built and devoid of comfortable fittings, and had presumably served as barn or stables. At the extreme end of it is an imperfectly excavated structure which may represent the bath-house.

As another instance of the composite type we may take the 'villas' at Mansfield Woodhouse in Nottinghamshire, explored and planned in the eighteenth century[2] (FIG. 57). A corridor house, 125 feet long and 48 feet wide, equipped with mosaic floors, hypocausts, painted wall-plaster and the like, formed perhaps the lord's residence. It is not so simple as the Frilford example (FIG. 52), although the central passage or corridor is quite plain. At the same time, it is a good deal less elaborate than that at Brislington (FIG. 53). To the north of it, more rudely built, is an oblong structure of 57 by 150 feet, containing a central courtyard and having at one end some rooms which, to judge from their simplicity, must have been intended for servants or labourers. At the other end are a stokehole, a hypocaust, a cold bath,

[1] *Vict. Hist. Hants* i, pp. 313 ff.
[2] See *Archaeologia* viii, pp. 363–76.

and some other bathing arrangements, possibly for use in the afternoon (the favourite time for bathing) by the dwellers in the so-called 'Villa Urbana'. The central courtyard is the characteristic feature. As I have hinted,[1] we may suspect that, though the eighteenth-century plan preserves no indications of this, there may once have been columns all down it. In other words, the plan may be identical with that of the house at Clanville (FIG. 55) or the northern building at Brading (FIG. 56).

As a general rule, the remains of these villas suggest only the housing of the landlord or farmer, and of his servants, beasts, and crops. But traces do occur here and there of manufactures. In particular, a large villa, dug in 1894 at Darenth in Kent, has been plausibly explained as given over largely to fulling, and the well-known villa at Chedworth has been thought to have been in one part adapted to the same industry.[2] We may in short suppose that the life and business of the dwellers in these houses was self-contained. They "baked their own bread and made their own beer", like the inhabitants of English country houses four or five generations ago; and further they sometimes combined with the management of a sheep-run the conversion of the raw material into a finished product.[3] In fact, they exemplified a phase of economic life which characterized the earlier and the latest periods of antiquity. German scholars have styled it '*Oikenwirtschaft*'. '*Oiken*' is a Germanized plural of the Greek *οἶκος*, a house, and the whole compound signifies that the house produced for itself and supplied its own needs.

[1] *Supra*, p. 228.

[2] So, too, a rural dwelling at Titsey in Surrey. On the whole subject see 'Notes on some probable traces of Roman Fulling in Britain' by G. E. Fox in *Archaeologia* lix, pp. 207 ff.

[3] Cf. '*Les villas étaient des ruches actives où de nombreux esclaves ou journaliers exerçaient tous les métiers utiles à l'exploitation du domaine et parfois des industries d'exportation*' (Cumont, *Comment la Belgique fut romanisée*, p. 43).

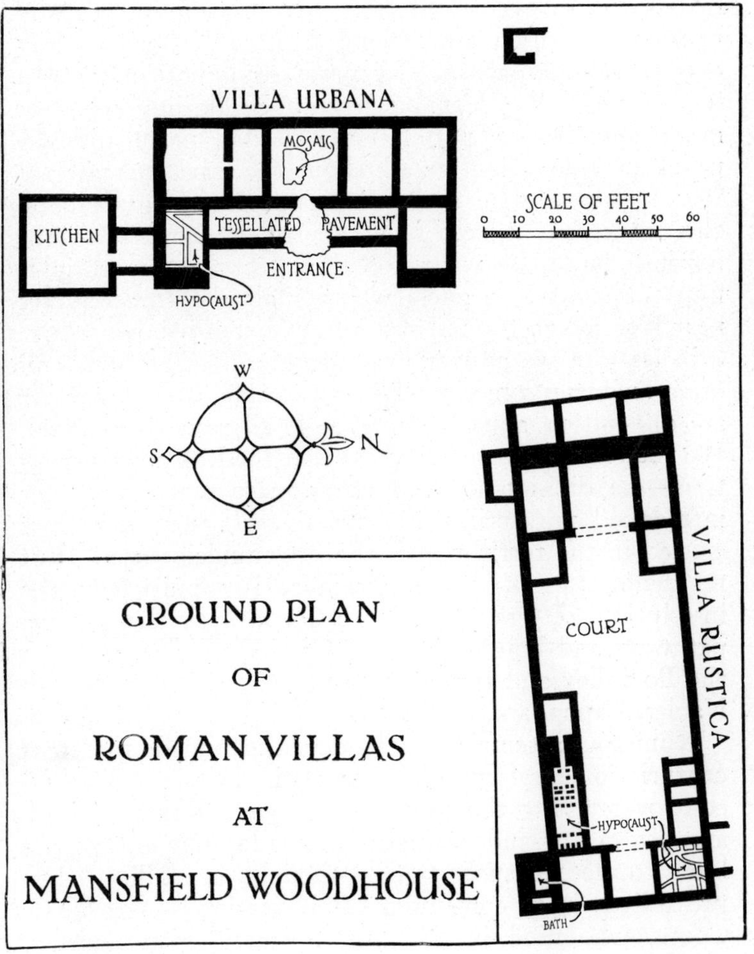

VILLA URBANA
MOSAIC
KITCHEN
TESSELLATED PAVEMENT
ENTRANCE
HYPOCAUST
SCALE OF FEET
0 10 20 30 40 50 60
W
S
N
E
VILLA RUSTICA
COURT
HYPOCAUST
BATH
GROUND PLAN
OF
ROMAN VILLAS
AT
MANSFIELD WOODHOUSE


Fig. 57.

The inhabitants of the villas were, so far as we can tell, Romanized natives of Britain. Here and there a settler from Gaul, or even from Italy, may have found his way to the island and acquired landed estate. There is, however, a singular absence of proof or indication of any such thing. We seem clearly to be dealing with an indigenous native population. A far more difficult problem arises when we ask about the legal character of these estates. The archaeological evidence gives little clue. We cannot even tell their sizes or how far neighbouring buildings went together. For instance, it is impossible even to guess whether all the three houses near Northleigh formed part of one extensive ownership. Still less can we answer legal questions. The legal and other analogies sometimes quoted to elucidate the matter are difficult to appraise, and are in all respects *a priori*. We need not, however, suppose that the Roman centuriation—the division of land into square plots—was ever introduced universally into Britain. It may well have existed in the territories of the five municipalities. But no definite proof survives such as is supplied by the inscriptions of Orange in south Gaul, or by the modern pathways and boundaries near Carthage, or by those in the Po valley and further south in the rich plain round Naples, Capua, and Caserta.

Numerous attempts have, indeed, been made to detect centuriation, or something like it, in Britain. The old controversy as to the continuity between Roman Britain and Saxon England has naturally made some antiquaries keen to detect such traces—though, in reality, they prove little as to continuity of civilization.[1] Mr. H. C. Coote, who died in 1885, in a treatise distinguished

[1] In Mediterranean countries the boundaries of the Roman *limitatio* have outlasted sweeping changes of race, civilization, law, and government. The *limites* or paths, which bounded the individual plots, seem to have been public paths and, perhaps for that reason, have survived in some cases almost beyond belief. Roman Africa provides a striking example: see, for a recent discussion of this subject, W. Barthel in *Bonn. Jahrb.* cxx (1911), pp. 39 ff.

rather by ingenuity than by sound scholarship, tried to collect evidence, especially from inscriptions, which he misinterpreted wholesale. For example, a stone found at Manchester[1] states that 'the century of Candidus'—that is, a company commanded by the centurion Candidus—built XXIIII feet of the rampart round the *castellum* there. It is an ordinary Roman military text, with hundreds of parallels, and is simply a record of building work achieved by soldiers. In Mr. Coote's hands it becomes "a stone showing the *numeri limitum*. The XX express the number of the decumanal *limes*, as the IIII is the number of the cardinal *limes* upon both which the *centuria* of Candidius was situate".[2] Since Coote wrote, many scattered endeavours in the same direction have been made. All of them, so far as I can judge, have failed. I do not think that even Mr. Montague Sharpe, the latest to enter the field, has succeeded any better than his predecessors; certainly his arguments on this point seem to me far less convincing than his attractive earlier theory concerning Brentford and the place where Caesar may have crossed the Thames, and I cannot consider that he has detected real traces of centuriation surviving in modern Middlesex.[3]

Again, we cannot feel sure that the relation between labourer and landlord was the same in Britain as in other provinces, or that the colonate was here universal. There were, it is true, *coloni* in Britain. That we know: for the Theodosian Code[4] contains a fourth-century

[1] *CIL.* vii. 215.

[2] *The Romans of Britain* (1878), p. 84. Cf. *Archaeologia* xlii (1867), p. 151.

[3] Cf. *Eng. Hist. Rev.* xxiii, p. 543. For a fuller examination of the whole question, with references, see 'Centuriation in Roman Essex' in *Eng. Hist. Rev.* xxxiii, pp. 289 ff., reprinted with Appendix in *Trans. of the Essex Archaeological Society* xv, pp. 115 ff. In this article F. H. draws attention to possible traces of centuriation near Great Dunmow and Braintree, in what may have been the *territorium* of Roman Colchester.

[4] xi. 7, 2.

ordinance concerning them. But the Roman Empire, as Mitteis [1] and others have well pointed out, was no realm of rigid uniformity in matters of law and of tenure. It is quite likely that the soil of Britain was largely owned by British nobles after the Roman conquest, and that their relations to their dependants were regulated by native customs. It is equally likely that, just as the cantonal magistrates became assimilated to those of the Roman municipality, the British peasant took—in some part, at least,—the position of the Roman *colonus*. But, so far as I can see, speculation on these points is at present unprofitable and even undesirable. In particular, we know too little of the villages and hamlets to be able to argue from them as to the status of the labouring population. One or two have been explored, notably by the late General Pitt-Rivers.[2] But the exploration, informative as it was in many ways, revealed nothing as to the legal position of the villager. We can only say that men did sometimes live in villages, that they possessed or were coerced into communal effort enough to enclose themselves within rather irregular ramparts and still more irregular ditches, and that the villages examined by Pitt-Rivers stand in no very obvious relation to neighbouring villas.

From this sketch of towns, villas, and villages let us now turn to the civilization which existed in them. About this our knowledge is perhaps as full as our legal information is deficient. The inferences to be drawn from this knowledge are what any student of western Europe might expect. Alike in town and in country the better classes in Roman Britain lived in Roman fashion. Their houses were indeed (if I am right) based on models native to Britain and north Gaul. But, as I have pointed out in speaking of the towns, the internal

[1] *Reichsrecht und Volksrecht*, p. 8.

[2] See *supra*, p. 218. Cf. the settlement on Rockbourne Down, excavated by Mr. Heywood Sumner: see 'Roman Britain in 1913' in *British Academy Supplem. Papers* ii, p. 23.

equipment of the houses—the whole fabric of life—was Roman-provincial, the monotonous, conventional, imitative fashion of the western Empire. Only, as Britain was small and remote, the equipment was less elaborate than even in many parts of Gaul. Normal in character, it was perhaps subnormal in amount. Thus, the masonry of house-walls exhibits none of the special features visible in Rome and in several provinces. That the characteristic brickwork should be absent is not to be wondered at; geological causes are responsible. But *opus reticulatum* is equally unknown to the British builder. His work is often enough very rough. It is possible to be rough and yet Roman, in more senses than one.

To make all this more definite, let me enumerate in rapid succession, and at the risk of some repetition, the Roman features which strike the eye on every Romano-British site. The architectural fragments, sometimes magnificent, as at Bath (PLATE V), sometimes poor enough, are all based on Roman originals. So, too, the frescoes on the walls, the glass in the windows, the mosaics adorning the principal rooms, the hypocaust chambers beneath the floors,[1] the bathrooms, the nymphaea and other devices for hours of ease and pleasure. The mosaics, of course, to take one instance, are not splendid. When we see them to-day, we admire them a good deal more than they deserve, just because they are novel to us, not because they are really beautiful. But, as I have said,[2] they are wholly Italian in design, in scenes, in ornamentation. I have never met on any Romano-British mosaic a single distinct reference to local British habits or a single bit of ornament which might not occur in Italy. And this Romanization was

[1] In view of current misconceptions, it is worth while pointing out that the heat did not pass through the floors into the rooms above; the floors were made specially thick in order to prevent that. Instead, the heated air from the hypocaust chambers was conveyed up through the walls by various pipes and passages, and thence let out into the rooms to any suitable extent, the pipes and passages serving in any case as radiators.

[2] *Supra*, p. 210.

not confined to the towns and to the ' villas ' of the well-to-do. It spread to the dwellings of the peasant poor. In plan the Romano-British villages—like Woodcuts, Rotherley, Wansdyke, Woodyates and the rest, dug up by Pitt-Rivers—are not Roman ; their round mud-huts and pits, their strange ditches, their shapeless enclosures, date from days before or early in the Roman occupation. But Roman civilization soon reached and absorbed them. The ditches were filled up ; hypocausts, odd but unmistakable, wall-plaster painted in Roman fashion, roofing of Roman tiles came into use.[1] There were in Britain splendid houses and poor ones. But a continuous gradation of all sorts of buildings and all degrees of comfort connected them ; there is no discernible breach in the scale. Throughout, the dominant element is the Roman provincial fashion which is borrowed from Italy.

If we turn from the structural remains to the smaller objects of daily life, our picture is again Roman and not British. The finer pottery is all of the ubiquitous ' Samian ' type which has already been noticed.[2] The glass jars, cups, and bowls are equally Roman. Some, no doubt, were made in the island, some very probably in northern Gaul. But none occur which might not have found a place in any Italian house. Even the villagers learnt to eat and drink from Samian dishes and cups of glass, and actually to keep their clothes in wooden chests of drawers. So, too, the bronze objects—brooches, the so-called horse-trappings, and other countless decorations sewn to leather or fastened to wood-work, the buckles and needles and buttons and smaller trifles. The enamelled work itself is principally Roman. Though the art of enamelling was thought by the Romans to be of Celtic origin, the largest and most ambitious pieces of

[1] Pitt-Rivers, *Excavations in Cranborne Chase, &c.*, iii. 3 ff. So Colt Hoare, *Ancient Wilts, Roman Aera*, p. 127 n. : "On some of the highest of our downs I have found stuccoed and painted walls, as well as hypocausts, introduced within the rude settlements of the Britons."

[2] *Supra*, p. 180. Cf. Oswald and Pryce, *Terra Sigillata* (London, 1920).

PLATE VII. ENAMELLED BRONZE SHIELD FROM THE THAMES AT BATTERSEA

enamelling as yet found in Britain are plainly Roman in style. In a word, all the smaller material circumstances of life in Britain were Roman—rude enough, but Roman and characteristic of a historic fact. We see here none of that hatred of foreign fashions—or at least of all foreign fashions except a few that are peculiarly useful—which characterizes populations still proud of their nationality and defiant of external inroads.

The result in Britain perhaps was not aesthetic. The new culture was conventional. It obviously had not the genuine artistic creativeness or the genuine artistic sense of well-chosen detail, nor had it any real delight in individually beautiful objects. That was not an artistic age; it was merely practical and administrative. Its spirit is alive to-day in the long streets of neat cottages and 'eligible residences' which have grown up round the west end of Reading or in our own east end at Cowley. Those houses with their monotonous conventionality, each like the pattern of its immediate neighbour, each ornamented—if ornamented at all—by meaningless devices, borrowed from three or four different periods of art, each (be it added) trim and sanitary and watertight, represent quite well one of the ideals of the Roman world, the ideal of good, prosaic, respectable, and orderly life.

But, however unaesthetic it may have been, the result is clear, and indeed all the clearer, as we shall see, because it is unaesthetic. Let us compare the character of the old native art which Rome drove out. We shall then be in a better position to understand the meaning of the change. That art had once been a feature in the world of central and western Europe. Right across the land, from the Severn to the Rhine and indeed to the Danube and the Black Sea, we find its relics. It appears to coincide with the original homes of the Celtic tribes; and, as it dates from the period just before the Empire, it has been christened Late Celtic. Its main features are a fondness for circles returning upon themselves and a tendency to trumpet-mouthed curves, a flamboyant and artistic treatment of plant and animal forms, a free use of enamel, and especially of red enamel, and with all this a genuine artistic delight in ornament. We can afford to dispense with

Fig. 58. BRONZE-MOUNTED TANKARD FROM ELVEDEN, SUFFOLK (½)

continental illustrations, for nowhere do we meet with finer examples of Late Celtic craftsmanship than in Britain. We may select three. The well-known bronze shield found in the Thames near Battersea, and now in the British Museum (Plate VII), displays in high perfection most of the characteristics I have enumerated. It was probably made in the first century B. C. Not less graceful are the returning spirals on a bronze-mounted tankard from Elveden in Suffolk (FIG. 58). Finally, a bronze mirror from Trelan Bahow in Cornwall may be taken as typical of a series (FIG. 59). The groups of engraved lines which are used to form a background represent a favourite device of Late Celtic art.

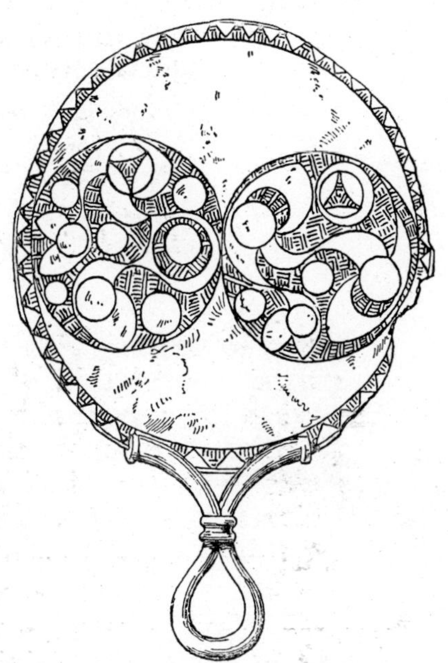

FIG. 59. BRONZE MIRROR FROM TRELAN BAHOW ($\frac{1}{3}$)

With the coming of the Romans this art vanished. But it did not vanish utterly. It survived in many details. We can trace its influence at work amid the predominance of Roman fashions. Its continued vitality may not be unconnected with the fact that, beyond the civilized area, the resistance to Rome was so stubbornly maintained.[1] Many of the brooches found in Britain, for instance, are peculiarly British. One of the commonest of Romano-British 'fibulae', commoner in the north than in the south of the island, is not only directly traceable to a Celtic ancestry, but is very rare on the Continent (FIG. 60). The examples which have been found in northern Gaul and Germany can almost be counted on the fingers of two hands; and, when a specimen once turned up near Frankfurt, it so startled the local archaeologists that they assigned it to Africa[2]. But the most

[1] See *supra*, p. 124.
[2] *Mitt. über röm. Funde in Heddernheim* ii. 40.

striking example is supplied by the richly enamelled 'dragon-brooches' (FIG. 61). Both their designs and their gorgeous colouring are Celtic in spirit; they occur not seldom in Britain; from the Continent only four or five instances are recorded.[1] Here certainly Roman Britain is more Celtic than Gallia Belgica or the Rhine valley. Yet a complete survey of the brooches used in

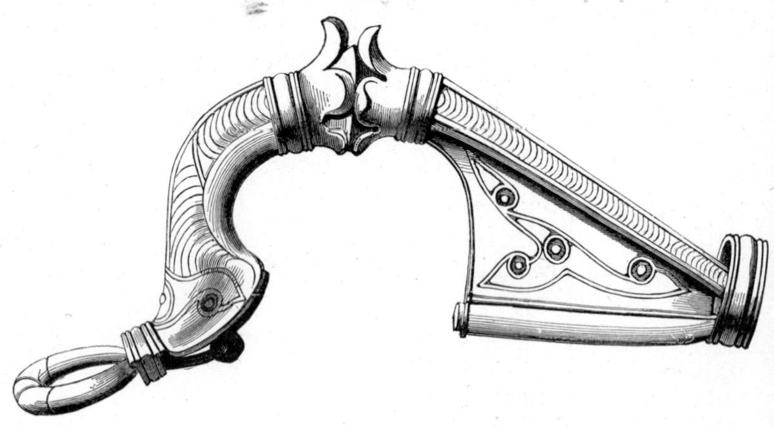

FIG. 60. SILVER-GILT 'BOW-FIBULA' FROM BACKWORTH, NORTHUMBERLAND[2] ($\frac{1}{1}$)

The trumpet-mouthed motive is conspicuous here. For the origin of the type, see Sir Arthur Evans in *Archaeologia* lv. 183; for further illustrations and for the distribution, J. Curle, *A Roman Frontier Post*, pp. 321 ff., and F. H. in *Arch. Ael.* (3rd ser.) v, pp. 400 f.

Britain would show, especially in the south, a dominant array of types which were equally common here and on the continent, and belong to the Roman provincial civilization. The 'Aucissa' and 'knee' and 'cross-bow' varieties may serve as examples.[3]

[1] For a list, see F. H. in *Arch. Ael.* (3rd ser.) v, pp. 403 ff.; see also J. Curle, *A Roman Frontier Post*, pp. 319 ff., and R. A. Smith, *P.S.A.L.* (2nd. ser.) xxii, pp. 61 f.

[2] The Backworth Find is described by F. H. in *Northumberland County History* ix, pp. 26–32.

[3] See F. H. in *Arch. Journ.* lx, pp. 236–46, and lxii, pp. 265–9, on 'Aucissa' and 'shield-shaped' fibulae, and in *Arch. Ael.* (3rd ser.) v, p. 402, on 'knee' fibulae. Cf. also *C. and W. Trans.* (n.s.) xix, pp. 1–16

But the survival is best seen in certain local pottery wares—the New Forest stoneware with its curious leaf-ornament, which was used a good deal in southern Britain,[1] and the more familiar and far more widely distributed Castor ware, made on the banks of the Nen some five miles west of Peterborough. Here, on the north and south sides of the river, were two Romano-British settlements of comfortable houses, furnished in

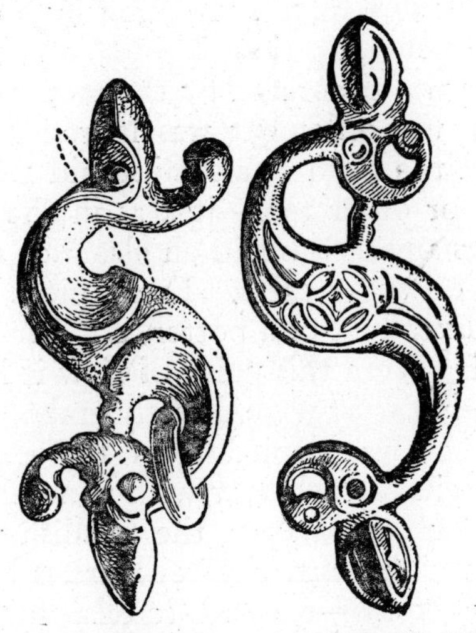

FIG. 61. 'DRAGON-BROOCHES' FOUND AT CORBRIDGE ($\frac{1}{1}$)

genuine Roman style. Round them stretched extensive pottery works, which seem to have been active during the greater part of the imperial period.[2] The ware, or rather the most characteristic of the wares, made in these works is generally called Castor (or sometimes Durobrivian) ware. It was not, indeed, peculiar to the potters of the Nen valley. There is evidence that, to

1 See *Romanization of Roman Britain*, pp. 48 f., and *Vict. Hist. Hants* i, pp. 326 ff. Cf. Heywood Sumner, *A descriptive account of the Roman pottery made at Ashley Rails, New Forest* (1919), and *A descriptive account of Roman pottery sites at Sloden and Black Heath meadow, Linwood, New Forest* (1921).

2 See *Vict. Hist. Northants* i, pp. 206 ff.

some small extent at least, it was made elsewhere in Britain, and it must have been produced freely in northern Gaul, though none of its kilns has been yet identified there; possibly it was produced there first and afterwards copied in Britain.[1] But Castor is the only attested centre of its manufacture on a large scale, and the cups and jars from its potteries seem to be not only more abundant but also more varied in decoration and sometimes more directly inspired by native elements than the continental fabrics.

Castor ware was decorated by the method often called 'barbotine'; the ornament was in relief and was laid on by hand in the form of a semi-liquid 'slip' with the aid of a tube or other tool—just as in the later Roman Empire the ornament was laid on glass,[2] or as in our own day it is put on sugar-cakes. Every piece is, therefore, the individual product of a potter, not a mechanical cast from a mould. From this point of view it is noteworthy that the British Castor ware directly embodies the Celtic tradition. If it was copied from the Continent, the island potters either took over with it an element which has all but disappeared from the Gaulish work, or else they added that element. Castor ware is based, indeed, on classical patterns—foliated scrolls, hunting scenes, gladiatorial combats, even now and then a mythological representation. But it recasts these patterns in accordance with its own traditions and also with the vigour of a true art. Those fantastic animals with strange outstretched legs and eager eyes; those tiny scrolls scattered by way of background above and below them; the rude beading which serves, not ineffectively, for ornament or for dividing line; the suggestions of returning spirals; the manifest delight of the artist in plant and animal forms—all these things are Celtic (Fig. 62).

When we turn to the scenes in which man is prominent—a hunting picture in which (exceptionally) the

[1] See J. Curle, *A Roman Frontier Post*, pp. 255 f., and also *Romanization of Roman Britain*, p. 50, foot-note.

[2] Kisa, *Glas im Altertume* ii. 475.

Fig. 62. CASTOR WARE FOUND AT CORBRIDGE

Fig. 63. CASTOR WARE IN COLCHESTER MUSEUM

huntsman appears,[1] or a chariot race, or a gladiatorial show (Fig. 63), or Hesione fettered naked to a rock and Hercules saving her from the sea-monster (Fig. 64), we do not always find the same skill and vigour. From of old the Celtic artist had been averse to representations

Fig. 64. CASTOR WARE FOUND IN NORTHAMPTONSHIRE

This is, of course, a fragment: the portion with the sea-monster is wanting.

of the human form. When with an initiative lacking to his continental rival—an initiative which it is fair to recognize—he added this to his repertory, he passed beyond his proper bounds. Now and then he succeeded; more often he failed; his Hercules and Hesione are not fantastic but grotesque. In taking in new Roman elements, his Celtic art lost its power and approximated to the conventionalism of Samian ware. We could want no better external instance of what Romanization meant.

Leaving the outer fabric of life, let us look for a moment at the internal activities of politics, literature, language,

[1] *Vict. Hist. Northants* i, p. 190.

and religion. We cannot, it is true, say much of these. Of politics there was little in Roman Britain. Of its literature we know nothing, save that a few Christian writers used Latin for their works. About language we are better informed. There is literary evidence, distinct if not abundant, as to the use of Latin in Britain. Agricola, as is well known, encouraged it, with the result (says Tacitus) that the Britons who had hitherto hated and refused the foreign tongue, became eager to speak it fluently.[1] A little before A. D. 83, one Demetrius of Tarsus, a 'grammarian', was teaching in Britain, as Plutarch mentions in his tract on the cessation of oracles, and his teaching is recorded as being nothing out of the ordinary course.[2] Rather later, in A. D. 96, Martial[3] boasts that he was read in Britain, and about A. D. 128 Juvenal[4] alludes casually to British lawyers taught by Gaulish schoolmasters. It is plain that by the second century Latin must have been spreading widely in the province, and we need not therefore feel puzzled about the way in which the British workman of perhaps the third or fourth century learnt his Latin. That it was the ordinary speech of men and women of all classes in Calleva Atrebatum (Silchester) is, I think, clear.[5] And, though our evidence for other towns is less than it is for Calleva, it tends in the same direction. I have spoken of Caerwent.[6] Similar indications have been noted in London, Leicester, and Dorchester.[7] All this is significant—far more so than we in uni-lingual England are apt to suppose. In point of speech the Roman Empire must have been very like what Austria-Hungary was

[1] *Agricola* 21.

[2] Plutarch, *De Def. Orac.* 2 (410 A). He may confidently be identified with the Demetrius whose name appears on a well-known inscription at York (*Ephem. Epigr.* iii, p. 312 = Dessau, *Inscr. Sel.* 8861). Cf. also *Ephem. Epigr.* ix, p. 560, and Dessau in *Hermes*, xlvi. 156. The identification was first suggested by C. W. King (*Arch. Journ.* xxxix (1882), p. 23).

[3] xi. 3. 5.

[4] xv. 3.

[5] *Romanization of Roman Britain*, pp. 29 ff.

[6] See *supra*, p. 212.

[7] *Romanization of Roman Britain*, p. 32.

before its final collapse. The men who were disloyal to Rome or ignorant of her civilization would no more have spoken the Latin language than the modern Czech would answer a German in the streets of Prague, or the Transylvanian Saxon in Hermannstadt would talk Hungarian, or the Ruthene peasant be able to use any tongue but his own.

When we turn to the population outside the towns of Roman Britain, the question of language is more difficult, since the evidence is deficient. The owners of the villas certainly spoke Latin, for they set up altars and gravestones inscribed in that language. But the language of the peasantry is entirely unknown. A scattered *graffito* here and there suggests an acquaintance with Latin,[1] and Britain—unlike Gaul—can show no single inscription in Celtic which can be referred to the Roman age. Beyond this, we are reduced to *a priori* considerations. It is hard to believe that if Gaulish lingered on in Gaul, as we have seen that it did,[2] British should have been forgotten even in the lowlands of our island. No doubt, the usual division of language in a bilingual land seems to be by social ranks. That the upper classes in town and country should ordinarily speak (let us say) Polish and the lower classes Ruthene, is more common, I fancy, than that the whole town population and the upper classes of the country should speak one language, and the peasants another. Nevertheless, such a division can, or could recently, be paralleled in some Slavonic districts of Austria-Hungary. Something very like it prevails today in the remoter parts of the Scottish Highlands. It may have prevailed in Roman Britain. That is, the townsfolk of all ranks and the upper class in the country may have spoken Latin with one another, while the peasantry may have used Celtic. No actual evidence has been discovered to prove this. But it is not in itself improbable.

[1] *Romanization of Roman Britain*, pp. 32 f.   [2] *Supra*, pp. 176 f.

Religion tells much the same tale as the other subjects which we have discussed. If the Celtic element seems to be more in evidence here, that is perhaps because Rome had so little in the way of religion to offer to anybody. Purely Roman dedications, such as an Italian might have set up in Italy, are common enough in the military area. There we meet altars to Iuppiter Optimus Maximus and other true gods of Rome, without any intermixture of non-Roman religion. But they are altogether rare in the towns and country districts. Nor do we hear more of the official worship of the Emperor. Dedications to his Divinity are frequent in forts and fortresses. Elsewhere they are scanty. The imperial cult not only had no religious value in Britain; it had not even the social importance which it enjoyed in Gaul. Romano-Celtic and native dedications are far commoner. Many of these are dedications to Roman gods with Celtic epithets, to Mars Belatucader, Mars Cocidius, Mars Corotiacus—not to Mars simply. We may infer that scattered, mostly local, cults crystallized round Roman names. It was, however, only a few Roman gods—in Britain, as in north Gaul, mainly Mars and Mercury—who attracted Celtic epithets to themselves at all freely. Apollo, Diana, Juno, Neptune and the rest appear comparatively seldom, or even never, with them. On the other hand, a long series of dedications concerns gods whose names are purely Celtic except for their Latin terminations. These are many. But they do not greatly differ from those just described; in fact, many Celtic deities appear now with, now without, the Roman prefix. Where Roman and native elements combine, the Roman appears to be predominant.[1]

If we proceed to scrutinize the Celtic cults of which

[1] See *Romanization of Roman Britain*, p. 73. This is a point on which F. H. was wont to insist. Some may be disposed to think that he pressed it too strongly. It might be argued that in Britain Roman forms are no more inconsistent with Celtic content than are Greek forms with Oriental content in the eastern provinces.

we meet remains in Britain, we must note first the absence of any hierarchy of great gods. Of Esus, Taranis, and Teutates,[1] sometimes styled the Celtic Trinity, no sign emerges. Instead, a crowd of lesser deities reveals a primitive religion in much the same rudimentary state as were the religions of Greece and Rome before the Olympian gods had become acknowledged as supreme. Some bear names which seem descriptive of character. Such was Belatucader, 'good at war', who was worshipped in the north and (as I have just said) coupled with Mars. Such, too, Maponus, kin somehow to the Welsh 'Mabon', a child, and habitually yoked with Apollo.[2] Others belonged to natural features. Verbeia at Ilkley was patron saint of a stream still called Wharfe; the Northumberland Cocidius (often Mars Cocidius) may have begun as god of the Coquet. Others with less intelligible names were clearly connected with special spots; such were Ancasta at Bitterne (near Southampton), Coventina, whose sacred water bubbled up within the shadow of Hadrian's Wall, and Antenociticus, whose shrine now lies beneath a suburb of Newcastle.[3] Sul or Sulis, thought to be by origin the Celtic female Sun and identified with Minerva, was goddess of the Bath waters.[4] Nodens, kin to or bearing the same name as an Irish hero, Nuada of the Silver Hand, was worshipped in west Gloucestershire at Lydney.[5]

[1] Best known from the lines of Lucan (*Phars.* i. 445 f.):

> '*Teutates horrensque feris altaribus Esus*
> *Et Taranis Scythicae non mitior ara Dianae.*'

In Britain Teutates occurs once, possibly twice, identified with Mars; the others are absent. Whether these gods were really so important is disputed; see Jullian, *Cambridge Medieval History* ii, p. 464 (for), and S. Reinach, *Cultes, Mythes et Religions* i, pp. 205 ff. (against).

[2] *C. and W. Trans.* xv, p. 463.

[3] *Ephem. Epigr.* ix, 1164.

[4] *Vict. Hist. Somerset* i, p. 220.

[5] See Bathurst's *Roman Antiquities at Lydney Park, Gloucestershire*, edited by C. W. King (1879), pp. 12 and 45, and *Bonn. Jahrb.* lxvii, pp. 29 ff.

These cults and others like them are British. Some Celtic dedications which occur in the province seem, on the other hand, to have been brought in from the Celtic mainland. Mars Leucetius (the lightning god), Mars Rigisamus (most royal), Mars Lenus,[1] Mars Olludius, Apollo Grannus, are from across the Channel; Grannus, god of healing waters, had a home at Aachen. A conspicuous example of imported Celtic worship may be found in the Mother Goddesses, the *deae Matres*, referred to in an earlier lecture.[2] Every one who has looked into museums in the north of England or along the Rhine will be familiar with the curious reliefs which show the Three Mothers seated stiffly side by side, clothed in long robes and strange head-dress, and often holding on their laps round baskets of fruit. Their cult was common in north Italy and south-eastern Gaul, and on the middle and lower Rhine, and in Britain. But in Britain it is limited mainly to the army; its monuments occur, with comparatively few exceptions, within the military area, and the worshippers, so far as they state their professions, are nearly all soldiers. Probably its birthplace was in the Celtic districts of northern Italy and south-eastern Gaul, where the earliest dedications have been found. There, during the early Empire, soldiers were recruited in large numbers for service on the Rhine and in Britain, and these soldiers took their native worship with them. Only, from the Rhine garrisons the cult spread to German and Gaulish tribes around, finding perhaps some native Triad of Goddesses with which it amalgamated, while in Britain it remained, for the most part, confined within its military habitat.

I have alluded to the absence from Britain of all sign of the so-called 'Celtic Trinity'. There are other points of contrast with Gaul. The strictly native monuments,

[1] See *supra*, p. 212.

[2] See *supra*, p. 176, and reference there, and also *Archaeologia* lxix, pp. 183 f. and 204 ff. An example recently found in Scotland is discussed in *P.S.A. Scot.* lii (1917–18), pp. 38 ff.

so far as I can check them, exhibit few or none of those curious un-Roman forms which occur in some parts of France—strange horned figures, frequently seated in attitudes that, outside of Asiatic India, recur only on the Gundestrup bowl[1]; or deities represented in animal shape, such as the bull Tarvos Trigaranus[2] or the bear of Artio; or gods with odd emblems, wheels and mallets and the like, or with three heads. Where indications of anything of the sort do occur, it is from the military area that they almost invariably appear to come. Cases in point are the horned representations from Bremenium (High Rochester)[3] and elsewhere, and the quaint earthenware mould (Fig. 65) found in 1909 at Corbridge. Probably, therefore, like the dedications mentioned in the preceding paragraph, and like the *colonne au géant* at Cirencester,[4] they are to be regarded as importations. Whether the animal forms be, as M. Reinach thinks,[5] traces of totemism, does not matter. The fact that they do not seem to be British is significant. It almost looks as if the native religion had lacked that strength and vigour which we meet across the Channel. Again we are tempted to feel that Britain was smaller and weaker, and the Roman influence within the civilized

[1] For an explanation of the appearance of this remarkable bowl in N. Europe, see Rostovtzeff, *Iranians and Greeks in Southern Europe*, pp. 138 f.

[2] On this obscure and difficult matter see S. Reinach, *Cultes, Mythes et Religions* i, pp. 233 ff.

[3] Bruce, *Lapidarium Septentrionale*, p. 305, Nos. 585–7. Examples from Uxellodunum (Maryport) and Burgh-by-Sands are now at Netherhall and in the Blackgate Museum at Newcastle. Another, from Kirby Underdale, NE. of York, is figured in *Yorks. Journ.* xxiv (1917), p. 321. Latterly, F. H. thought it possible that these figures may represent "some horned British deity, akin to the horned Cernunnos of Celtic Gaul" (*C. and W. Trans.* xvi (n. s.) (1915–16), p. 285). Even if they be native, however, they are so rare that the argument set forth above is not seriously weakened.

[4] *Archaeologia* lxix, pp. 190 f.

[5] *Les survivances du totémisme chez les anciens Celtes* in *Rev. Celtique* 1900, pp. 269 ff., reprinted in *Cultes, Mythes et Religions* i, pp. 30 ff.

Fig. 65. EARTHENWARE MOULD FROM CORBRIDGE

The wheel is characteristic. So, too, is the crooked stick, which may possibly represent a thunderbolt, although no obvious parallel can be cited. The plaques made in this mould were probably affixed to the outside of large vases and similar surfaces, in the manner of *reliefs d'applique*. See *Arch. Ael.* (3rd ser.) vi (1910), p. 224.

area perhaps more crushing than in the wider plains and forests of northern Gaul.

The evidence as to the growth of Christianity points in the same direction.[1] I had occasion in the last lecture to mention the three British bishops who attended the Council of Arles. Other references in literature confirm the inference that an organized church existed in our island at the outset of the fourth century. By the close of that century it was able to produce men like Pelagius the heretic, and Faustus, abbot of Lerins in 434 and bishop of Riez in 461. The church at Silchester,[2] small objects found in many places, town and country, show that the early bishops had flocks to care for. It is plain indeed, that by A.D. 400 or 420 Christianity had made vast progress in Britain. Here, as throughout the western Empire, it spread first and fastest in the great centres of city life. It was not, however, confined to the largest towns; its traces can be detected both in the smaller towns and in the villages of southern and central England. What proportion of the population accepted it, we do not know. The toleration shown by Constantius Chlorus, the direct protection accorded by Constantine, doubtless favoured its growth in Britain and Gaul at the end of the third century, and there is good reason to think that at least in the latter half of the next century Christians must have been in a majority in some parts of Britain. One class, however, seems to have been wholly uninfluenced. We have no clear sign of Christianity in the army. Throughout the military area the presence of the new religion is almost imperceptible. In this Britain resembles the rest of the Empire. The imperial army, recruited from peasants and barbarians, *pagani* and *gentiles*, contained few Christians.

[1] See 'Early British Christianity' in *Eng. Hist. Rev.* xi (1896), pp. 417 ff., for a fuller statement of this evidence. Cf. also 'Early Northumbrian Christianity' in *Arch. Ael.* (3rd ser.) xv, pp. 22 ff., and H. Williams, *Christianity in Early Britain* (Oxford, 1912).

[2] See *supra*, p. 206.

On the other hand, the haunts of the soldiers gave shelter to a great variety of foreign worships. Some of these (we have seen) were imported from Gaul. Others were non-Celtic. One group, in its way an interesting group, consists of Teutonic cults brought over by German soldiers serving in the northern British frontier garrisons. Sometimes these Germans accepted the gods whom they found in their new quarters; thus, a little band of men who bear German names and expressly call themselves 'Germani', is found erecting an altar to Maponus close by Hadrian's Wall.[1] But they did not forget their Teutonic deities—Mars Thincsus and the two Alaisiagae[2], Garmangabis,[3] Viradecthis, the Unseni Fersomari[4], and many like them. Far more momentous to the Empire as a whole than these little Teutonic cults were the immigrant religions from the east, the worships of Mithras and Dolichenus and Cybele and Isis and others. They were very powerful. But in the Atlantic provinces, in Spain and western Gaul and Britain, their power was limited. They were confined to special areas, and in particular to military areas. Mithraism, the greatest of them all, overran Italy and central Europe and the Rhone valley which so closely copied Italy. But farther west and north it went only where the troops went—to the Rhine frontier, to northern Britain, to the legionary fortresses. So, too, with the cult of the Semitic Dolichenus and the barbaric rites of Cybele. The latter, although (perhaps in mitigated form) they invaded southern Gaul, made little headway in the west and least of all in Britain.[5] If we would find eastern cults in Britain, we must go to the military posts. At Corbridge-on-Tyne was, as we know, a military depôt with

[1] *CIL.* vii. 332.

[2] See Profs. Bosanquet and Siebs in *Arch. Ael.* (3rd ser.) xix, pp. 185 ff., where it is pointed out (p. 186) that 'Thincsus', rather than 'Thingsus', is the proper form.

[3] See *Arch. Journ.* l, p. 316, and *Arch. Ael.* (2nd ser.) xvi, pp. 321–7.

[4] See *C. and W. Trans.* (n.s.) xi, pp. 470 f., and xiii, p. 187.

[5] A. von Domaszewski, *J.R.S.* i, pp. 54 f.

some sort of settlement round it, where all manner of military men collected. There altars were set up to Astarte (Ashtoreth), to Hercules of Tyre, to Dolichenus, to Sol Invictus, to Panthea (Isis ?), as well as to the British Brigantia and Maponus and the German Veter[1]. Nothing of the sort occurs in the towns or country-houses of the civilized area. The influence of the Roman garrisons in Britain was limited to themselves.[2]

One more feature has still to be added to the picture of the lowlands—the industries other than agriculture and pasturage. They are few and confined to minerals, and a brief summary will exhaust them.[3] Tacitus indeed tells us that the island yielded " gold and silver and other metals ", which would be the reward of a successful invasion.[4] But for the Roman world Britain was not the rich mineral country which the discovery of steam power has made it. Its mines were much less important than those of Spain and of Dacia.

Of gold there was but little in Britain in Roman days, nor is there absolute proof that the Romans ever attempted to dig for it. The strongest evidence comes from south-west Wales, where supposed traces of actual Roman gold-mining have been found in the secluded valley of the Cothi—among the hills dividing the Tivy from the Towy—near the hamlet of Dolaucothy, twenty-two miles north-east of Carmarthen, and ten miles north-west of Llandovery, on the line of a Roman road which connected Carnarvon and Carmarthen. Some, however, hold that certain technical features in the adits and passages of these workings indicate not Roman but later

[1] See *Northumberland County History* x, pp. 496 ff.

[2] For a fuller discussion of the religion of Roman Britain, see *Romanization of Roman Britain*, pp. 67 ff.

[3] For a more detailed account, see the Appendix on 'Minerals in Early Roman Britain' in the revised edition of Furneaux's *Agricola* begun by F. H. and completed by J. G. C. Anderson (Oxford, 1922).

[4] '*Fert Britannia aurum et argentum et alia metalla, pretium victoriae*' (*Agricola*, c. 12).

activity.[1] The question must be left undetermined until further investigation has taken place. As matters stand, however, it seems on the whole to be probable that the Dolaucothy workings may be Roman in origin.[2] The likelihood, then, is that gold was worked in Wales—perhaps with as much success as to-day. Silver must have yielded a perceptible revenue. But it was not directly won. Though it is found in a native state, it has in that state a very limited distribution, being usually embedded in mineral veins in mountain regions. Roman metallurgy was incapable of extracting it except where it occurred in combination with ores of lead.[3]

Of lead Roman Britain had abundance. It could spare some for export as early as Nero's reign.[4] Roman lead mines are known to have existed in Somerset, in Shropshire, in Flintshire, in south-west Yorkshire, and in mid-Derbyshire, and there is reason to believe that the lead deposits of south Northumberland were also drawn upon.[5] The lead of Mendip in Somerset was probably the earliest to be worked. I have already cited [6] an inscribed 'pig', which can be dated to A. D. 49 (FIG. 66 *a*), as proof that mining had begun there within six years after the Claudian invasion. Others show that it lasted for perhaps two centuries.[7] Similar inscribed 'pigs' bearing the name of the Emperor Hadrian (FIG. 66 *d*) indicate that the Shropshire mines were specially active in the first half of the second century.[8] They also imply that the metal was regarded as an imperial monopoly, as, indeed, there is other reason to believe. The north-east

[1] *Royal Commission on Hist. Mon. in Wales and Monmouth*, *Carmarthenshire Inventory*, pp. 25 ff.

[2] See F. H. on 'Roman Dolaucothy' in *Trans. of Carmarthenshire Antiq. Soc.* v (1909–10), pp. 14 ff.

[3] Gowland, *Archaeologia* lvii, pp. 359 f.

[4] *CIL.* xiii. 3491 (Dessau, *Inscr. Sel.* 8709), and F. H. in *Arch. Journ.* xlvii, p. 258.

[5] Bruce, *Roman Wall* (1867), p. 433; *Arch. Ael.* (1st ser.) iv, p. 36.

[6] *Supra*, p. 108.

[7] See *Vict. Hist. Somerset* i, pp. 338 ff.

[8] See *Vict. Hist. Shropshire* i, pp. 263 ff.

corner of Wales contains much lead, especially in Halkin mountain and near the town of Flint. Here was a district called by medieval men Tegeingl, a name which perhaps preserves an echo of the old tribal name, Decangi or Deceangi, known from Tacitus[1] and otherwise as the name of a British tribe living in this quarter. Many traces have been noted here of Roman mining, and 'pigs' of lead have been found, some here (or near) and some elsewhere, which bear inscriptions showing that they come from the district of the Deceangi (or whatever the true spelling of the name was),[2] and that Roman miners were busy there in A. D. 74[3] and later (FIG. 66 *b*).[4] The Yorkshire supply of lead ore is fairly plentiful, and it was worked by the Romans. Two 'pigs' found in 1734 on Heyshaw moor, eight miles from Ripley, bear the name of Domitian and the date A.D. 81 (FIG. 66 *c*)[5].

But the limestone hills of Derbyshire provided perhaps the chief stock of lead ore in Roman Britain.[6] Roman lead-mining in Derbyshire has left many traces, notably between Wirksworth and Castleton and around Matlock, near to which latter town five 'pigs' of Roman lead have been dug up. These 'pigs' seem to have been found near where they were smelted; one was actually lying in its mould, and we may suppose generally that

[1] *Annals* xii. 32. 1.

[2] See *Arch. Journ.* xlix, pp. 221 ff., and *Ephem. Epigr.* ix, p. 642, from which it will be noted that F. H., who originally inclined to DECEANGI, ultimately came to prefer DECEANGL, a reading which recent rubbings of the 'pigs' amply confirm. Cf. *Flints. Hist. Soc. Trans.* ix, pp. 58 f.

[3] *Chester Journ.* vii, Nos. 196 f.

[4] The example illustrated was found in Staffordshire. It can be dated to A. D. 76, and has DECEAG on the side. *CIL.* vii. 1205 reads DE CEA, and the *B. M. Guide to the Antiquities of Roman Britain* gives the inscription as DE CEA(N)G(IS). But there is no space between E and C and, while there is room for two ordinary letters between A and G, there is no indication that the mould there had ever been other than perfectly smooth.

[5] *CIL.* vii. 1207, and *Ephem. Epigr.* ix, p. 643.

[6] See *Vict. Hist. Derbyshire* i, pp. 227 ff. For the Weald, see *Arch. Review* i, pp. 436 and 438 (Chitcomb, Maresfield, Sedlescombe).

*a*

IMP·VESP·VII·T·IMP·V·COS· *b*

IMP·CAES·DOMITIANO·AVG·COS·VII *c*

IMP·HADRIANI·AVG *d*

IMP·CAES·HADRIANI·AVG·MET·LVT *e*

L·ARVCONI·VERECVND·METAL·LVTVD *f*

C·L·TRL·LVT·BR·EX·ARG *g*

FIG. 66. INSCRIBED 'PIGS' OF BRITISH LEAD (1/5)

the ore was smelted where it was unearthed. The inscriptions resemble those on the 'pigs' from elsewhere. In one or two cases Hadrian's name appears (FIG. 66 *e*), proving that in his reign the Derbyshire lead mines were, as we should have expected, crown property.[1] But in others we have the names of private individuals (FIG. 66 *f* and *g*), who had presumably leased mining rights from the emperor through his *procurator*, or had perhaps prospected on their own account. All the Derbyshire 'pigs' seem to bear the name **LVTVDARES** (short for *Lutudarenses*), usually in an abbreviated form, **LVTVD** or **LVT** or **LV** (FIG. 66 *e*, *f*, and *g*). Apparently some place in the mining-district, or the mining-district itself, was called in Roman times Lutudarum or (as Ravennas gives it) Lutudaron.[2] The occurrence here and elsewhere of the letters **EX ARG** for *ex argentariis* (FIG. 66 *g*) implies that the lead had been through silver works for desilverization, and analysis shows that other 'pigs' not so stamped have been similarly treated.[3]

Lead, then, and the silver which it yielded were the chief mineral products of Roman Britain. Iron was worked in the Weald behind Pevensey and in the Forest of Dean, and chance smelting was doubtless carried on elsewhere.[4] But the abundance of iron ore in Spain, in parts of Italy and Gaul and in Noricum would make the distant British supplies seem little worth to a Roman. Nor was tin in better case, despite popular ideas to the contrary. Before the days of the Empire, British tin was certainly worked, and the product was conveyed overseas to a western Gaulish port and thence, probably by the pass of Carcassonne, to the Mediterranean.[5]

[1] See *Chester Journ.* iv, pp. 80–95.

[2] *Rav.* p. 429, 2.

[3] *Vict. Hist. Derbyshire* i, p. 233.

[4] As, for instance, at Corbridge: see *Arch. Ael.* (3rd ser.) viii pp. 207 ff., and *Journ. of Iron and Steel Institute* lxxxv (1912) pp. 118 ff.,

[5] Diodorus, v. 22. 2; 38. 5. On the theory that the 'tin-islands' of the ancients were to be sought in Britain, see F. H. in Pauly-Wissowa's *Real-Encyclopädie*, x, s. v. Κασσιτερίδες.

Under the Empire, Britain no longer appears as an important reservoir of tin, and it has been suggested that at some period other tin districts eclipsed it. Pliny, certainly, writing of tin about A. D. 75, refers to north Spain as the principal source of the metal in his day.[1] The Roman remains found in Cornwall are consistent with this view. Innumerable vestiges of ancient tin-mining exist there, but little is definitely of Roman date. Coin-finds suggest that Roman traders had pushed as far west as Bodmin, and perhaps even to Penwith, in Nero's reign. But of mining activity by the Romans, then or later, there are few distinct signs. Only one block of Cornish tin has been discovered which bears a Roman stamp, and that shows the much worn head of a fourth-century emperor.[2] The industry cannot have been at all considerable where it has left so few traces. Even the Roman coins found in Cornwall, though several belong to the reign of Nero, are mostly of a latish date. We may infer that, while the Romans were not indifferent to Cornish tin, the extensive deposits in north-west Spain made the more distant ores seem unimportant. Still these were worked, even in the later Empire. It cannot be an accident that most of the Romano-British vessels and objects of tin and pewter are connected with the period A. D. 205–400.[3]

[1] *Nat. Hist.* xxxiv. 16. 156.

[2] *Ephem. Epigr.* ix. 1262. Cf. F. H. in *Mélanges Boissier* (Paris, 1903), p. 249. The well-known St. Hilary milestone (*CIL.* vii. 1147) is of the reign of Constantine the Great. Cf. *Ephem. Epigr.* ix, p. 632.

[3] See F. H. in *Num. Chron.* 1900, pp. 209 ff., and *P.S.A.L.* (2nd ser.) xviii, pp. 117 f. An account of Roman Cornwall by F. H. will appear in a forthcoming volume of V. C. H.

PLATE VIII

NORTH GATEWAY OF CAERWENT

With entrance narrowed

# LECTURE VI

## ROMAN BRITAIN AND SAXON ENGLAND

My subject to-day is the effect of the Roman occupation on the later history of our island. This means that the course of lectures is coming to an end. You must not be too confident that I shall arrive at a conclusion. To tell the truth, conclusions are here almost impossible. In every detail and department the subject cries out against any pretence of definitive treatment. The period of time which is involved, that of the fifth and sixth centuries, is often styled one of the most puzzling and ill-understood periods in history. I do not know whether it ought to be called a period at all. One of its peculiar difficulties consists in the fact that it forms a transition between other periods. It is one of those borderlands of knowledge which invariably tax to the uttermost the resources of research, since they demand an acquaintance with two or more provinces of knowledge which are not easily and not usually studied by one and the same man. In the case before us three worlds meet—Roman, English, and Celtic. Each of them has its own special characteristics and interests. It is rare for one man to control two of these worlds. Most of us cannot properly understand and criticize arguments adduced from more than one of them. But this is not the only nor the worst difficulty to be faced. If information existed in abundance about these three worlds, inquiry would be possible, though hard. We have no such information. The whole subject is at present extraordinarily little known to us. If for one reason it is not to be called a period, for another reason it can hardly be called history. Like the Bronze Age or the Early Iron Age, it lies outside the ordinary range of historians. An American writer has, I think, best described it in the title chosen for a book which is otherwise of doubtful value—' The Two Lost Centuries of Britain '.

Of the three worlds, two are practically unexplored. The early history of the English has been written often enough. But it is mostly fiction. Few facts or sequences of facts, still fewer dates, can be established earlier than 597, the year when Augustine landed in Kent. Few laws or institutions, few social and economic customs can be pointed out which unquestionably existed in known and determinate forms in (say) 500. The seeming minuteness and precision of the Saxon Chronicle has hidden the blank from our eyes. But that kind of precision characterizes the authorized version of the ' prehistory ' of every nation, whether it be Roman or Jewish or another. It ought indeed to set inquirers on their guard and to arouse scepticism instead of satisfying curiosity. The Celtic world is equally unhelpful. For the fifth and sixth centuries no contemporary narrative exists ; we have only a series of unreliable dates, compiled years too late, and the writings of Gildas, which may best be characterized as Lamentations. Celtic philology is at present little better than a maze of shifting lights. Our knowledge even of the old Celtic vocabulary is very small, and parts of the earliest Celtic literature are practically unintelligible to us. The same passage is sometimes so differently construed by different scholars that the English renderings can hardly be recognized as referring to the same original. Thus, one piece has been variously explained as relating to a Pictish soldier on service with a copy of the Christian poet Juvencus, a Frankish servant, and a copper kettle ; or to an inspired bard refusing to sing until he has had his dinner ; or to Llywarch of Argoed, left to an evil fate with a single companion.[1] I have quoted, perhaps, an extreme instance. But I do not think I have exaggerated the

[1] Skene, *Four Ancient Books of Wales* ii, p. 2. The passage is ' translated ' and discussed *ibid.*, pp. 311 ff.

general uncertainty which overhangs large parts of Celtic studies. Here assuredly is no place for a respectable historian.

Fortunately, there remains the third or Roman world. The student of Roman Britain *can* make some approach to certainty. Here ancient history comes to the rescue of modern. I think I am entitled to claim that the inquiry into the history and character of Roman Britain, with all its defects and imperfections, has been carried much farther than the inquiry into Celtic or Saxon Britain, much farther too than the inquiry into any other Roman province; and that our scientific knowledge of the island, however liable to future correction and addition, stands by itself among the studies of the Roman Empire. Roman Britain may be taken as a real fact. And the results of the examination carried out in the preceding lectures have made the nature of that fact quite plain. A genuine Romanization took place in the island, not unlike the Romanization of Gaul or of Spain. The Roman influences in Britain were not confined to the army or the frontier fortifications. Nor did they merely traverse the land, like an eastern river crossing a half-desert plain and affecting only the immediate neighbourhood of its own banks. They permeated the whole civilized area; they made it Romano-British in speech and thought and external life. But they were less intense than in provinces nearer the Mediterranean; they affected only the lowlands; they varied in their results even in different parts of those lowlands. The Romanization was genuine. But it had limits, which we shall find decisive of its fate.

This civilization was only reaching its maximum when the Roman occupation neared its close. We can trace the history of its growth with some approach to accuracy. Let me go back to A. D. 43 and briefly recapitulate. The first conquest, it seems, was followed by an outburst of Romanization in the south-east. In this connexion the early grant of municipal rights to Verulamium is significant. The movement was cut short abruptly by the revolt of Boudicca and the massacre of thousands of Romanized Britains by their patriotic and anti-Roman countrymen. It revived in the Flavian age. Then, as Tacitus tells us, Latin began to be spoken, the toga was worn, and temples, town halls, and private houses were built in Roman fashion. Then, as archaeological remains prove clearly, towns like Silchester, Bath, Caerwent, took definite shape; two *coloniae*, Lindum and Glevum, were founded; civil judges (*juridici*) were appointed to deal with the presumably growing business;[1] and the garrison of the province was permanently reduced to suit the growing pacification.[2] In short, the same development occurred as marks the last thirty years of the first century in many provinces. The second century probably maintained the tendency. Frequent revolts in the north seem indeed to have checked the work of peace and progress, but in the south at least it went forward.

So, too, the third century. Little as we know of Britain during that troubled epoch, we can see that our island was then perhaps less disturbed than the continent. The development of the countryside by means of farms and country houses must already have begun before its opening years. We meet early traces of this in Kent and the south-eastern part of the island generally, and sometimes outside these limits. Even in Oxfordshire, a site such as Northleigh has yielded pottery which can hardly be later than the first half of the second century. In the latter half of the third a new era dawned, at least for rural life. After 280, villas began to be built in greater numbers, and the half century, 300 to 350—the opening age of modern history according

[1] *Iuridici provinciae Britanniae* are mentioned, *CIL.* iii. 2864 (cf. p. 1062), vi. 1336 and 1509, and ix. 5533 (Dessau, *Inscr. Sel.* 1015, 1151, 1123, and 1011).

[2] According to Ritterling (see *supra*, p. 118, foot-note 1), the Legio Secunda Adjutrix was withdrawn and sent to Pannonia about A.D. 85. Filow ('Die Legionen der Provinz Moesia' in *Klio*, vi. Beiheft, pp. 39 f.) prefers A.D. 88.

to the latest Oxford ideas [1]—marks the zenith of ancient history in Britain. It was then that the villas of the lowlands were most numerous, that corn was exported to the Rhine and cloth to Asia Minor, and that skilled workmen were fetched from Britain to supply the deficiencies of Gaulish builders.[2]

No Golden Age lasts long. The prosperity of Britain was soon threatened—perhaps indeed before 350. On one side were Picts and Irish; as early as 343 the aspect of affairs on the northern frontier was so menacing that Constans had to cross the Channel and take command in person.[3] On the other were German sea-robbers. As in later ages, the pirates obviously attacked the Gaulish coast earlier and more fiercely than the British; but Britain suffered quickly enough. The assaults were made all the more dangerous by the internal difficulties. Hitherto, it seems, the British garrison had been maintained in good order and strength. Now it attracted the notice of statesmen wanting troops and of pretenders wanting thrones. Mr. Rudyard Kipling has sketched the result with much literary power, and his general picture of depleted garrisons, endangered frontiers, and ambitious generals is not amiss. The effect is indeed produced by the employment of several improper elements, but, if Mr. Kipling had not taught us to expect photographic accuracy in his sketches, we should hardly even trouble to notice that in a work of the imagination.[4]

Primarily these troubles concerned only the frontiers. But they cannot have been without their effects upon the lowlands. The *Mosella* of Ausonius, written about A. D. 371, no doubt makes it plain that Gaul had not by then suffered gravely from barbarism. For a perfect

[1] The reference is to the prescription of A. D. 285–604 as the earliest of the periods of General History which may be taken by candidates in the Final Honour School of Modern History.

[2] See *supra*, p. 220.

[3] See Ammianus, xx. 1.

[4] The allusion is, of course, to *Puck of Pook's Hill*, which appeared shortly before the lectures were originally delivered.

picture of a smiling land there is nothing in literature to surpass it. Similarly, among the great cities of the world which the same poet celebrates (a select group that rank with Rome and Alexandria and Athens) as many as four are in Gaul—Trier and Bordeaux, Arles and Narbonne. If the continent, with its Alamannic and Frankish and other dangers, could still be happy, Britain must have prospered also for a while. But it can hardly be a mere deficiency in our evidence which shows in many villas no later coins than those of the third quarter of the century. Though others remained occupied till about 385 or even later, the rural districts, it is plain, began then to be no longer safe; the discovery of occasional fortified farms is eloquent of the conditions that prevailed;[1] some houses were burnt by marauding bands, and some forsaken by their owners.[2] In the crisis of 367–8 the ravages seem to have spread over almost all the lowlands.[3] The twilight was already deepening.

Darkness fell soon. The respite secured by the victories of the great Theodosius was short-lived. In 402 Stilicho withdrew troops—the '*legio praetenta Britannis*' of Claudian, which does not necessarily mean legionaries[4] —from Britain, just as he did from the Rhine frontier. Three years after, in the winter's night that divided 406 and 407, a barbarian flood broke finally and irretrievably into Gaul and Spain. A host, composed mainly of Vandals, crossed the frozen Rhine on foot at Mainz, and burst like a whirlwind on the peaceful provinces, bringing red ruin in its train.[5] In 410 Rome itself was sacked.

[1] *E. g.* at Cwmbrwyn, which F. H. dated to *c.* A.D. 300 (*Roman Wales*, pp. 10 f.), and at Ely near Cardiff, which Dr. R. E. M. Wheeler assigns to the same period (*J.R.S.* xi, pp. 67–85).

[2] See *Vict. Hist. Hants* i, pp. 293 ff., for coin-finds of the 'villas' at Thruxton, Abbots Ann, Clanville, Holbury, Carisbrooke, &c. The Croydon hoard, deposited about A. D. 351 (*Num. Chron.* 1905, pp. 36 ff.), may have a similar significance, and there is much evidence of the same kind from Kent among the unpublished *Vict. Hist.* material.

[3] Ammianus, xxvii. 8. 7.

[4] *De Bello Pollentino*, 416. See *Class. Rev.* xxi (1907), p. 105.

[5] '*Uno fumavit Gallia tota rogo*' (Orientius, *Commonitorium* ii, 184).

When the storm cleared, Britain was found to be cut off from Rome. The precise character of the severance has not been recorded. Our chief authority, Zosimus, probably lived two generations later than the events now in question and, like many historians in all ages, he died before he had completed his work. In his last and least-finished section he alludes thrice to the fortunes of Britain. None of the passages is very clear. But they can be made to yield some coherent idea of what happened.

The first states that in 406–7 barbarian menaces made the British garrison elect an emperor Constantine, who presently crossed the Channel and made himself master of Gaul.[1] The second adds that about 408 other barbarian invasions compelled Britain and part of Gaul (including Armorica) to separate from "the Roman Empire" and to set up for themselves: they did this, and then drove out the barbarians from their own lands.[2] What exactly the 'compulsion' was, or what the relation of these districts to Constantine, Zosimus does not say. But (unless he has duplicated one event in two forms) it would seem that the great invasion of 406–7 sundered Britain and northern Gaul from Rome, while further troubles sundered them from Constantine and drove them to self-protection. Five chapters later, he adds that Honorius—apparently in 410, while Constantine still ruled in the west—sent dispatches to Britain, bidding the British states or cities (πόλεις) look after themselves.[3] That is, the central Government appears to have acquiesced in the situation. At all events, it henceforward ceased to send officials or recruits to Britain, and the rule of the province passed (as we should expect

[1] Zosimus, vi. 2 f.

[2] *Ibid.* vi. 5.

[3] *Ibid.* vi. 10. It is possible that 'Britain' in this passage may be a copyist's mistake for 'Bruttii': see *Romanization of Roman Britain*, pp. 78 f., foot-note. Even so, the general position would remain as described above. On a possible colleague of Constantine, a second Carausius, see Sir Arthur Evans in *Num. Chron.* 1887, pp. 210 ff.

from continental analogies) to the *civitates*, or cantonal units of local administration centred in the country towns, which I have described in a previous lecture. It is noteworthy that this severance of Rome from Britain did not (in the eyes of Zosimus) imply any 'departure of the Romans' or any withdrawal of troops or any anti-Roman feeling among the provincials. As Mommsen puts it, it was not Britain which broke loose from the Empire, but the Empire which gave up Britain.[1] The Romano-Britains merely accepted the inevitable, as men were doing at the time all over Europe. It is no less noteworthy that, when thus left alone, they did not submit to the barbarian like some of their fellow provincials elsewhere.

It is thus dimly that we discern the separation of Britain from Rome. The sequel is buried in still deeper obscurity. Written and unwritten evidence alike fail. It is doubtful whether even a single coin has ever come to light in our island which can be dated to any part of the fifth century except the few first years while Honorius was on the imperial throne. The common version of the course of events is derived mainly from the British priest Gildas, who wrote about 540.[2] But it may be questioned whether he has not introduced more error than truth into our conceptions. Stripped of rhetoric and of reproaches, his account shows three successive and similar scenes, leading in artificial style to a final catastrophe. The first scene is placed after the departure of Maximus with his troops to try his chances of empire, about 388. The Picts and Scots assail Britain; an embassy goes to Rome; a legion is sent in aid, and a wall of turf built by it to defend the north.[3] The second scene is not dated. The Picts and Scots resume their inroads; Britain again appeals to Rome; again aid is sent and stronger defences are built—a stone wall in the north and towers

[1] *Roman Provinces*, i. 194.
[2] On the date of Gildas, see W. H. Stevenson in *Academy*, 26 Oct. 1895.
[3] *De Excidio*, c. 15.

along the southern coast.[1] In the third scene the Picts and Scots return to their prey. The islanders send a third appeal to Rome, couched in a curious rhythmical strain which may be Gildas's own devising, and addressed '*Agitio ter consuli*'.[2] Agitius must be Aëtius, the only '*consul ter*' of this period bearing any such name, and if so the date is A. D. 446. No help now comes from Rome; the Britons at first defend themselves and then call in the Saxons.[3]

In all this the dramatic effort is plain. But dramatization is always dangerous—whether to a novelist or to an historian; had Tacitus been less richly dowered with the dramatic instinct, we should have known a good deal more about the early Roman Empire. Equally plain is the absence of the historical element. Even the more recent events are misconceived. The Saxons, for example, are first introduced in 446. But they began their attacks long before that. They had given their name to the Saxon Shore by 300; it was apparently either Diocletian or one of his colleagues or immediate successors that was responsible for the reorganization of the coast defences of the Channel[4] and the appointment of a *comes litoris Saxonici*. No less erratic is the earlier history. The turf and stone walls here attributed to builders between 388 and 446 are the walls of Pius and Hadrian and Severus, built in the second and perhaps the third centuries.[5] One of them, the wall of Pius, was actually abandoned before 200. The other, the wall of Hadrian and Severus, though held till about 400, reveals no trace even of reconstruction subsequent to the Constantinian period. The south coast 'towers'—Brancaster, Burgh Castle, Reculver, Pevensey, Porchester, and the rest—were erected about 300.[6] One solitary item of coast fortification

[1] *Ibid.*, c. 18.

[2] *Ibid.*, c. 20.

[3] *Ibid.*, c. 23.

[4] See *supra*, pp. 164 f.

[5] See *supra*, pp. 158 f., for the theory as to the building of the Tyne and Solway Wall, which underlies this sentence.

[6] See *supra*, pp. 165 f.

can indeed be dated to the early years of the fifth century (*c.* 406), a fort or signal station that stood high on the lofty cliff at the south end of Robin Hood's Bay, crowning the promontory of Peak, close to what is now the Ravenscar Hotel. But that seems to have been built (or rebuilt) later than the other members of the system to which it belonged.[1] Moreover, unfortunately for Gildas, it is not in the south of the island. It is beyond question that he here preserves only a confused memory of facts three-quarters forgotten. The significance of the confusion we shall see later. For the present we need only conclude that in 540 the Britons knew too little of what had occurred a century or a century and a half before to record it rightly. Only the latest item of Gildas, the appeal to Aëtius, may be genuine.

The stories of the *Historia Brittonum*, of Bede, of the Saxon Chronicle and of the Celtic annals are still further removed from the truth. In large measure they depend on Gildas. The Chronicle, as Mr. H. M. Chadwick has lately tried to show,[2] may contain one or two details drawn from early sources. The *Historia Brittonum* may date in parts from the seventh century. But it is plain that in all this literature we deal with legends, and it is as legends that we must interpret them. Legends generally embody truth. But they embody it so successfully as to hide it altogether. Recent investigations into legendary regions have, however, indicated what is, so to say, the law of legendary analysis. Archaeological or legal or political inquiries have revealed the truths underlying the stories of Minos, of Troy and Mycenae, of Antenor, Evander, and Aeneas, of the Etruscan race, of Romulus and Remus; and these all tell us plainly what to expect. Legend is history personified in fiction. When we can test legends, the general history—clues to

[1] See 'Notes on the Roman Coast Defences of Britain, especially in Yorkshire' in *J. R. S.* ii, pp. 201 ff., for a discussion of this series of stations and a detailed account of one of them (Huntcliff, near Saltburn). The sites at Scarborough and Filey there referred to are being excavated at present (1923).

[2] *The Origin of the English Nation* (1907), pp. 22 ff.

migrations of peoples, or great wars, or the rise and fall of states—proves usually to be true. The picturesque and moving narratives of kings, their feuds and battles, their personal characters and their names, are left unproven, or even disestablished. The heroic age remains —without the heroes. Legends are excellent clues for historical inquiry, as notably in Crete. But they are in themselves only the decorations by which later ages have sought to give meaning to the lifeless-seeming events.

It is the same with our British legends. The tale, as a whole, may be true and yet the personages—Hengist and his colleague Hors or Horsa, Hengist's fair though nameless daughter, Vertigern the King of Kent, Cerdic the West Saxon, and the rest—may all be fictions. Hengist and Horsa are certainly an odd-named pair, and their names are not only odd but uncommon. Hengist is nearly unique and Horsa apparently unparalleled. Vertigern is a good Gaulish name, tolerably common and actually compounded of two well-understood Celtic elements, the second of which is said to survive in the name of the French statesman Thiers.[1] A British noble may well have borne such a name in the early fifth century. Probably the use of native personal names never died out in the Roman provinces, and the experiences of the later Empire certainly tended to revive it. Even in the third century a Roman officer and would-be Emperor of Britain was called Carausius. Later, in the fifth century, it is no more strange that a British noble should be called Vertigernus than that a Gallo-Roman mathematician, friend of Sidonius Apollinaris, should be called Iulianus Vertacus. But the silence even of Gildas about these names suggests only too plainly that, here as elsewhere, legend has put on personal shape. It may be pleasing, but it is not history.[2]

[1] Mr. W. H. Stevenson notes that this is true, only if the name of the statesman is derived from the village of Thiers-en-Auvergne, the *Thigernum castrum*, *Tigernense castellum* of Gregory of Tours.

[2] An opposite view is maintained by E. Windisch, *Das keltische*

On the other hand, the general tenor of the Saxon invasion seems to stand firm. In all the barbarian invasions into the Empire, the first attacks were delivered by freebooters, the serious assault by immigrants. So here. We already know that early plunderers gave their name to the Saxon Shore by A. D. 300. Later on, in the fifth century, a real immigration set in. Before or during this, at an uncertain date, a stray body of 'exiles', that is, emigrants from Germany, were bidden, in the fashion of the age, to help the British provincials against the other barbarians, and apparently to guard in particular the Saxon Shore—not the northern defences—against the Picts. It was all a long process, and we cannot date it well. A contemporary Gaulish chronographer, preserved to us by chance, puts the Saxon conquest of Britain at 441–2.[1] It is of course impossible to determine what point in the conquest the chronographer selected. But his choice fits in well with the "groans of the Britons" assigned by Gildas to the third consulship of Aëtius. Indeed it supplies an additional reason for them. The appeal to Rome is, however, significant enough. Britain, it is plain, still counted itself a part of the Empire, though fate had broken it off. We have not yet reached the notion of an independent, un-Roman Britain.

Turn now to the ensuing struggle between Saxon immigrant and Romano-British provincial. Our legends tell us of a war of extermination, lasting through several generations. The famous instance which they give of this extermination, the siege and annihilation of Andredsceaster, assigned to 491, may be mere invention. "This

*Britannien bis zu Kaiser Arthur* (Abhandl. der philol.-hist. Klasse der kön. sächs. Ges. der Wiss., Bd. xxix, No. VI, 1912, pp. 53 ff.). He admits that certain details, such as the meeting with the wonderful fatherless boy and his prophesying, may be legendary, but holds that, in the main, we can trust Nennius, Bede, Geoffrey, and the Saxon Chronicle.

[1] *Monumenta Germaniae Historica: Auct. Ant.* ix (*Chronica Minora Saec. iv, v, vi, vii* vol. i), p. 660—*Chron. Gall., A. ccccclii,* 126. Prof. Bury suggests that this was really the date of the Roman evacuation: see *supra*, p. 157, foot-note 3.

year Aelle and Cissa besieged Andredsceaster, and slew all that dwelt therein, so that not a single Briton was left."[1] But, if (as is usually supposed) Andredsceaster be identical with Pevensey, the Anderida of the *Notitia Dignitatum*,[2] it was only a fort ten acres in area, and can hardly have suffered a massacre worthy of especial record. So, too,—though it is nearer in date of composition to the probable time of the event—it is most unlikely that there is any historical or traditional warrant for the description of the storming of Bath (if it be Bath) contained in a curious and beautiful eighth-century poem called 'The Ruin'.[3] The defences, according to the poet, were carried by assault after a stout resistance, the buildings razed to the ground, the inhabitants put to the sword: "death destroyed all." The poet, however, seems to be merely giving rein to his fancy. Yet, if those literary details fail, real evidence, general and particular, supports the tenor of the legends.

In the first place, a long and desperate war is what we should expect in Britain. The invaders came from homes remote from Roman civilization. They can hardly have shared the desire of many barbarian invaders to acquire the culture of the conquered. Even town life, we read, was hateful to them. For some parts of the Empire we might repeat, with a little change, Horace's famous '*Graecia capta ferum victorem cepit*'. No one could say that of Britain. On the other hand, the balance of forces on each side is curious. The invaders, if fiercer, were also less numerous than the hosts which poured over Gaul or the Danubian provinces, and less able to win an instantaneous triumph, while the provincials whom they attacked were less powerful and wealthy than those of the mainland. The struggle in Britain was on a small

[1] *Saxon Chronicle* (Rolls Series) i, pp. 24 f.

[2] See F. H. in Pauly-Wissowa, *Real-Encyclopädie* ii A, 332.

[3] See Thorpe, *Codex Exoniensis*, p. 476; Earle, *Bath Field Club* ii, p. 266; Grein and Wülcker, *Bibliothek der angelsächsischen Poesie* i, p. 296. Cf. *Vict. Hist. Somerset* i, pp. 224 f.

scale, and for that reason (if for no other) little noticed by foreign chroniclers. But it was evenly balanced and fiercely disputed.

These general considerations are backed by some interesting archaeological details. The examination of Roman sites in Britain has thrown a little light on the character of the conquest. The conquerors were destroyers. They did not, like their contemporaries on the continent, settle down beside the conquered or occupy their cities. So far as our evidence extends—in many cases the facts are still unsifted—the towns of Roman Britain came to an end. Some are desolate to this day; since the Briton passed away, no man has dwelt in Verulam, hardly any man even near to Silchester or Wroxeter or Kenchester or Caister-by-Norwich or Alchester in our own neighbourhood. Others have been reoccupied because natural advantages or roads or piles of hewn stone attracted settlers; such are Chester and Bath and Canterbury and very probably York. The country houses met the same fate as the towns.[1] On them one brief sentence will suffice. No case is known where Saxons dwelt in a Roman villa.

We can distinguish two different methods by which the destruction came to pass. Often the place was burnt. This apparently happened at Canterbury and Wroxeter and at many of the villas—though some of these may have been destroyed by accident, or by robbers earlier than 441. On such sites excavators have discovered frequent traces of general conflagration and skeletons of town and farm folk slain in fight or flight.[2] Silchester, on the other hand, was not burnt.[3] It was evacuated. The town seems to have passed through a period of decay before it ceased to exist. Some, if not

[1] The destruction of the Llantwit Major villa is a case in point (*Athenaeum*, Oct. 20th, 1888; *Cardiff Naturalists' Soc. Trans.* xx, pp. 50 ff.; and *Arch. Cambr.* (5th ser.) v, pp. 413 ff.

[2] See *Vict. Hist. Shropshire* i, pp. 217 f.

[3] See 'The Last Days of Silchester' in *Eng. Hist. Rev.* xix, pp. 625 ff.

all, of its gates were partly walled up—presumably because they could thus be more easily defended—and the material employed for the purpose includes worked stones from large buildings in the town. Such blocking of gateways has been found in other places, as in Caerwent[1] (PLATE VIII) and Colchester[2] and in the forts on Hadrian's Wall, and everywhere it seems to signify increasing danger or decreasing strength. Then at some time or other, we know not precisely when, the inhabitants found the stress of war too great. They arose, packed (we may think) their goods, and set out for some western region where no English had yet come to trouble.

We have almost an exact parallel from the same period in central Europe, in a part of the Empire where the Roman civilization perished as completely as in England. The Romanized population of the Danube bank east and west of Passau—the province of Noricum Ripense—found themselves in the later part of the fifth century grievously oppressed by the Rugi, a tribe of the same wildness and perhaps even of the same north German stock as the invaders of England. The frontier forts and some of the towns had been destroyed in the course of the barbarian invasions, but the inhabitants had still held on to their walled settlements and, as the Empire could not help, they had accepted the protection of the Rugi, on the opposite bank of the Danube. This availed little The Rugi, like Hengist's people, were dangerous friends; other barbarians were as dangerous enemies. Life was hardly safe inside the towns, and those who ventured outside were liable to be caught up by marauders. As the conditions grew insupportable, the remnant retired from one town to another, from Quintana to Batava, from Batava to Lauriăcum and thence to Fafianae, thus gradually concentrating from the west to the east of the district. They left their old homes desolate and uninhabited; no man dwelt in them, no trader found there

[1] *Archaeologia* lix, p. 92.

[2] *J. R. S.* ix, p. 143.

any one with whom to traffic. A very few here and there declined to leave their native soil and attempted to occupy still the deserted towns; their immediate fate was death or slavery at the hands of the barbarians. At last about 488 Odoacer, unable to protect the survivors, deported them in a body to securer homes in Italy.[1]

We know that the general character of the Saxon conquest was similar, but we cannot date its progress. The traditions of the English give years for all the chief events. But they cannot be trusted. Indeed, they often seem impossible, and even the sequence of events (which Mr. Chadwick wishes to retain while sacrificing the dates) is not always intelligible. A little light can be won from Gildas. He wrote, as I have said, about 540. He was more concerned to lament than to relate. Most of his work is taken up (as sermons so often are) with verbatim extracts from the Bible. But he gives a few facts, and he mentions three British place-names in connexion with his own time. One, Mons Badonicus, is unknown. Even Bede knew no tradition about it, and the general idea that it was near Bath is based on a mere similarity of sound which will not stand philological test.[2] Gildas only alludes to it as the scene of a siege and a great slaughter, which took place in the year of his own birth.[3] The other two are the names of the Demetae, the Celtic tribe of Carmarthen, and Damnonia which is Devon and Cornwall.[4] Of towns he names none; only, he says rhetorically that they had all been destroyed by the English. It is hardly credible that London and Silchester, Bath and Leicester and York, were still British while he wrote.[5]

The general impression made by the few attested facts is that, in the Saxon as in the Roman conquest, geography

[1] *Eugippii Vita Severini* (ed. Mommsen, 1898).

[2] See W. H. Stevenson in *Eng. Hist. Rev.* xvii, p. 633.

[3] *De Excidio*, § 26.

[4] *Ibid.*, §§ 28 and 31.

[5] '*Ne nunc quidem, ut antea, civitates patriae inhabitantur; sed desertae dirutaeque hactenus squalent*' (*Ibid.*, § 26). For London see *J. R. S.* i, pp. 170 f.

had its say. Eastern Britain offered few physical obstacles to Saxon advance. Even the fortified places could not be held if the lands were lost around them. These country towns were small and weak. They could not play the part of Athens facing Deceleia, or of Ravenna in the fifth century, or of the Italian cities of Hannibal's wars or in the Middle Ages. The natural strategy of the conquest might as safely leave them alone as after the Moscow campaign the Allies could leave Napoleon's eastern fortresses to fall one by one. The English probably made themselves masters of the lowlands comparatively soon. Their advance was doubtless far slower than that of Claudius, three hundred years before. They were less organized and, for a time at least, far fewer in numbers than his three armies. Where Rome took five or six years, they may have taken fifty or sixty. But their advance went on to the same point as did Rome's. Like Rome's, it came to a stand at the foot of the hills. Perhaps we may interpret that term more liberally than in the case of the Romans. Towns near the Welsh border and within easy reach of the hills, such as Viroconium, may have long remained in British hands, and the south-western frontier must always have been uncertain and changeable. The great post-Roman earthwork called the Wansdyke, which stretches from the Marlborough and Devizes Downs right on to the hills south of Bristol, may have been at one time or another a British-English frontier.[1]

This of course conflicts violently with the dates in the Chronicle. According to that venerable document, the English took Aylesbury and Benson and Eynsham in our own neighbourhood in 571, Bath and Gloucester and Cirencester in 577, and Bradford on Avon, six miles south-east of Bath, in 652.[2] This is hard to credit. The archaeological remains of Bath, for instance, reveal no token of occupation after the Romano-British period,

[1] On the Wansdyke see *Vict. Hist. Somerset* i, p. 371.

[2] *Saxon Chronicle* (Rolls Series) i, pp. 32 and 50.

and antiquaries and geologists are alike agreed that it lay waste for many years before the English occupied it. The baths fell in and choked up; their pools were overgrown; the wild birds came to nest in the thickets, and one of the eggs remains in proof in the local museum.[1] Nowhere is there trace of human life. But, if the Britons held it for a hundred and seventy years after their severance from Rome, some trace of this period ought to survive. Even savages use pots and pans and live in houses and bury their dead, and in a hundred and seventy years a good deal accumulates. In a hundred and seventy years, too, fashions change. The Romano-British pottery of the early fifth century would have given way to some newer, perhaps ruder, but certainly distinguishable style. The coot's egg tells of the age of desolation. Nothing testifies to Britons in the supposed hundred and seventy years of life. One can only conclude that Bath was lost to the Britons long before 577. If the events ascribed to that year have any historical value, they must belong to a period of fluctuations, when Briton and Saxon (in modern language) played 'a give and take game', and when a walled site, such as Aquae Sulis probably was, might be sometimes held by the one and sometimes by the other, without being permanently inhabited to any appreciable extent. I may add that the chronology towards which I incline suits best with the long pause in the Saxon advance between 510 and 560, attested by Gildas, and indeed provides a reason for it.

The details of the struggle matter less than the results. By 600 at latest, the Britons had lost the lowlands. They held only the hills. The whole area of Romano-British civilization had been wrested from them. This fact has not, I think, been properly recognized by most writers. Ignorant of the distinction between the occupation of upland and of lowland in the Roman period, they have been equally ignorant of its result. Yet the significance is clear. As the Romano-Britons lost the south and west,

[1] *Vict. Hist. Somerset* i, p. 224.

as a Silchester was abandoned in despair and a Wroxeter was stormed and burnt, the centres of Romanized life were destroyed. During the disaster many of the Romano-Britons must have fallen by disease or the sword. Many must have fallen into slavery and been sold into foreign lands, like the later English slaves whom Gregory saw at Rome about 586. Many fled overseas. A remnant escaped into the west; but, in doing so, it exchanged the region of walled cities and houses, of town life and Romano-British culture, for districts occupied hitherto only by soldiery, ill-provided with roads, unsuitable to wealth or agriculture. Misery destroys the habits of civilized life equally among states as among individuals, and it makes sadly little difference whether the misery is due to fault or to misfortune. J. R. Green has pictured the plight of the Britons in a passage of singular eloquence which seems to me to describe extraordinarily well a general process, whilst needing correction in detail.

In its special application, to be sure, the passage is unhistorical. Almost without exception the human remains found in the caves of Britain belong at latest to the second and third centuries. They are two hundred years older than the Saxons.[1] But the picture of decivilization is true and noteworthy:

> The caves of the Yorkshire moorlands preserve traces of the miserable fugitives who fled to them for shelter. Such a cave opens on the side of a lonely ravine, known now as the King's Scaur, high up in the moors beside Settle. In primaeval ages it had been a haunt of hyænas, who dragged thither the mammoths, the reindeer, the bisons, and the bears that prowled in the neighbouring glens. At a later time it became a home of savages, whose stone adzes and flint knives and bone harpoons are still embedded in its floor. But these too vanished in their turn, and this haunt of primitive man lay lonely and undisturbed till the sword of the English invaders drove the Roman provincials for shelter to the moors. The hurry of their flight

[1] Cf. *Vict. Hist. Derbyshire* i. pp. 241 f., where other necessary corrections will be found, and *Vict. Hist. Somerset* i, pp. 368 (Uphill) and 369 (Wookey Hole).

may be gathered from the relics their cave-life has left behind it. There was clearly little time to do more than to drive off the cattle, the swine, the goats, whose bones lie scattered round the hearth fire at the mouth of the cave, where they served the wretched fugitives for food. The women must have buckled hastily their brooches of bronze or parti-coloured enamel, the peculiar workmanship of Celtic Britain, and snatched up a few household implements as they hurried away. The men, no doubt, girded on as hastily the swords, whose dainty sword hilts of ivory and bronze still remain to tell the tale of their doom, and hiding in their breast what money the house contained, from coins of Trajan to the wretched 'minims' that showed the Empire's decay, mounted their horses to protect their flight. At nightfall all were crouching beneath the dripping roof of the cave or round the fire that was blazing at its mouth, and a long suffering began in which the fugitives lost year by year the memory of the civilization from which they came. A few charred bones show how hunger drove them to slay their horses for food; reddened pebbles mark the hour when the new vessels they wrought were too weak to stand the fire, and their meal was cooked by dropping heated stones into the pot. A time seems to have come when their very spindles were exhausted, and the women who wove in that dark retreat made spindle-whorls as they could from the bones that lay about them.[1]

Romano-British elements no doubt survived. It cannot be for nothing that names like Emeritus, Tribunus, Protector occur on British Christian inscriptions of the sixth and seventh centuries, and Protector even in the Celtic genealogies.[2] Some relics of the Roman military system must have survived with them. Nor is it an accident that Roman words appear to have made their way into Celtic speech. Celtic scholars indeed refuse as yet to agree either as to the actual words which survived or as to the probable date of their introduction into Celtic.[3] But survivals do seem to have occurred and,

[1] Green, *Making of England* (1885), pp. 67–8.

[2] See Hübner, *Inscriptiones Britanniae Christianae*, 13 and 102; Rhys in *Arch. Cambr.* (5th ser.) xii (1895), pp. 311 ff.

[3] See Loth, *Les mots latins dans les langues brittoniques* (1892), and more recently H. Pedersen, *Vergl. Gramm. der kelt. Spr.* i, pp. 189 ff.

when Welsh philology reaches the stage of certain knowledge, we shall doubtless be able to point them out in detail. Such items fit in with the records of Gildas. Note, for instance, the names of Ambrosius Aurelianus, who apparently lived in the fifth century, and is expressly described as '*Romanae gentis*' and of imperial origin; of Constantinus, British chief, contemporary of Gildas, and nicknamed "the tyrannical whelp of the unclean lioness of Damnonia"; of Aurelius Caninus (or Conan), another chief, contemporary with and enemy of Gildas.[1] Note, too, personal names in the Welsh genealogies—Agricola, Tacitus, Arthur (apparently the not uncommon Latin Artorius), Maximus, Eugenius. They appear in Celtic form—Aircol, Tegid, Owen, and the rest. But their Latin origin is plain, and it is not due merely to Latin Christianity.[2]

No less plain is the political position. Gildas, though his Roman feeling is somewhat overrated by Mommsen, is largely a Roman. He quotes Vergil and is capable of calling Latin '*nostra lingua*'.[3] He was also not unfriendly

[1] *De Excidio*, §§ 25, 28, and 30.

[2] Professors Pedersen and Morris Jones think *Owein* may be a genuine Celtic name. On the whole question Mr. W. H. Stevenson writes "*Owen* is not certainly an adaptation of Latin-Greek *Eugenius*, and it is not certain that it is a native Celtic name. It is compared, on the one hand, with Gaulish *Esu-genus*, supposed to mean 'born of the God Esus'. But the *e* of *Esus* seems to be long, and Zimmer has pointed out that its length is fatal to this derivation of the Welsh name. The alternative is the assumption that there was a Celtic *esus*, 'good', corresponding to Greek εὖ from *esu-s*, but the evidence for this is very weak. Lloyd (*History of Wales* i, p. 88) cites Ambrosius (Emrys), Aeternus (Edern), Agricola (Aergol), Tacitus (Tegid), and Donatus (Dunod) as personal names showing Roman influence, but suggests that their popularity was chiefly due to the influence of Christianity. This must be the case with *Meurig*, from *Mauricius*, for this name was popularized by the story of the Theban Legion, which seems to have arisen in the fourth century. But there are several other names of Roman origin of which the Christian source is not obvious."

[3] *De Excidio*, §§ 23 and 25. See Mommsen, *Monumenta Germaniae Historica: Auct. Ant.* xiii (*Chronica Minora Saec. iv, v, vi, vii* vol. iii), pp. 9 f.

to the Roman party among the Britons, and not unaware what the Roman Empire was and what its relation to Britain. Still, we meet in him a stage beyond that noticeable in the appeal of 446. His atmosphere is Celtic. For him the '*tempora imperatorum Romanorum*' belong to the past. We see that the Britons are not only become conscious of their severance from Rome, but have drawn the natural conclusion. A distinction is now visible between Briton and Roman. Such a phrase as '*ita ut non Britannia sed Romania censeretur*' implies a sense of contrast. But for that there is a further reason to which we may now pass.

While Roman elements subsisted in what was left of Roman Britain, another force was growing up to oppose them. The end of the Empire was not merely an age of continental invasions. Other barbarian nationalities, tribes that had no fear of Hun or Tartar, that had never heard of Attila or called him the scourge of God, now began to move. Among these tribes were the Celts in Ireland. For whatever reason, they sent out emigrant hosts who conquered southern Scotland and gave it its present name. They sent waifs and strays to the western and southern coasts of Britain and especially into Wales. One chief of the Desi clan thus settled in Demetia (in South Wales),[1] at a date which is given commonly as near the end of the third century—on what precise grounds, I cannot say. Other Celts went farther afield—even to the Alps, the Celtic poets boasted—thus providing Geoffrey of Monmouth with a convenient precedent for the continental triumphs of Arthur. Such were Cúrói, whom Professor Rhys is tempted to identify with Carausius,[2] Dathi, and Niall. Mere names they all

[1] Zimmer, *Nennius Vindicatus*, pp. 86 ff.; Kuno Meyer, *Cymmrodorion Soc. Trans.* 1895–6, pp. 55 ff., and *Eriŭ* 3, pp. 135 ff.; Rhys in *Arch. Cambr.* (5th ser.) ix, pp. 65 f. Dr. R. E. M. Wheeler (*J.R.S.* xi, p. 82) is inclined to connect with this inroad the fortification of the villa at Ely (*supra*, p. 266, foot-note 1), and, more doubtfully, the destruction of that at Llantwit Major (*supra*, p. 274, foot-note 1).

[2] *Celtic Britain* (ed. 1904), p. 286; *Arch. Cambr.* (5th ser.) ix, pp. 67 f.

are to us. But the legends about them indicate real migrations of tribes or families.

It may be difficult to tell precisely where and when these newcomers affected Britain. Even the archaeological evidences of their presence are doubtful. The Winsford monument of the clan of Caractacus (Caratācus) [1] and the Silchester Ogam [2] may be due as easily (on the theory of Professor Rhys) to west Britons as (on the view of Professor Bury) to Irish immigrants.[3] But the effect of the Irish upheaval can only have been to fortify Celtic influences in Britain. The Roman element in the province had been uprooted, destroyed or exiled. The barbarian invasions had cut the island off from Rome. No further cause is required to explain why Celtic is now spoken in Wales, and why Celtic numerals (as Mommsen somehow discovered) are still employed in the sheep-scoring of Westmorland and north-west Yorkshire. There remains the question with which I set out. What was the effect of the Roman conquest on later England? I am not quite sure that the question has not by implication answered itself.

No statements are universally true—except perhaps the one which I have just made. We shall not therefore expect the statement that the Britons were exterminated to be without exceptions. And as a fact evidence exists, though not very satisfactory, which indicates that some

[1] *Ephem. Epigr.* ix. 982 and references there, to which add *Somerset Trans.* lxiv, pp. xxxviii f. Cf. *J. R. S.* ix, pp. 208 ff.

[2] *Archaeologia* liv, pp. 233, 441, and F. H. in *Eng. Hist. Rev.* xix, p. 628, with references.

[3] Rhys (*Arch. Cambr.* (5th ser.) ix (1891), p. 73, and elsewhere) minimizes the Irish invasions of southern Britain. Bury (*Life of St. Patrick*, p. 288) emphasizes them. The decision of the question seems to depend upon whether we should regard the Goidelic elements in Britain as due in part to an original Goidelic population or ascribe them wholly to Irish immigrants. At present philologists do not seem able to speak with certainty on this point. But the evidence for some amount of invasion seems adequate. A fuller discussion of this and some other matters touched on in the present lecture will be found in *Romanization of Roman Britain*, pp. 80 ff.

Britons remained while the main population disappeared. The names of certain early west Saxon leaders—Cerdic (Coroticos), Ceadwalla, Mul, Cada—if authentic, suggest that some Celtic chief or noble had joined or even headed Saxon invaders. The 'Wealas' who occur very occasionally in some parts of later England suggest that here and there other British fragments of less high rank may have been spared or survived. All this is credible enough, if only it rested on better proof. Similar indications can be discovered in the occurrence of both Celtic and English place-names together, in works like the *Historia Brittonum* or Asser's *Life of King Alfred*. Thus the *Historia* records events as occurring at a place known as Episford in Saxon and Rithergabail in Celtic[1], and again an island called in British Ruoihm and in Saxon Thanet[2]. This last example is double-edged. Thanet, as we know well, was the name of the island long before the Saxons first left their German homes, and the writer of the *Historia*, or his authority, must be speaking at second hand and perhaps using a name known to him only on paper and as a matter of learned knowledge. But other instances are less open to cavil, and they seem to introduce—to a very limited extent—a bilingual stage in the English development. In short, the bulk of the native population and culture vanished at once, although scattered elements remained to be absorbed imperceptibly in the succeeding years.[3]

This is a very natural result and not devoid of analogies. The amalgamation of native chiefs with invaders, the general destruction of native elements, the slow absorption of a few survivals can be paralleled, for example, from the conquest of Mecklenburg by the Germans in 1170–1280. The country was before 1170 purely Wendish (Slavonic). In 1160 Henry the Lion conquered it. There

[1] *Hist. Brit.* c. 44. [2] *Ibid.* c. 31.

[3] For a recent and very full discussion of the linguistic evidence of contact, see Max Förster, *Keltisches Wortgut im Englischen* in *Texte und Forschungen zur englischen Kulturgeschichte* (*Festgabe für Felix Liebermann*, 1921), pp. 119–242.

followed a German immigration, and in a hundred years the land appeared to contemporary observers to have become German. The process—which can be followed by fairly extensive documentary evidence—included the adherence of a few Wendish nobles to the Germans, the general destruction of the Wends by death, persecution, or banishment, and the survival of scattered items which were gradually absorbed in the following centuries down to 1400 and 1500. Such total absorption of alien elements by the dominant race is common enough. Roman *coloniae* in Asia Minor, Huguenots and Flemish weavers in England, and hundreds of other examples can be cited from all ages. In each case the alien element has merged in its surroundings without appreciably affecting them.

Between Roman Britain and Saxon England, then, there is a great gulf fixed. And Rome itself is even more completely sundered from the Britain that we know. In Britain Rome had passed beyond her proper limits. Rome was a Mediterranean Empire. Its politics, its civilization, its trade, its whole life, were based on that inland sea. The lands in which it wrought most successfully lay round its shores or at least within easy reach. Wherever the Empire stretched out its frontiers beyond those bounds, its work was imperfect; for the most part it was merely military. No man realized the Empire's natural limits more clearly than its founder, and his wisest successors laid to heart his often-quoted precept—'*coercendum intra terminos imperium.*' Nevertheless occasional advance was natural, perhaps unavoidable. Great empires often blunder in fixing their extreme borders; conquest leads to conquest, and each seems a tiny step. The masters of southern Gaul had good reason to want northern Gaul; the peace of northern Gaul called for the annexation of southern Britain; thence it was obvious to go on to York, to the Tyne and Solway isthmus, to the Forth and Clyde. But the annexations which began in one world ended in another. Not because Britain is more than eight hundred miles from Rome, but because the Italian climate and sky and manner of life are wholly un-British, the Emperors of Rome had little business here. And now they have all gone, like an insubstantial pageant faded, and from the Romans who once ruled in Britain, we Britons have inherited practically nothing. Here and there Roman roads still linger on in modern use. For the rest, the Roman has passed from Britain as though he had never been. He has left no name on hill or river; he has not even bequeathed a few drops of Roman blood. Racially, topographically, culturally, ancient Rome has nothing to do with modern Britain.

In history, however, as in human nature, that which you turn out by the front door often comes in again speedily by a less conspicuous entrance. The Roman armies abandoned Britain beyond all question and quite publicly. Yet in a less obvious and less public, but still a very real, manner ancient Rome has much to do with modern Britain. He who essays the huge task of estimating the work of the Roman Empire, finds two achievements above all others worthy of his notice.[1] One, which affected the Empire as a whole, also matters most to later generations, for it ended in the civilization of Europe. I do not know whether it is a useful metaphor to say that nations have their missions. Certainly it is true that every nation which has counted for anything in history has contributed some definite element of its own to the growth of the world. The mission, the destiny, the contribution—call it what you like—of Rome, as an Empire, was to teach the practice of social duties, to discipline the diverse peoples, whether wild Celts or wilful Greeks, into a social order, and to institute the common life of well-organized cities. That mission it accomplished. It maintained the longest and most orderly government that has yet fallen to the lot of any portion of the Old World. It diffused one common speech through Europe

[1] See *Some Roman Conceptions of Empire* (Occasional Publications of the Classical Association, No. 4, 1916).

and north Africa. It opened freedom of trade and intercourse over the whole of the then civilized world. It planted and fostered towns far and wide—each regularly planned, each constitutionally ruled by a municipal council. It conciliated its citizens by a prudent system of local autonomy, which hastened the voluntary adoption of Roman speech and Roman manners.

Thus—based (shall I say ?) on Free Trade and Home Rule—it assimilated the provincial populations in an orderly and coherent civilization which was strong enough to survive even the Empire's fall and to conquer its barbarian conquerors. Vergil, writing in the infancy of the Empire, outlined its destiny in well-known lines :[1]

> '*Tu regere imperio populos, Romane, memento*
> *hae tibi erunt artes—pacisque imponere morem,*
> *parcere subiectis et debellare superbos.*'

They are among his stateliest verses ; they are full of a proud national consciousness. But for once the noblest of Italian poets missed the true ideal. The work of Rome was greater than conquest and greater than the *pax Romana* ; it taught men not merely to live quietly but to live in social harmony together as citizens and as individuals. A later and lesser poet, Claudian of Alexandria, writing at the very end of the western Empire, knew better: '*haec est in gremium victos quae sola recepit*'—

> 'Alone she gathers to her bosom those
> whom late she vanquished ; citizens, not foes,
> she calls them now. Their conqueror they proclaim—
> mother, not mistress. So her general name
> enfellowships mankind, makes fast, with bands
> of love devout, the far-off daughter lands,
> that, wheresoe'er we range, 'tis all one race,—
> debtors to her by whose peacemaking grace
> no place is strange but everywhere a home,—
> one world-wide family all akin with Rome.'[2]

So, too, under the Emperor Marcus a couple of centuries earlier a Greek of the East, the rhetorician Aelius

[1] *Aeneid* vi. 851 ff.

[2] Claudian, *De consulatu Stilichonis* iii. 150 ff. The translation is by Professor Phillimore of Glasgow.

Aristides, in his *Praise of Rome* had called her *πάντων μήτηρ* and had spoken of the Empire as *μία χώρα συνεχὴς καὶ ἓν φῦλον*. Rome perhaps did not herself at first recognize her own achievements; it was left to others, to Greek-born men, to understand them. It would be well if all subjects of the British Empire always spoke as loyally of it.

But it is not enough to encourage a civilization. If the world is to be the better permanently for it, it must be given strength to survive. This was the second work of Rome. By a system of defence drawn round her frontiers in Europe, Africa, and Asia she kept safe the early growth of her Roman-provincial culture till it had waxed and won strength, till it was capable (as I have said) of conquering the barbarians who broke down the Empire. I am not sure that this will, at first blush, seem a very necessary or a very great feat to a modern mind. The whole trend of present politics leads men to believe in fleets and armies mainly as a means for securing the independence of some one nation against the aggression of its neighbours. It is not likely that any modern nation will ever stand in quite the place that Rome then held. Our civilization seems firmly set in many lands; our task is rather to spread it further and develop its good qualities than to defend its life. If war destroy it in one continent, it has other homes. But the Roman Empire was the civilized world; the safety of Rome was the safety of all civilization. Outside roared the wild chaos of barbarism. Rome kept it back, from end to end of Europe and across a thousand miles of western Asia. Had Rome failed to civilize, had the civilized life found no period in which to grow firm and tenacious, civilization would have perished utterly. The culture of the old world would not have lived on, to form the groundwork of the best culture of to-day, while the invaders themselves would not have learnt, by hard contact and many long struggles, to reverence the organization, the solidity, the coherence of the Empire.

# APPENDIX

## THE XXVIII CITIES OF BRITAIN

GILDAS, in the third chapter of his Lamentations '*de excidio et conquestu Britanniae*', describes Britain as containing twenty-eight *civitates* and some *castella*, and the statement is repeated verbally at the opening of the *Historia Brittonum* and in the second paragraph of Bede's *Ecclesiastical History*. In none of these passages are the names of the cities given; nothing is recorded about Roman Britain from which we might attempt conjecturally to restore them, and it must remain unknown what cities Gildas had in mind or why he reckoned that there were twenty-eight. His book contains, indeed, not a few historical assertions for which we have no other and confirmatory evidence.

But the omission of the names has been supplied by another writer. In one of the appendices to the *Historia Brittonum* there is a list, entitled '*nomina omnium civitatum quae sunt in tota Brittannia, quarum numerus est xxviii*'. This list, as edited by Mommsen [1] from the best manuscripts, is as follows:

Cair Guorthigirn. Cair Guinntguic. Cair Mincip. Cair Ligualid. Cair Meguaid. Cair Colun. Cair Ebrauc. Cair Custoeint. Cair Caratauc. Cair Grauth. Cair Maunguid. Cair Lundem. Cair Ceint. Cair Guiragon. Cair Peris. Cair Daun. Cair Legion. Cair Guricon. Cair Segeint. Cair Legeion Guar Usic. Cair Guent. Cair Brithon. Cair Lerion. Cair Draitou. Cair Pensa vel Coyt. Cair Urnarc. Cair Celemion. Cair Luit Coyt.

The origin of this list is not at all clear. Plainly it belongs to a Celtic and not to a Roman world: it is neither a list handed down from Roman times, nor the translation of such a list. On the other hand, the retention of the intervocalic 'g' in the names Legion, Segeint, and the rest, induces philologists to ascribe it to a fairly early age, and Zimmer [2], for various reasons,

[1] *Monumenta Germaniae Historica: Auct. Ant.* xiii (*Chronica Minora Saec. iv, v, vi, vii* vol. iii), pp. 210 ff.

[2] *Nennius Vindicatus*, pp. 108 ff.

some of which are perhaps better than others, is inclined to consider it as composed between the time of Gildas and the end of the eighth century. The list itself does not seem to be exactly what it professes. It claims to give the names of all cities in all Britain, and antiquaries who have used it have in general accepted its own account of itself. But, so far as we can identify its names, it appears to refer more particularly to Wales and to other parts of western Britain which remained in Celtic possession for some time after the English invasion. The first name, Cair Guorthigirn, is Welsh, according to a statement in the text of the *Historia Brittonum*, and is represented by one or two later place-names, in especial Gwrtheyrnion in Brecknock and Radnorshire. Cair Guricon is Viroconium (Wroxeter), Cair Segeint is Segontium (Carnarvon), Cair Legeion Guar Usic is Caerleon on Usk, Cair Guent is Caerwent close by it, and Cair Legion is probably Chester. Cair Luit Coyt, again, appears to be Letocetum (Lichfield) [1]. Professor Rhys tells me that Cair Urnarc belongs to the Snowdon district, and Cair Peris possibly to the neighbouring Llanberis. Further, Cair Ligualid seems to be the old Luguvallium [2] advancing on its way towards Caerluel; and if Pensa vel Coyt is not Penselwood in Somerset, it is a very odd coincidence—though I do not mean, by saying this, to pronounce on the late Mr. Kerslake's theories. On the other hand, only three names refer with any probability to the eastern half of England. Cair Ebrauc is obviously York. Cair Colun should denote one of three other Romano-British *coloniae*, Colchester, Lincoln, or Gloucester, and Cair Lundem may be London. Of the other sixteen I can say nothing worth saying. But the details which I have enumerated are perhaps adequate to suggest that the list may have been composed, about the seventh or eighth centuries, by a Celt who knew Wales well, who perhaps knew the other Celtic districts of Britain a little, and who shared the notorious ignorance of his fellows concerning the eastern English districts.

Once composed, the list was destined to a long life and many developments, in the course of which it has influenced historians more than they have always been aware. In the first place it was increased from 28 to 33. Some one read xxviii into xxxiii, and

[1] See *supra*, p. 191, where it is pointed out that the proper Roman form of the name was 'Letocetum', not 'Etocetum'.

[2] The phonetic history of the development of British *Lugu-balion* or *-valion* to Welsh *Lliwelydd*, corresponding to the *Ligualid* of the list, has been demonstrated by Zimmer in *Gött. gel. Anz.* 1890, p. 527, and Sir J. Morris-Jones in *Y Cymmrodorion* xxviii (1918), p. 59.

had in consequence to find five additional names. These are Cair Merdin, Cair Gloui, Cair Ceri, Cair Gurcoc, Cair Teim (or Cei)—that is Carmarthen, Gloucester, and three names not now identifiable with certainty[1]. The man who made these additions obviously knew Wales, but his date cannot be fixed. As the enlarged list occurs first in an eleventh-century manuscript of the *Historia Brittonum* (Mommsen's M), we can only say that the enlargement is older than that century. It may well be much older.

Next, the enlarged form was again reduced to xxviii. Henry of Huntingdon,[2] writing about 1130, quotes from Bede the statement that Britain had twenty-eight cities, and appends to it a list of twenty-nine. One of these is his own invention—to which we shall return below. The other twenty-eight are obtained by striking five names—four of the original and one of the added names—off the enlarged list. Whether Henry struck the five off himself or found them struck off by some predecessor, there is nothing to show but, as we have reason to credit him with the addition of a name, we may also credit him with subtraction. His source was some manuscript of the *Historia Brittonum* like Mommsen's M, to which allusion was made in the last paragraph. In orthographic details he resembles most closely a manuscript kindred to M, which Mommsen calls N. That, however, belongs to the twelfth century, and it does not seem possible to decide whether it is carlier or later than the composition of Henry's list.

Henry was not contented merely with reproducing this forgotten list of cities. He went on to provide English equivalents for the majority of the Celtic names. His identifications appear to be his own devising, and, on the whole, they possess very little value. Some few were correct, York for Kair-Ebrauc, Gloucester for Kair-Glou, Carmarthen for Kair-Merdin; but these were obvious, even in the twelfth century. Others are plainly wrong: Kair-Lion is not Carlisle, nor Kair-Loitchoit Lincoln,[3] nor is Kair-Guent in this case Winchester. Others are mere arbitrary guesses. There is no reason for identifying Kair-Gorangon with Worcester (Wigornia), except that both contain the same consonants in

[1] Mr. W. H. Stevenson suggests that Cair Ceri (Cirencester) is probably taken from Asser's *Life of King Alfred*, c. 57.

[2] *Hist. Angl.* i. 3 (Rolls Series, p. 7).

[3] Mr. W. H. Stevenson adds: "This identification of the *Cair Luit Coyt* of the Welsh list is obviously based upon misreading *Luit* as *Lint*, which suggested Lindsey and Lincoln, O.E. *Lindcylene*. Similarly Henry perverts *Cair Brithon* into *Kair Bristou* in order to identify it with Bristol, O.E. *Brycg-stow*."

different orders. There is no reason for converting Cair Grauth into Kair-Grant, except to assimilate it to the Grantchester and Grantebridge (Cambridge), which lay within the area of Henry's own personal knowledge. And it can hardly be doubted that Henry invented himself Kair-Dorm, the one city in his list which appears in no earlier list. He calls it '*Dormeceastre, quae sita in Huntendonensi provincia super flumen quod vocatur Nen, penitus destructa est*'. This is the Romano-British Durobrivae, known in the twelfth century by the name which Henry gives, Dormeceastre, but, if we may argue from Henry's language, something more than a mere name to him. And, indeed, the place, like Cambridge, lay well within the area of Henry's personal knowledge.

It is noteworthy and has not hitherto been noticed that Henry's list of cities and identifications is not quite the same in his first and in his later editions. In the latter, one city name has been altered and three identifications have been added, of which one concerns the altered name. First, the twenty-fifth name, Kair Peris, has no identification in the first edition; afterwards Henry added Porcestre, that is, Porchester in Hampshire. Secondly, the twenty-sixth name in the first edition was Kair-Lerion, without any appended identification; afterwards Henry substituted Kair-Legion and added the note: '*in qua fuit archiepiscopatus tempore Brittonum, nunc autem vix moenia eius comparent ubi Usca cadit in Sabrinam.*' Thirdly, the last name, Kair-Segent, stands in the first edition without comment; afterwards Henry added the words: '*quae fuit super Tamesin non longe a Redinge et vocatur Silcestre.*' If we now go on to ask why Henry made these alterations, the reason can be given with some confidence. In the interval between his first and his later editions, Henry became acquainted with the 'History' of Geoffrey of Monmouth, and in that history he would find mentions of Porchester as a famous fortress anciently called Kaerperis (iv. 12, 14; v. 8), of Caerleon as a British capital and archbishopric (iii. 10, 12; iv. 19; vii. 3; viii. 10; ix. 1, 12), and of Silchester as a British city and bishopric (vi. 5; ix. 1, 15). This fact alone makes it highly probable that Henry followed Geoffrey in these details. The probability is heightened by the fact that Henry's note on Kair-Legion is almost a verbal echo of Geoffrey's mentions of Caerleon (iv. 19; ix. 12), and still more by the fact that in other passages Henry seems to borrow from Geoffrey, as, for instance, in his account of the parentage of Helena, wife of Constantius (Geoffrey, v. 6; Henry, i. 37).[1]

[1] See *supra*, p. 61, foot-note.

Geoffrey himself appears to have known of the list of xxxiii cities. He mentions several names which occur in it, Kaerebrauc (ii. 7, &c.), Kaerleir (ii. 9), Kaerguen (ii. 9, &c.), Kaerglou (iv. 15), Kaerpen-Huelgoit (iv. 16), Kaercolvin (v. 6), Kaerperis (v. 8), Kaercaradauc (vi. 15; viii. 9) and perhaps others, and, as he appears to have known of the *Historia Brittonum* and its appendices, we may imagine that he derived these names from the appendix. He does not, however, ascribe them to any special group of xxviii or xxxiii, nor does he allude to such a group except once (i, 2), and there he is quoting from Gildas and Bede. He simply mentions them as he mentions many other Kaers—some apparently of his own invention—and in the history of the list of the xxviii cities he plays no direct part.

That history goes on from Henry of Huntingdon. The list of xxix cities which he gives was copied (immediately after its appearance) by Alfred of Beverley (fl. 1143) in its fullest form, i. e. with the three alterations made subsequently to Henry's first edition.[1] From Alfred of Beverley it was copied by Ranulf Higden, and thence passed into the stream of English chronicle writing. From the chronicles it became known to Camden,[2] and through him to a host of modern writers, who have quoted freely its items, often without any idea of their origin. It has had a long history which it did not deserve, and has wasted the time of many men.

[1] Dr. J. G. Evans collated for F. H. the list in the Peniarth MS of Alfred (Pen. MS. 384 = Hen. MS. 145), which is said to be the best. It is now in the National Library of Wales, Aberystwyth.

[2] Mr. W. H. Stevenson writes: "The prominence given by Camden to the names of these British cities is mainly due to the work of Humphrey Llwyd (Lhuyd), *Commentarioli Britannicae Descriptionis Fragmentum*, published at Cologne in 1572 but written in 1568 [see *supra*, p. 68, foot-note 2]. He remarks (fo. 28 r.) that the Welsh applied the word *Caer* not only to walled towns but to other places that were defended by walls and ditches. As we learn from Giraldus Cambrensis, towns were unknown in Wales. The identification of *civitas* with entrenched camps was no doubt due to the use of *caer* to describe the Roman stations or walled towns as well as the entrenched camps. Llwyd seems also to be Camden's authority for identifying groups of counties with the British names mentioned by Ptolemy and others."

# INDEX

*While the Index is primarily intended to cover the Lectures, a number of references to the Bibliography have been added. Each of these is followed by a date within parentheses.*

Printed in England at the Oxford University Press